770

Monochrome darkroom practice

Monochrome darkroom practice

A manual of black-and-white processing and printing

Jack H. Coote

Focal Press

London & Boston

Focal Press

is an imprint of the Butterworth Group
which has principal offices in
London, Sydney, Toronto, Wellington, Durban and Boston

First published 1982

British Library Cataloguing in Publication Data

Coote, Jack H.
  Monochrome darkroom practice.
  1. Photography – Processing
  I. Title
  770'.28'3   TR287

  ISBN 0-240-51061-5

Photoset by Butterworths Litho Preparation Department
Printed in England by Mackays of Chatham

Contents

Introduction

At times during recent years there have been those who predicted the demise of most forms of black-and-white photography, believing that colour processes would become as simple and cheap to operate as the black-and-white process. In some ways the prediction has proved correct, for example in the large-scale production of snapshots by the photofinisher or the widespread use of colour transparencies as originals for reproduction on the printed page; but when it comes to the essential business of using an enlarger to make a print, real differences remain.

Give any black-and-white negative to half a dozen good printers, and four or five minutes later (less than that if they process by machine) you will see six different but perfectly satisfactory black-and-white prints. Do the same with a colour negative the printers have never seen before, and after half an hour or more the chances are that you will have six prints that differ in colour balance and an argument about which is correct!

One thing that widened the gap between the relative ease of black-and-white printing and the complexity of colour printing was the introduction of waterproof or resin-coated papers, allowing high-quality black-and-white prints to be developed, fixed, washed and dried within a few minutes. Resin-coated papers were originally intended to reduce the processing time for colour prints, but quickly led to machines producing black-and-white prints in a 'dry to dry' time of little more than a minute. For optimum control, though, no machine can replace developing by inspection, one of the great advantages of black-and-white printing.

There are applications where the use of resin-coated papers is still considered unacceptable – by photographers who sell their prints to collectors, for instance. For these perfectionists, who want their prints to last for the longest possible time, new fibre-based papers have been introduced and revised processing procedures are recommended.

Whenever it is necessary to compare the cost-effectiveness of monochrome and colour photography, it should be remembered that in the majority of cases almost as much information is conveyed by a monochrome representation as by a colour photograph of the same subject. This is not so surprising if one considers the many visible characteristics that describe an object, most of which can be quite adequately indicated in black and white. Shape, relative size, position, surface, angle of view, transparency or opacity, fine or coarse detail – all of these can be perfectly well recorded and reproduced with black-and-white materials. The addition of colour, while often appealing, is frequently superfluous to the everyday purposes of photography.

During the earliest days of photography, before the turn of the century, a photographer had to prepare all his own sensitive materials. When using the wet collodion process that held sway for several decades, he would first clean a sheet of glass and coat it with collodion. Then, after moving into some kind of darkroom or tent, he would sensitise it by immersion in a tank of silver nitrate solution before the collodion had time to dry. After exposure, development would be in a solution of ferrous oxalate, prepared just before use. The plate being large, it would be contact-printed on to a sheet of albumen-treated paper that had been previously floated on a bath of silver nitrate. By the time he had exposed his print (using the sun or the sky as a light source) and had washed, toned and fixed it, the photographer of those days could truly say that he had 'made' a photograph.

Even after the introduction of gelatino-bromide emulsions, many photographers used their favourite formulae to coat their own plates. But gradually convenience won the day and the gelatin dry-plate became an everyday commodity. Home-made silver and platinum papers also gave way to the far more convenient chloride and bromide papers produced by the many small manufacturers that sprang up around the turn of the century.

From that time there has been no need for a photographer to know anything about the manufacture of negative or print materials. Yet some understanding of how the materials are made often enables the user to choose the product best suited for a particular job or to recognise the limitations of the material he has to use. Neither is it essential to know anything about the process of development, since the photographer can produce perfectly good negatives and prints simply by following instructions; but a reasonably good understanding of the principles of photographic processing will help him to recognise and rectify the occasional fault or shortcoming that might otherwise continue to trouble him.

The first two chapters of the book are therefore devoted to the construction and properties of black-and-white sensitised materials and the process of development by which they are rendered useful. The remaining chapters, comprising most of the book, deal with the practice of making negatives and prints.

By introducing their Annual £1000 Print Awards in 1969, Ilford Limited recognised the profound influence that a printer can have in creating a winning picture from a negative that might, if it were printed straight, command no special attention. Gene Nocon puts it another way: 'The excitement felt by a printer in his darkroom when he produces a special photographic print can equal the photographer's experience in taking the original picture.' As a tribute to printers who work in monochrome, most of the illustrations used in the book have been selected from entries to the Ilford Competitions.

I would like to thank my friends from the Technical Service departments of the Ilford Group, particularly Philip Jenkins, Mike Gristwood and Michael Waldon, for their willing and frequent help during the preparation of the book; any mistakes there may be, however, certainly remain mine. The staff of Focal Press also deserve my thanks for their ready understanding and for showing me that fewer words often serve just as well and sometimes better.

1 Monochrome photographic materials

It has been estimated that during the relatively short period of the development of the photographic process, the sensitivity of photographic layers has been increased by 20 million times.

When Fox Talbot began experimenting in 1834, he was forced to give exposures of ten minutes in his camera obscura to obtain any kind of image. His method of producing a light-sensitive paper was to dip a sheet of it in salt-water solution and, after drying, to paint it with a solution of silver nitrate, thereby forming a layer of silver chloride. In September 1840 Fox Talbot made his biggest breakthrough, increasing the sensitivity of light-sensitive paper by 100 times. This discovery, together with his negative-positive method of obtaining a print, seems to justify William Henry Fox Talbot as the inventor of photography as we know it.

Fox Talbot made ordinary sheets of paper sensitive to light by an impregnating rather than a coating procedure as used nowadays. The prints he made were known as calotypes. Because they were printed through the paper base of the negative images he obtained in his camera, calotypes were not at all sharp, which was one of the reasons why many photographers of that time preferred the much greater detail obtainable in the directly recorded positive image of a daguerreotype.

The first practicable way of using glass as the support for a light-sensitive layer was disclosed by Frederick Scott Archer in 1851, and it became known as the wet collodion process. It was called wet because all the preparation and exposing procedures had to be carried out without allowing the collodion to become dry. Despite its great inconvenience, the wet collodion process soon replaced both the daguerreotype and the calotype processes for producing a photographic image.

Dry plates

The next significant change in photography came with the introduction of 'dry' gelatin-bromide plates, the invention of which is usually attributed to an amateur, Dr R. L. Maddox. Maddox described his method in 1871. It involved suspending silver bromide particles in a solution of warm gelatin, and coating some of the mixture on to glass while still warm. Then, after chilling to solidify the gelatin, the coated plates were dried and stored until required for exposure. After exposure the plates were developed, fixed and washed, before being dried once again.

In fact, dry plates made according to Maddox's recommendations were not as sensitive to light as wet collodion plates. It took some years and many more experiments by a variety of amateur and professional photographers before the dry plate became competitive in speed with the wet collodion plate. Significant improvements came from Burgess in 1873, when he began to use an alkaline solution of pyro as a developer; from King in the same year when he proposed to wash the set and shredded emulsion to remove unwanted salts; from Johnson in 1877, when he recommended the use of ammonia in the emulsion; and above all from Bennett, who discovered in 1878 that sensitivity could be greatly increased by heating or 'ripening' the emulsion before coating.

The early photographic recording processes (daguerreotype, calotype, wet collodion and the first dry plates) could only 'see' blue and blue-violet light, the inherent sensitivity range of all the silver halides. In 1873, however, while trying to reduce halation by introducing dyes into the emulsion layer of his plates, H. W. Vogel noticed that one of the dyes had extended the sensitivity of the emulsion into the green and yellow regions of the spectrum.

Vogel's discovery had no immediate effect on the manufacture of dry plates because the dye he had used produced a low-speed emulsion that was prone to fog. It was not long, however, before better sensitising dyes were found – particularly erythrosin, which J. M. Eder discovered in 1889 and which gave better green sensitivity than the dye used by Vogel. Then, in 1905, Homolka discovered pinacyanol, a dye that extended the sensitivity for the first time into the red end of the visible spectrum, and made it possible to produce panchromatic plates.

Today's emulsions

Today, more than a hundred years after many of these early discoveries, silver bromide is still the principal light-sensitive component in films. But there is much more to making a modern film such as Ilford HP5 than suspending silver bromide crystals in gelatin, adding some dye and coating a layer of the resulting emulsion on to a transparent film support. Today's high-speed camera films are the result of a century of continuous progress that has gradually yielded ever higher sensitivity, lower granularity, better resolving power, greater consistency and improved keeping properties. These things have not come as the result of any one technological breakthrough but from continuous and patient research.

If it seems surprising that the silver halides have not been replaced as essential ingredients in high-speed emulsions, it is equally remarkable that gelatin has remained the indispensable medium in which the silver salts are suspended. Gelatin is obtained from a variety of uncontrolled sources, including bones, skins, hides and slaughterhouse trimmings, not the most promising of origins for an important component in a photographic emulsion.

Alternatives to gelatin, such as polyvinyl alcohol, can be and are used in emulsion making, but they always result in a relatively slow emulsion. Gelatin is thought to form an elastic 'shell' around

Don Fraser, frequent winner and sometime judge of the Ilford Photographic Awards, used HP5 rollfilm for this shot, 'The Earth's ears'; it typifies the dramatic nature of so much of his work

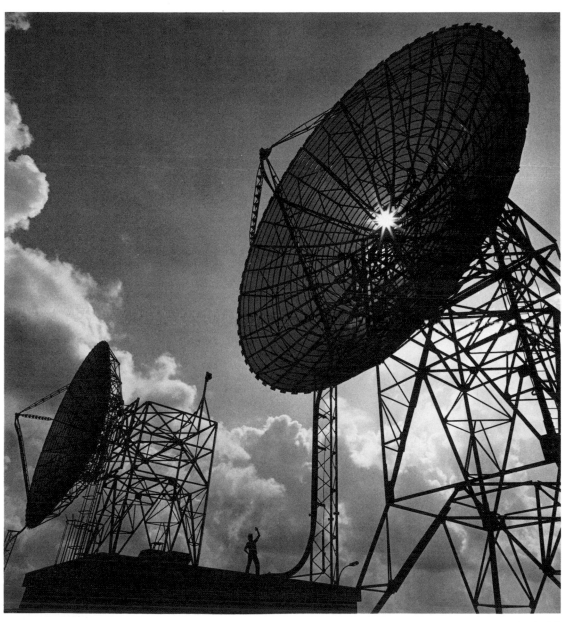

the silver halide grains when the emulsion is ripened, allowing the grains to grow in size and become more sensitive to light; polyvinyl alcohol and other gelatin substitutes are more rigid, and therefore prevent or restrict the growth of grains during the digestion process.

As long ago as 1925, S. E. Sheppard, a colleague of C. E. K. Mees, discovered that a sulphur-containing compound (allyl mustard oil or some compound closely related to it) was present in some gelatins and acted as a valuable sensitiser.

Some photographically active components are present in gelatins in concentrations no greater than a few parts per million, and vary according to the source of gelatin. Consequently, for many years the unpredictable nature of gelatin forced the makers of photographic emulsions to test every batch submitted to them before accepting it. Even then it was necessary to blend a number of batches of gelatin together to average out their differences. Nowadays, in order to have better control over their performance in an emulsion, gelatins are often rendered relatively inert by removing any photographic impurities before replacing them with precisely controlled amounts of synthetic sensitisers. To achieve the desired emulsion characteristics, it is still often necessary to blend several different gelatins.

It is not only the chemical properties of gelatin that make it a necessity in most types of photographic emulsion. Its physical properties are also particularly well suited to the requirements of coating and processing emulsion layers. Warm gelatin solutions of 2 per cent concentration or more will set to a rubbery consistency when cooled to below 30°C. It is therefore possible to apply a liquid emulsion layer to a glass, film or paper support, and then to set the layer before drying it and subsequently cutting and packing the finished product.

When placed in cold water or a developing solution, gelatin swells. If the gelatin has been coated on to a support that has been prepared with some kind of 'subbing' layer to ensure adhesion of the emulsion, the swelling will be in one direction only: away from the support. When dried, the swollen gelatin shrinks to approximately its original size. In its swollen state, gelatin can be thought of as a kind of sponge that is readily penetrated by aqueous solutions. This means that the suspended silver halide grains can be reached easily by developer and fixer, and with similar ease the subsequently formed silver image can be washed free of residual chemicals.

A greatly swollen gelatin layer is soft and easily disturbed by contact with anything rigid; it would be difficult, therefore, to process negatives or prints by hand, and impossible to put them through a roller processing machine, if the swelling could not be restricted in some way. The process that restricts the swelling of gelatin is called hardening. There are several junctures in the photographic manufacturing and processing sequence where hardening treatments can be introduced. The emulsion itself will contain a hardener when it is coated, and the exposed emulsion layer can be further hardened either before or during development, or during or after fixing.

The earliest hardeners were based on aluminium or chromium, but these have been largely replaced by more effective and more suitable organic compounds such as formaldehyde and glutaraldehyde. Hardening techniques have become so effective that processing can now be conducted at much higher temperatures than before, without the previous risk of reticulation caused by a gelatin layer 'slipping' on its support.

The control of fog in an emulsion, particularly a high-speed one, has also steadily improved over the years. Most of the early anti-foggants reduced the speed of an emulsion as well as its tendency to fog, but modern stabilisers do not have this adverse effect and are used successfully in the fastest emulsions to control fog and improve keeping properties. The long shelf-life of modern films (several years with films such as FP4 or HP5) is one of the most valuable achievements of emulsion technology.

Principal stages in emulsion making

The emulsion-making process involves four main stages: emulsification, ripening, washing to remove excess soluble salts, and after ripening or 'digestion'.

Most emulsions require a mixture of two or more silver halides. For example, a high-speed film emulsion depends mainly on silver bromide with a small proportion of silver iodide, while a paper for enlarging may require a mixture of silver chloride and silver bromide. However, the precise formulations used in emulsions almost always remain secret. In fact, apart from one in Russian, the only books written on emulsion making were published in the twenties and thirties. Some additional information became available after World War II, when the formulations and methods used by German manufacturers were disclosed in a number of British and American intelligence reports.

Emulsification It is not only the composition of an emulsion in terms of its gelatin and silver halide content that determines the properties of the resulting photographic material. The precise way in which the silver halide grains are precipitated in the very first moments of the emulsification process is also extremely important.

15

In the single-jet method of precipitation, a solution of silver nitrate is 'jetted' into a warm gelatin solution that already contains dissolved halides. The rate of addition, the temperature and the manner of stirring are all carefully controlled. Alternatively, both the silver nitrate and the halide solutions can be added to the warm gelatin from two separate jets, but again the sequence and rates of addition and the temperature of all the component solutions must be precisely controlled.

These initial stages of precipitation determine the basic characteristics of an emulsion. Broadly, the quicker the silver nitrate and the halide solutions are mixed together, and the lower the temperature at which this is done, the smaller the grain and the lower the sensitivity of the resulting emulsion.

Ripening Whatever the grain size distribution immediately after precipitation, the size of the grains and their subsequent sensitivity to light can be changed by later heat treatment of the emulsion, as Bennett discovered in 1878. Such treatment is referred to as ripening. During this process, physical changes take place in the emulsion; in particular, the larger crystals of silver halide grow at the expense of smaller ones. Since the speed and contrast of an emulsion are largely determined by the size and distribution of the silver halide grains, the mechanisms of the precipitation and ripening stages of emulsion making are critically important.

Washing If an emulsion were coated on a glass plate immediately after ripening, it would display a crystalline surface when dry. The crystals would not be silver halide, but ammonium nitrate or some other by-product of the emulsion-making process. Had the same emulsion been coated on a paper base, the by-products might have been largely absorbed by the paper base, but this cannot happen when an emulsion is coated on glass or film or on a resin-coated paper. Consequently it is necessary to remove the unwanted by-products in some way.

One method is to set the emulsion by chilling it immediately after the desired period of ripening, and then to shred or otherwise cut up the solidified emulsion so that it can be washed in water until the concentration of soluble halides drops to the required level. But washing an emulsion in this way is time-consuming and rather uncontrollable, so it is now more usual to coagulate the gelatin by a process called flocculation. This can be achieved by adding inorganic salts (such as sodium sulphate) or other coagulants (such as methanol or polystyrene sulphonate) to the liquid emulsion. The tough, rubbery precipitate of gelatin that results from flocculation contains the silver halides and can be redispersed in a fresh solution of gelatin.

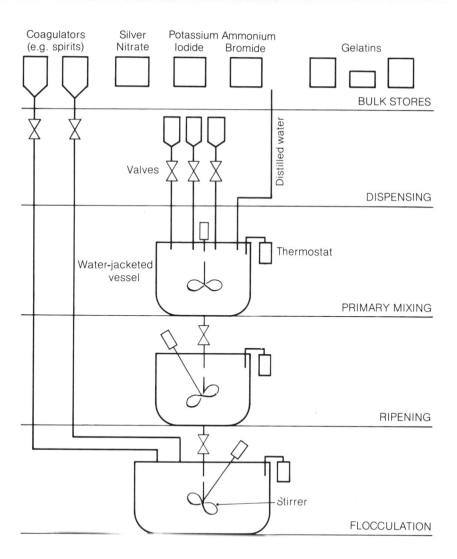

Coagulators (e.g. spirits) | Silver Nitrate | Potassium Iodide | Ammonium Bromide | Gelatins

BULK STORES

Valves

Distilled water

DISPENSING

Water-jacketed vessel

Thermostat

PRIMARY MIXING

RIPENING

Stirrer

FLOCCULATION

Schematic diagram of emulsion-making layout

After-ripening   This is a heating process during which chemical sensitisers, such as certain sulphur compounds or even some forms of gold, are added to increase the sensitivity of the emulsion. The period of after-ripening can be relatively long (30 minutes to one hour) but it must be stopped before the onset of fog. This is done by dropping the temperature and by adding a stabiliser.

A freshly made emulsion could, if necessary, be coated on to a support immediately following after-ripening, but in practice it is usually stored in a cool room until it is required.

Final additions   When an emulsion is re-melted in preparation for coating, several other additions are made to it. If sensitivity is to be extended to include green and red light, the appropriate sensitising dye or dyes will be added. A disinfectant such as phenol may also be used to ensure that the gelatin layer will not be attacked by bacteria if it is stored in very humid conditions. Some kind of gelatin hardener will also be added at this stage. These miscellaneous additions are sometimes referred to as 'finals'.

Chromogenic monochrome film   The emulsions used for XP1–400 film contain colour couplers to produce a printable negative image after all silver has been removed from the developed film. Strictly, there is no need to generate more than a yellow image to make prints on bromide paper, but in practice the image would be difficult to see. The final negative image on XP1 appears reasonably neutral, and can easily be focused in an enlarger since it is a composite of three or four different dyes, including yellow, magenta and cyan.

In addition to the image-forming colour couplers, a development inhibitor release (DIR) coupler is added to XP1–400 emulsion to produce the enhanced edge effect that gives a negative a subtle quality sometimes called 'sparkle'.

Emulsion supports

The earliest forms of photography used metal (daguerreotype), paper (calotype) or glass (wet collodion) as supports for the light-sensitive layers. Film, which was to become by far the most important material on which camera-speed emulsions are coated, was adopted quite rapidly by the amateur but more slowly by the professional photographer, particularly in Europe.

The advantages of a flexible material on which a series of exposures could be made were recognised from the earliest days of photography. Melhuish made a paper-negative roll holder for calotype prints in 1854. Paper was also used as a support, albeit a temporary one, for the 'film' that George Eastman used in his earliest Kodak camera. The first practicable photographic film base was made by Carbutt in the United States in 1888, and by the following year a cellulose nitrate film was being cast on long glass tables by Eastman in Rochester.

All the early photographic film bases were cellulose nitrate, a highly inflammable material. After 1920 this was gradually replaced by the less dangerous cellulose esters, particularly cellulose acetate. Cut sheet films, especially those used for graphic arts and for X-ray recording, are now made with the stronger and dimensionally more stable polyester (polyethylene terephthalate) base. Motion-picture films and most of the films used for amateur photography are still coated on cellulose acetate, butyrate or triacetate material, because it will tear before the camera or projector mechanism is damaged whenever there is a mechanical jam.

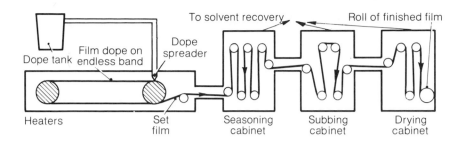

Schematic diagram of triacetate base casting

To solvent recovery

Roll of finished film

Dope tank

Film dope on endless band

Dope spreader

Heaters

Set film

Seasoning cabinet

Subbing cabinet

Drying cabinet

Film base can be made by casting or by extrusion. Cellulose acetate films are made by casting or spreading a viscose solution on to a highly polished moving surface, such as a large wheel or an endless metal band. The solvents in the 'dope' are driven off by heat and are recovered. The resulting film is stripped from the wheel or band in a continuous process. The thickness of the film can be adjusted by controlling the speed of the casting wheel or band, and is usually 90 μm (0.0035 in) for roll film, 130 μm (0.005 in) for 35 mm film and about 180 μm (0.007 in) for cut sheet film.

Polyester film base such as Mylar or Melinex is produced by extrusion and stretching. A relatively thick and narrow strip of polymer is extruded and then stretched, first longitudinally by means of over-driven rollers and then laterally by means of a side-gripping but divergent 'stenter', until it is about sixteen times its area when first extruded. A roll width of 1.4 metres (54 inches) is quite usual in the photographic industry today. For a given strength, the thickness of a polyester layer can be less than is possible with cellulose acetate base, which is why 72-exposure

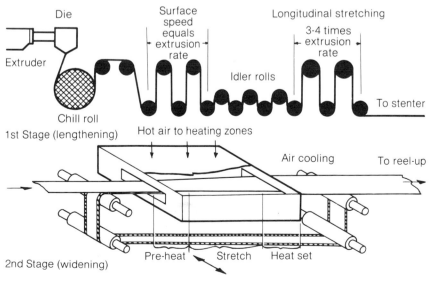

Schematic diagram of polyester base casting and stretching

Die

Surface speed equals extrusion rate

Longitudinal stretching

3-4 times extrusion rate

Extruder

Idler rolls

To stenter

Chill roll

1st Stage (lengthening)

Hot air to heating zones

Air cooling

To reel-up

2nd Stage (widening)

Pre-heat   Stretch   Heat set

19

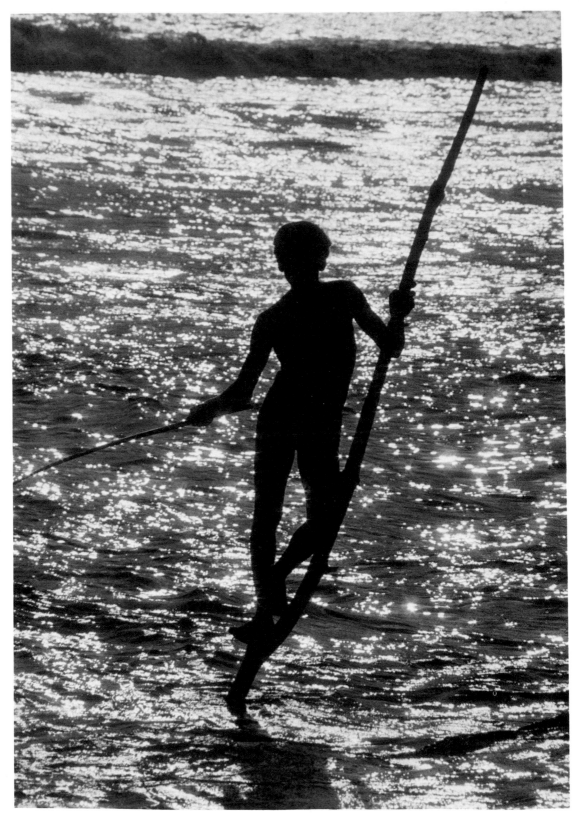

Ilford Autowinder film can be accommodated in a standard 35 mm cassette.

If a gelatin emulsion were coated directly on to untreated glass or film, it might remain attached while dry but would certainly come off the base during processing. To make an emulsion layer adhere to the surface on which it is coated, it is necessary to prepare the base by coating it with a substratum or 'subbing' layer.

To reduce the effects of halation when extreme highlights are recorded on a negative, suitable light-absorbing dyes or pigments are used. These can be incorporated in an emulsion layer, can be used in an underlayer between the emulsion and the base, or can be applied to the back of the film. For most black-and-white motion-picture negative films and for 35 mm still-camera films, the base itself incorporates a non-dischargeable neutral dye that has an optical density of about 0.20.

All photographic emulsion layers are prone to develop either dark or light areas wherever their surface is knocked or scratched. This tendency to become either sensitised or desensitised by mechanical stress is reduced if the emulsion is protected by a super-coat of hardened gelatin.

Thin films, such as those used in roll-film cameras, need to have an anti-curl layer of gelatin coated on the back of the base to counteract the swelling and shrinking tendencies of the emulsion layer. Even though motion-picture and 35 mm still-camera films are slightly thicker than roll films and their negative sizes smaller, they, too, require an anti-curl treatment.

Emulsion coating methods

Very little is ever written about the coating methods used by photographic manufacturers. Most of what is generally known has been gleaned from the patent literature, which is not necessarily a reliable guide to what is actually happening. Those few text books that attempt to provide some kind of schematic illustration of a film or paper emulsion-coating machine usually depict a moving web of base material being transported round a roller. The roller is either dipping into a trough of emulsion or is in close proximity to another roller rotating in the trough and transferring emulsion to the base by a liquid bead. No doubt film and paper used to be coated in this way, but now other methods, permitting much higher coating speeds, have been adopted.

One of the limitations of the relatively simple early methods of emulsion coating was that any attempt to speed up the rate of travel of the web of base material resulted in an unavoidable increase in coating weight. This problem can be solved by using an air-blade (air-knife) located just above the coating point to cut

21

back the surplus emulsion picked up by the web. Quite high coating speeds and predictable coating weights can be obtained by adjustment of the velocity of the air leaving the blade.

With the advent of multi-layer photographic materials and the desirability of applying the multiple emulsions in one pass through a coating machine, a quite new method of emulsion coating was introduced and described by Russell, Wilson and Sanford in a US patent in 1956. In this method, variously known as 'slide-hopper' or 'cascade' coating, liquid emulsion is fed at a controlled rate

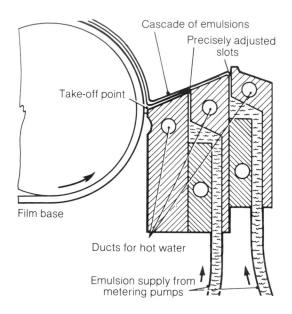

Cascade of emulsions
Precisely adjusted slots
Take-off point
Film base
Ducts for hot water
Emulsion supply from metering pumps

Schematic diagram of cascade coating head for two emulsions

through a precisely machined slot, so that all the emulsion supplied to the slot is transferred to the moving support. The slide hopper can incorporate slots for more than one emulsion; the slots can be arranged so that two or more liquid emulsion layers reach the coating point as a lamination, and as such are transferred to a web of paper or film without change in their spatial relationship. High-speed films, such as HP5, owe their speed and exposure latitude to the fact that they comprise two emulsion layers, both of which can be coated in one pass by means of a slide-hopper or cascade coating head.

Uniform coating thickness, in terms of both silver and gelatin, is essential for both sensitometric and economic reasons. The thickness of each coating must be consistent to within a few milligrams per square decimetre across the width of the web and throughout the many thousands of metres of film or paper that constitute a production run.

When a web of film or paper has been coated with a layer of liquid emulsion, it must be set as quickly as possible. This is done

22

either by passing the web into a 'chill box' through which refrigerated air is circulated, or by bringing it into contact with chilled drums. After setting, the drying process can begin. Since the rate and the conditions of drying can have a profound effect on both the sensitometric and physical properties of the product, this is an important stage in photographic film and paper manufacture.

The earliest emulsion-coating machines used an ingenious device, known as a 'festoon' dryer, to translate the continuous passage of the web past the coating point into the slower movement of the coated web while it was being dried. Loops of film or paper were suspended from cross-members or 'sticks', which moved slowly in a horizontal direction as new loops, with freshly coated base, were formed at the coating point. One of the problems with the festoon method is that the sticks, remaining stationary in relation to the loops they support, are likely to have a local effect on the rate of drying, which in turn may change the sensitivity of parts of the film. One answer to this is to use a spiral drying track on which the coated material travels continuously from the outside to the centre of a large spiral drying chamber, through which warm air is blown at right angles to the direction in which the web is travelling. However, it is more usual today for coated film or paper to be dried in what is sometimes called a straightaway or flat-bed track, running horizontally for quite a long distance. With the web supported on rollers or a cushion of air, the drying air can be applied uniformly from above the coated surface. Drying speeds, like coating methods, are not generally revealed, but the patent literature suggests that nowadays they may reach 150–180 metres (500–600 feet) per minute.

Finishing and packing films
According to the application for which they are intended, coated rolls of film may be slit and chopped into flat film sizes; slit and combined with backing paper to make roll films; or slit, perforated and inserted into cassettes for use in 35 mm cameras. Probably the most difficult of these jobs is the production of 35 mm film in cassettes, since there are several operations involved. After being slit and perforated, 35 mm rolls must be edge-signed with frame numbers and film type, and this has to be done for 20-exposure, 36-exposure and even 72-exposure lengths. Perforators that combine an illuminated signing drum and a tongue-notching punch can be used, or the perforating and edge-signing can be done as separate operations.

The most difficult jobs to automate fully are the spooling of roll films and their backing papers, and the loading of each length of 35 mm film into its metal cassette. Yet the rate at which these

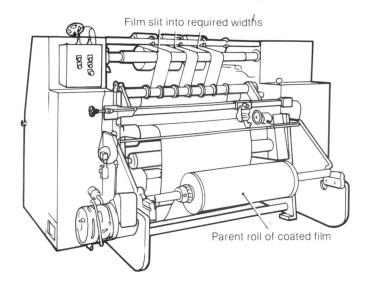

Film slit into required widths

Parent roll of coated film

Film-slitting and rewinding machine

operations are carried out can reach 50 units per minute. (Those who have loaded 35 mm cassettes from bulk rolls of film will realise how many operations are involved and how long the job takes when done by hand.)

To extend its useful life, the emulsion layer of a film should be maintained for as long as possible in the controlled atmospheric conditions under which it was packed. With this in mind, finished films are often enclosed in hermetically sealed, metal-foil wrappings. This method of protection has the disadvantage that it takes some time to remove the foil wrapping before the film can be loaded into a camera. For a press photographer a better alternative is to buy the film in airtight plastic tubs with easily removable 'press-on' caps.

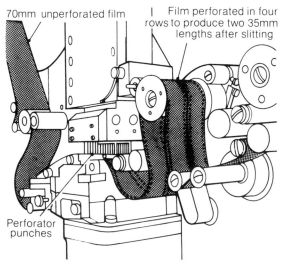

70mm unperforated film

Film perforated in four rows to produce two 35mm lengths after slitting

Perforator punches

Film-perforating machine

Photographic papers

The negative-positive form of photography began with paper-based sensitive materials for both camera and printing exposures. That paper is not really a satisfactory support for a negative image was indicated by the fact that Fox Talbot had to render his paper negatives translucent by treating them with wax. In his patents, Fox Talbot described how he selected 'the best writing paper' for sensitisation by brushing with a solution of silver nitrate in distilled water.

It is quite understandable that Fox Talbot used only the best paper he could find. The same principle applies today. Virtually flawless, fine-textured paper is essential for photographic use, and the paper manufacturer goes to great lengths to ensure that no contaminants are present in the pulp when it starts its long trip through the paper-making machine.

Although mechanisation and the scale of operations now employed make the fact difficult to appreciate, paper is still made in basically the same way as it was when the first hand-made sheets were produced in China more than ten centuries ago. Very briefly, an aqueous suspension of cellulose fibres (usually a mixture of hardwood and softwood fibres for photographic paper base) is spread uniformly on a travelling wire screen through which much of the water from the slurry drains away. More water is removed by vacuum suction until a fibrous wet mat remains, which can then be transferred to compacting rollers to squeeze out still more water. The web is heated to drive off the last of the moisture before the paper is calendered to impart the required surface finish. Paper base intended for photographic use is treated to enhance its wet strength so that it will withstand processing.

Photographic printing papers range in weight, or thickness, from around 100–150 grams per square metre for single-weight papers to 200–250 grams per square metre for double-weight papers. The lighter papers are used for most commercial and press applications, while the heavier papers are necessary for large prints intended for exhibition or display.

If a photographic emulsion were coated directly on to untreated paper, as it was when Fox Talbot was making his calotypes, the density range of the resulting prints would be limited because of poor reflection from highlights and poor absorption of light in the shadows. Some kind of highly reflective layer is needed between the paper and the emulsion. A paper of this kind was produced as early as 1866, and comprised a collodion emulsion on paper that had been previously coated with a layer of barium sulphate mixed with an adhesive. Similar 'baryta' coatings have been used in photographic papers ever since.

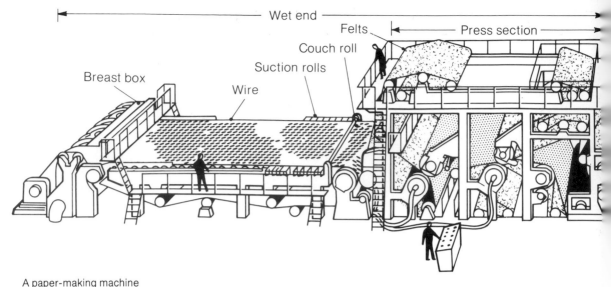

A paper-making machine

Today, for photographic uses, uncoated paper can be treated in one of two ways. It can be given a coating of a mixture of barium sulphate and gelatin, or it can be laminated between two thin layers of polyethylene, one of them colourless and the other pigmented white. Either of these two treatments serves to separate the emulsion layers from the paper base, and both permit the surface characteristics of the finished photographic print to be determined at the time the baryta layer or the polyethylene layer is calendered.

In order to enhance the apparent 'whiteness' of a photographic paper, optical or fluorescent brighteners are sometimes added to the paper or to its baryta coating. These brighteners (widely used in washing powder) are colourless substances that convert ultraviolet light into fluorescent energy in the visible region of the spectrum. Sometimes, additional brighteners are added to the subsequently coated emulsions to augment the effect of those included in the paper base or baryta layer.

Baryta-coated (fibre-based) papers, such as Ilfobrom and Galerie, quickly absorb aqueous solutions through both their coated and uncoated surfaces. This has several disadvantages that are nevertheless accepted by many photographers who still prefer to use a 'traditional' type of paper for prints that their customers may wish to keep for many years. Removal of residual processing chemicals from the fibres of a paper base requires a fairly long period of washing, and the subsequent removal of the water absorbed by both the emulsion and the paper base also takes quite a long time. A further disadvantage is that a baryta-coated paper,

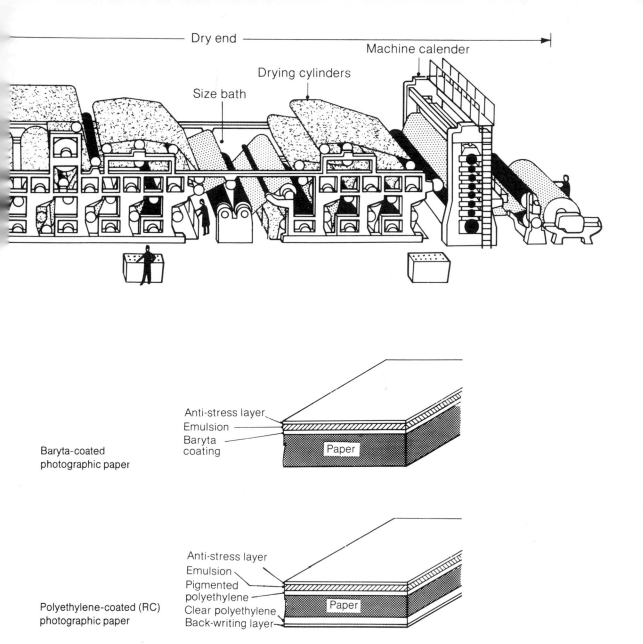

Dry end

Machine calender

Drying cylinders

Size bath

Baryta-coated
photographic paper

Anti-stress layer
Emulsion
Baryta
coating

Paper

Polyethylene-coated (RC)
photographic paper

Anti-stress layer
Emulsion
Pigmented
polyethylene
Clear polyethylene
Back-writing layer

Paper

even when the baryta layer has been calendered to a very smooth surface, produces finished prints that are not usually considered glossy enough without being glazed on a heated metal sheet or drum, a process that is less popular now that a high gloss can be obtained in much less time by putting RC prints through a hot-air dryer. Furthermore, a print on a baryta-coated paper base will expand significantly during processing and shrink to less than its original size if dried without glazing, making it difficult or impossible to predict the final dimensions of an image.

Resin-coated papers

A few specialised graphic arts materials were produced on polyethylene-coated paper during the early sixties in order to achieve image stability; but it was really the urgent need to reduce the processing times required for colour papers that accelerated the introduction of so-called resin-coated or 'waterproof' papers. Before resin-coated (RC) colour paper was introduced around 1970, it was quite common for the processing time for a colour print material to be 30 minutes or more, which entailed the use of very large processing machines to meet the rapidly increasing demand for colour prints. With RC paper the processing sequence could be reduced to about 10 minutes, and a photofinisher could double or treble the output from the same machine, without the bother of glazing the paper.

So much attention was given to the urgent requirements of the photofinisher that the advantages of a black-and-white RC paper were largely overlooked until Ilford introduced the Ilfospeed system in 1974. Since then, more and more photographers have come to realise the great convenience of polyethylene-coated papers.

Producing a paper laminated on both sides with thin layers of polyethylene is a difficult manufacturing job, requiring quite different methods and equipment from those used for the liquid coating of baryta and gelatin, or for that matter from the solvent coating of lacquer that had sometimes been used to produce earlier 'waterproof' photographic paper base. Polyethylene was chosen for a number of reasons, including the facts that it is impermeable to water, is relatively cheap and readily available, can be coated by extrusion, is inert to most chemicals and solvents, is flexible, and can be made to adhere to both paper and an emulsion layer.

In manufacture, both sides of the paper are coated with polyethylene in one pass through the laminating machine. The web of paper first runs beneath a slot through which molten polyethylene is extruded, and is drawn over a cooling roller to solidify the resin and impart the required surface texture to facilitate writing on the back of finished prints. The web then passes to the second extrusion head, where another layer of polyethylene, this time containing a white pigment such as titanium oxide, is applied to what will be the emulsion side of the paper. This second polyethylene layer is solidified on a cooling roller, which also adds one of the characteristic glossy, silk or 'pearl' textures to the surface.

As produced by the manufacturer, the surfaces of a polyethylene-coated paper base are hydrophobic and would not accept an aqueous photographic emulsion layer. This problem has

28

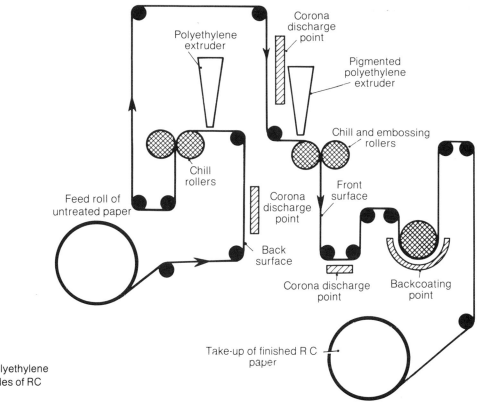

Polyethylene extruder

Corona discharge point

Pigmented polyethylene extruder

Chill and embossing rollers

Chill rollers

Front surface

Feed roll of untreated paper

Corona discharge point

Back surface

Corona discharge point

Backcoating point

Take-up of finished R C paper

Application of polyethylene layers to both sides of RC paper

been solved not by application of any intermediate subbing layer but by irradiating the surface of the polyethylene layer with a high-voltage electrical discharge. This 'corona' discharge is thought to create superficial oxidation of the surface of the polyethylene, producing a layer of hydrophylic oxides to which the emulsion can bind.

In many respects a print made on RC paper is likely to have a longer life than one made on baryta-coated paper. The removal of residual chemicals, particularly the by-products of the fixing process, can be achieved much more easily when the base paper itself has not absorbed any of the fixing solution. This fact led many people, including the photographic paper manufacturers, to believe that the use of RC papers would provide prints with a longer life than could be obtained with other papers processed in the same way. However, after RC papers had been in use for a few years, signs began to appear that under certain circumstances black-and-white prints made on RC paper could deteriorate in unexpected ways. The image could discolour or 'bronze' in local areas, and the image layer and the underlying polyethylene layer could crack in much the same way as an old oil painting will sometimes craze.

29

Although not by any means widespread, these unexpected and at first unexplained effects with RC papers naturally caused a great deal of concern among both users and manufacturers. Investigations into the causes of the two forms of deterioration commenced immediately, and Ilford were soon able to understand the mechanism causing the occasional bronzing of RC prints and to introduce improvements to minimise the risk of any recurrence of the problem. In collaboration with Wiggins Teape, Ilford also investigated the causes of cracking of image/polyethylene layers under some conditions of display. Here again, corrective modifications were made, this time to the polyethylene, and it can now be said that on the evidence of very severe accelerated-ageing tests, the modified base does not deteriorate. See also page 276.

Emulsions for paper

Printing papers made with a silver halide emulsion were first introduced as long ago as 1874, although the product made by the Liverpool Dry Plate Company was reported to be rather unsatisfactory. This is not altogether surprising since they used the same emulsion as for their dry plates. A slower paper called 'Alpha' was introduced by Ilford in 1886, and its less sensitive gelatino-chloride emulsion would have made it more suitable for contact printing.

Most paper emulsions contain a significant proportion of silver chloride together with silver bromide, the ratios commonly varying between 75 per cent chloride and 25 per cent bromide and vice versa. Although less sensitive than silver bromide, silver chloride develops more quickly and is therefore more suitable for printing papers.

In general, photographic papers use much finer-grained emulsions than are necessary for camera-speed films. Since a high speed is not normally required of papers, the emulsion-making procedures differ in several ways from those used for negative emulsions. A paper emulsion is designed to have optimum performance at exposures of about 10 seconds, while a camera-film emulsion is optimised at exposures of about one-hundredth of a second.

The method of precipitation of halides for a paper emulsion will usually require much shorter addition times than are used for a negative material requiring a wide range of grain sizes (see page 16).

Some paper emulsions are made without a washing stage, since baryta-coated base paper can serve as a 'sink' for any excess salts left in the emulsion. Now that so much paper is laminated with polyethylene, however, it is necessary to remove the soluble

30

chlorides or bromides. In any case, most emulsion-making procedures now involve a flocculation stage after which the supernatant liquid, containing most of the excess salts, is simply poured away.

Paper emulsions have a much higher gelatin-to-silver ratio than film emulsions because of the surface characteristics required in a print. A proportion of latex can be used to replace some of the gelatin in a paper emulsion, to lessen the tendency for the paper to curl (see below).

These differences between positive and negative emulsions do not necessarily make it easier to produce a good emulsion for a printing paper than one for a negative material. In fact, there are a number of important requirements associated with paper emulsions that need not concern the maker of camera-speed emulsions. For example, with the exception of variable-contrast papers, a series of different contrast grades must be produced for each type of paper; Ilford was the first manufacturer to accept the condition that all grades (except grade 5) should have the same effective printing speed.

In the case of a printing paper, contrast is the rate at which density increases with exposure, and is largely determined at the time of precipitation of the silver halides, shorter addition times producing higher-contrast results. Fortunately, even with a given grain-size distribution, the contrast of an emulsion can be further modified by the addition of a variety of substances, including copper, cadmium or rhodium salts. Rhodium, for instance, has a preferential desensitising effect on large grains, thereby increasing effective contrast when added to an emulsion.

Variable-contrast papers used to depend upon the use of two emulsions with different colour sensitivity and different contrast characteristics. In the case of Ilfospeed Multigrade, one emulsion was blue-sensitive and high-contrast, the other was green-sensitive and low-contrast. (The idea would of course still work if either the contrast or the colour sensitivity characteristics were changed over). The two emulsions could be coated as superimposed layers, but in the case of Multigrade they were mixed together and coated in one layer. When blue light is used to expose a print the result is a high-contrast image (roughly equivalent to grade 4 paper), while if green light is used the resulting image is soft (much the same as it would be on a grade 0 paper). By varying the proportion of blue and green exposing light, with the aid of suitable filters, any contrast between the two extremes can be obtained. The two emulsions used for Multigrade not only provided the required contrast range but were also designed to produce the same image colour throughout that range.

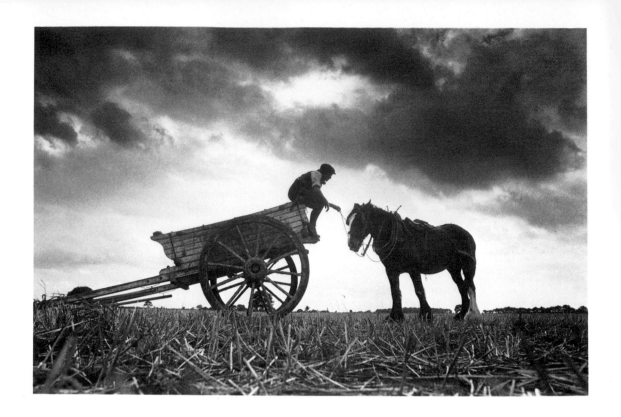

Another way of ensuring a constant image colour with a variable-contrast paper is to use the same basic emulsion for both components, and to depend upon a difference in speed rather than a difference in contrast to provide the necessary contrast range. If part of an emulsion is sensitised to green light while the other part remains blue-sensitive, the sensitised component is effectively faster than the other part and their characteristic curves are separated along the exposure axis. Then, by using filtered light to control the proportions of the faster and the slower components that are exposed, different combinations of their characteristic curves combine to produce 'hard' or 'soft' results.

The image colour of a finished print must be carefully chosen to suit the preferences of each particular market. The colour of the image is partly determined by the grain size of the emulsion, which in turn depends very much upon the choice and ratio of the halides used and the conditions of their precipitation. Image colour can also be modified by the addition of selected organic stabilisers.

In addition to Ilfospeed being made in six grades of contrast, five of them at the same speed and all of them having the same image colour, there are several other characteristics that must be built-in to such a product. In order to ensure good keeping properties, an organic stabiliser is added to the emulsion. To

Larry Bartlett used Multigrade paper for this print of John Downing's picture 'At the end of the day'

32

permit handling in dishes or trays as well as in automatic roller processors, the emulsion must be hardened with a hardening agent that is effective fairly quickly but does not make the emulsion brittle on storage. To ensure good spreading on the base during coating, and quick wetting when sheets are first immersed in a developer, a wetting agent is added to the emulsion and the supercoat.

Although the surface character of a printing paper is largely determined at the time the baryta or polyethylene layer is added to the paper base, it is sometimes necessary to add starch or fine silica to the supercoat and the emulsion layer to produce a sufficiently matt surface on finished prints. Addition of a supercoat of gelatin to the emulsion layer does, of course, slightly increase the paper's tendency to curl. For this reason, both the emulsion and the anti-stress layers are kept to a minimum thickness and some of the gelatin may be replaced by latex. There is close collaboration between the paper-base maker and the photographic manufacturer to ensure that the back coating applied to the paper at the time of manufacture counteracts the swelling and shrinking characteristics of the emulsion layer as much as possible. There was a time when photographic papers could curl so badly that they sometimes burst the lid of their box when stored under very dry conditions. Modern papers such as Ilfospeed remain flat enough for many printers to use them without a paper easel.

So-called 'stabilisation' papers, such as Ilfoprint, were introduced around 1960. The advantage of processing a print by activation in an alkaline solution followed by treatment in a stabilising solution is the extremely short time it takes (about 20 seconds) and the very compact processing machine used. The disadvantages are that the prints are slightly damp when they emerge from the processor, and they are not stable. Nevertheless, where speed of access is important and the prints will be used promptly and only once, the activation/stabilising system is very attractive. A paper that can be 'developed' by a short immersion in an alkaline solution (usually based on sodium hydroxide with a pH of 14) is coated with an emulsion containing a developing agent such as hydroquinone. (Small amounts of hydroquinone are, in fact, often added as a stabiliser to ordinary printing papers but the quantities included in the emulsion of a stabilisation paper are much greater.) Ilfoprint emulsions are coated on a baryta-surfaced paper base so that residual processing chemicals, particularly ammonium thiocyanate from the stabiliser, can remain absorbed in the fibres of the paper and will not crystallise out in the surface of the print as they would if a polyethylene-coated paper base were used.

Apart from the fact that paper emulsions are not usually panchromatic and can therefore be coated under useful levels of safelighting, there is not much difference between the coating methods used for papers and those used for film, particularly now that so many papers are produced on non-absorbent base that behaves in many respects like film.

For many years, paper was coated by simply dipping one of its surfaces into a trough of emulsion as the web passed round a roller, but this method cannot be used at high speeds. Nowadays it is usual to coat paper either with an 'air-knife' to control thickness of the layer or with a 'slide-hopper' of the type used for film coating. The parent rolls of paper on which emulsion is coated are usually 600 metres (2000 feet) long and up to 1.4 metres (54 inches) wide. Coating speeds may reach 90 metres (300 feet) per minute.

After drying, samples are taken from each coated roll and tested sensitometrically before the roll is sent to the finishing department. There it is slit and chopped to the required sizes, and packed in envelopes or boxes. Samples of each coated batch are stored for future reference and can be referred to in the event of a complaint, provided that the customer can quote the batch number of the paper he was using.

Characteristics of plates and films

Strictly, an emulsion is a fine dispersion of one liquid in another, so the term photographic emulsion is really a misnomer. When the silver halide is initially precipitated in liquefied gelatin, it is in suspension; later, when the 'emulsion' is coated and dried, the silver halide crystals are dispersed in the gelatin; after processing, the solidified gelatin contains particles of reduced silver. Sometimes gelatin is replaced or augmented by synthetic alternatives such as polyvinyl alcohol or a latex, but all the negative and print materials considered in this book use emulsions that are wholly or mainly dependent on gelatin.

A grain of silver bromide can be thought of as a lattice-like arrangement of millions of silver and bromide ions. When such a silver halide grain is exposed to the light, no visible change takes place. Nevertheless, it is believed that a number of atoms of silver are formed, although millions of unreduced silver ions may remain in any single grain. The silver atoms are thought to catalyse the reduction of the remaining silver ions in any 'triggered' grain when the emulsion is developed. This tremendous 'amplification' caused by development is the key to the outstanding superiority of the silver-halide recording mechanism over any other photo-chemical system.

Bill Cross of the *Daily Mail* had no chance of a second take of this shot, for which he used HP5 in a Nikon camera

34

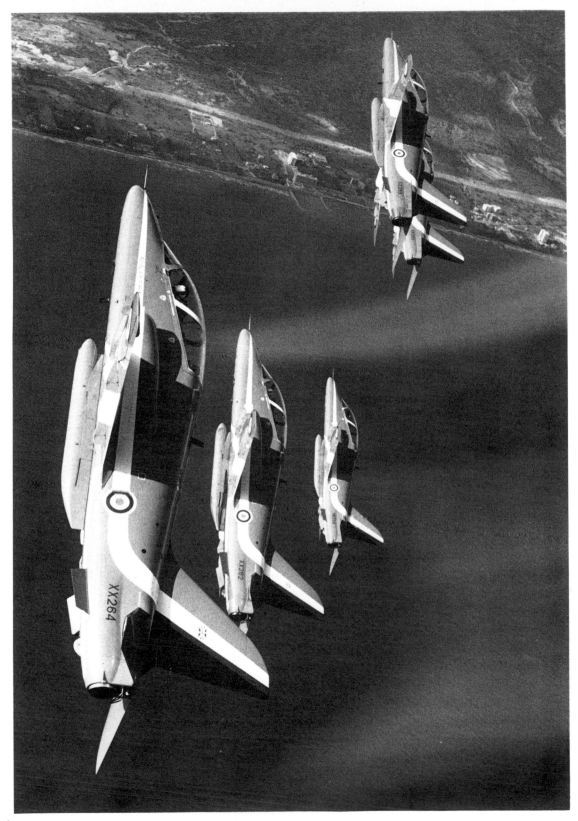

Gelatin is a very suitable vehicle in which to disperse silver halide grains for photographic purposes: it swells when immersed in aqueous solutions, thereby allowing the reacting chemicals easy access to the silver grains, and facilitating washing. A typical gelatin emulsion layer may swell to some ten times its original weight after immersion in a slightly acid (pH5) solution, and would swell almost twice as much in strongly acid (pH3) or alkaline (pH12) solutions. However, even though most developers are quite strongly alkaline, and most fixers quite strongly acid, the presence of dissolved salts in them tends to restrict swelling. Nevertheless, it is sometimes necessary to add a gelatin hardening agent to one of the processing solutions.

Temperature also affects the swelling of wet gelatin. This means not only that emulsion layers will melt in processing solutions that are too hot, but also that the temperature during the early stages of drying must be controlled if the whole emulsion layer is not to melt and even slide off its support.

Photographic negative materials depend upon there being a strong enough attachment between the emulsion layer and the glass or film support to resist the tendency of the gelatin to swell laterally during processing. If the bond between an emulsion layer and its support is not strong enough to withstand movement between the two, reticulation may occur. Reticulation can vary in degree from a just discernible 'matting' of the surface to large-scale 'crinkling' through the whole thickness of the emulsion layer. A frequent cause of reticulation is the use of washing water at too high a temperature in relation to the temperature of the preceding processing solutions.

Characteristics of the glass or film base   Assuming that the bond between an emulsion layer and its support does not break down, the dimensional stability of any image in the layer is dependent on the characteristics of the base on which it was coated. When it is essential for there to be the least possible difference between the size and shape of the optical image formed in the camera and the subsequent photographic image, glass should be used as the emulsion support. Lateral stability is sometimes not in itself sufficient to fulfil certain scientific requirements for which flatness of the emulsion surface may be critically important. In such cases, specially selected glass must be used.

When flexible film was first used as a support for photographic emulsions, it was made from cellulose nitrate. This had poor chemical stability and was flammable. It was largely replaced in the 1920s by the safer cellulose acetate. However, bases made from cellulose esters also have disadvantages; in particular, they

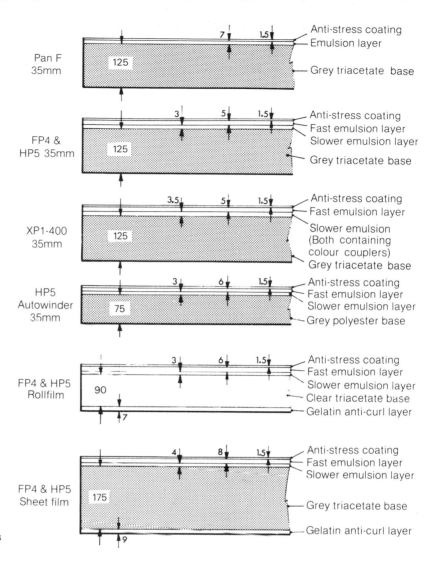

Pan F
35mm

Anti-stress coating
Emulsion layer
Grey triacetate base
125
7
1.5

FP4 &
HP5 35mm

Anti-stress coating
Fast emulsion layer
Slower emulsion layer
Grey triacetate base
125
3
5
1.5

XP1-400
35mm

Anti-stress coating
Fast emulsion layer
Slower emulsion
(Both containing
colour couplers)
Grey triacetate base
125
3.5
5
1.5

HP5
Autowinder
35mm

Anti-stress coating
Fast emulsion layer
Slower emulsion layer
Grey polyester base
75
3
6
1.5

FP4 & HP5
Rollfilm

Anti-stress coating
Fast emulsion layer
Slower emulsion layer
Clear triacetate base
Gelatin anti-curl layer
90
3
6
1.5
7

FP4 & HP5
Sheet film

Anti-stress coating
Fast emulsion layer
Slower emulsion layer
Grey triacetate base
Gelatin anti-curl layer
175
4
8
1.5
9

Cross-sections (not to
scale) of the Ilford range of
black-and-white films;
dimensions in micrometres

are not sufficiently stable for use in applications where precision of
image size is important. A much more stable base can be made
from a polyester such as polyethylene terephthalate, which, in the
form of a fibre, we know as Terylene. This material was first used
as a support for emulsions in the graphic arts business, where the
increasing demand for colour reproduction required the accurate
registration of the separated images. While not as resistant as glass
to dimensional changes after processing, polyester base is a great
deal better in this respect than cellulose triacetate.

Another property of the polyester base that distinguishes it from
earlier film base materials is its great strength, often an advantage
but sometimes a disadvantage. A 72-exposure length of Ilford HP5
Autowinder film has such great tensile strength that it cannot be
torn by hand, even though it is only 75 μm (0.003 in) thick.

Because of this, there has been a reluctance to use polyester-based film in either cinematography or 35 mm still photography: such a strong film could cause damage to camera mechanisms if it should jam, and could also cause trouble in certain kinds of continuous processing machines by not breaking when under excessive tension. Nevertheless, it seems likely that in time fail-safe clutch mechanisms will be incorporated in both cameras and processors so that polyester film base can eventually become standard throughout photography.

One great advantage that all film supports have over glass is their freedom from accidental breakage. On the other hand, only one surface of a glass plate is likely to be damaged by scratching, whereas both surfaces of a negative on a film base are susceptible to abrasion. While the emulsion surface of a photographic film is usually more prone to be scratched than the base itself, the fact remains that it is all too easy for 'tram-line' scratches to occur on the back of a 35 mm film because particles were trapped between the film and the pressure plate of the camera. Roll films do not suffer in this way because they are protected by a backing paper, although they can still be scratched during processing or even in an enlarger. Damage to the emulsion side of a film often occurs during processing, when the gelatin is swollen and soft so that accidental digs or scratches can even remove part of the image. Hardening the gelatin layer during processing goes some way towards improving its scratch resistance, although some hardeners have a limited effect until the layer has been dried.

When a film or a plate is to be dried after processing, it is usually only the water retained in the emulsion layer that has to be removed. Roll and sheet films, with their clear gelatin backing layer, are the exception. The drying process can be accelerated in several ways. The usual method is to direct a flow of warm air across the surface of the negative. In special cases it is also possible to replace the water in the gelatin layer or layers with a more volatile liquid, such as methyl alcohol. The rate at which a processed film is dried and the conditions during drying can affect the density of the final image; this can be particularly noticeable if there is any interruption or abrupt change of conditions during the course of drying.

Characteristics of negative emulsions It is fairly well understood that the characteristics of a photographic negative material, in terms of its speed, contrast and resolution, can be accurately predicted only if it is exposed and processed in a precisely specified way; but if it is to be judged by the kind of print it produces, the performance of a negative also depends upon the way it is printed.

38

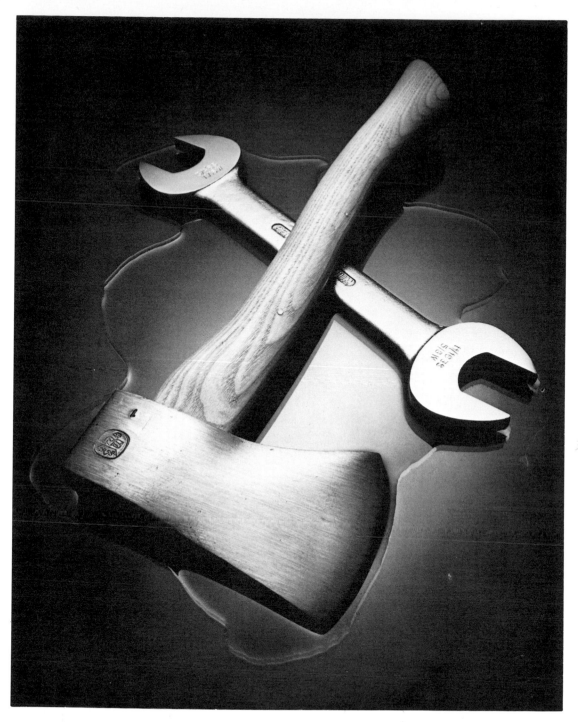

Frank Farrelly used Pan F
film in a Hasselblad camera
to ensure the textural
quality that makes this
picture

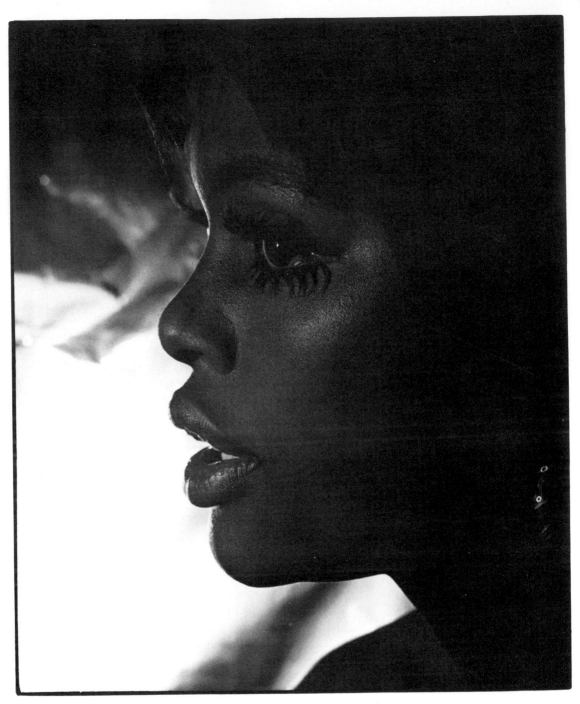

This close-up profile is
skilfully lit by Michael
Barnett, and the skin of the
girl is beautifully rendered;
FP4 rollfilm was used

40

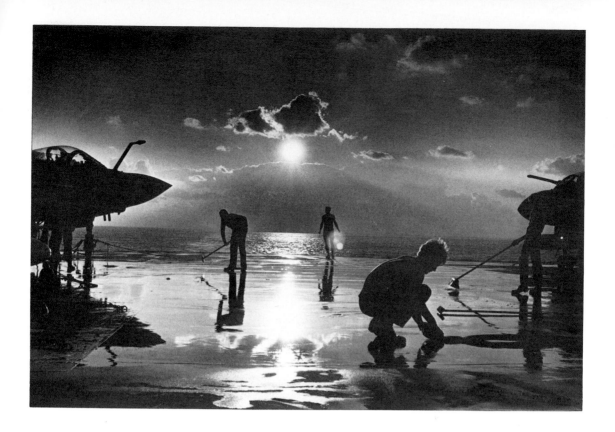

Only when you have a good printer behind you can you be sure that a shot into the sun like this will be translated into a successful print. Larry Bartlett did the printing from John Downing's negative on 35 mm HP5 film

Nevertheless, because most camera films are exposed, processed and printed in similar ways, a useful idea of the characteristics of a silver-image black-and-white film can be gained simply from its rated speed.

The introduction of Ilford XP1–400 film has dramatically altered the traditional relationship between speed and graininess. But leaving aside for the moment the special properties of XP1 film, silver-image negative films have, over the years, divided themselves into three broad groups. The Ilford products in these groups are Pan F (ISO 50/18°), FP4 (ISO 125/22°) and HP5 (ISO 400/27°).

What does an ISO speed rating of 400/27° really mean? To understand any of the several methods of assessing emulsion speed and sensitivity, it is necessary to have some understanding of the ways in which the image-forming characteristics of photographic materials are measured.

Sensitometry   Manufacturers assess their emulsions by making sensitometric measurements of the processed photographic image. Put simply, sensitometry is the measurement of the relationship between cause (exposure) and effect (density) in a photographic system.

41

During the decade between 1876 and 1886, photography underwent a complete revolution owing to the introduction of gelatin dry plates. The great variety of speeds of these new emulsions made them so different from the collodion wet plate, with its predictable sensitivity, that the problem of estimating exposure suddenly became much more difficult.

Dissatisfaction with its imprecision was one of the principal reasons given by Vero Charles Driffield for his partner, Dr Ferdinand Hurter, remaining interested in the photographic process. Driffield explained: 'In 1876 I induced Dr Hurter to take up photography as a recreation, but to a mind accustomed like his to methods of scientific precision, it became intolerable to practice an art which at that time was so entirely governed by rule-of-thumb, and of which the fundamental principles were so little understood. It was agreed that we should jointly undertake an investigation with the object of rendering photography a quantitative science.' This they did, and the evidence is to be found in their collected papers entitled *Photographic Researches of Hurter and Driffield*. One section of this, 'Photo-chemical Investigations and a New Method of Determination of the Sensitiveness of Photographic Plates', laid the foundation for photographic sensitometry.

Having constructed an actinometer with which to assess the amount of light available for exposure, Hurter and Driffield turned their attention to devising an apparatus with which they could measure the light-stopping capacity of any part of a developed silver image. They chose to express their measurements in terms of density rather than transmittance, because density can be considered as a measure of the amount of silver deposited.

So what is density? Suppose a piece of material (an optical filter for example) allows only one-tenth of the light reaching one side of it to emerge on the other side. If we lay another sheet of the same material on the first one, we find that only one-hundredth of the incident light emerges from the combined layers. Adding a third sheet allows only one-thousandth of the light to pass through all three layers. These figures, which disregard such secondary

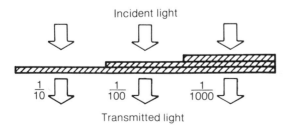

Incident light

Transmitted light

Reduction of light after passing through one, two and three layers of filter effects as scatter and intersurface reflections, can be presented and extended in tabular form:

Number of layers	Ratio of transmitted to incident light (transmittance)	Relative light-stopping power (opacity)	Logarithm of opacity (density)
1	1/10	10	1
2	1/100	100	2
3	1/1000	1000	3

The first column of the table can be considered as being directly proportional to the amount of silver deposited in a photographic image. The second column shows the light-passing power (or transmittance) progressively decreasing as the amount of silver increases. The third column shows the reciprocal of transmittance, i.e. the light-stopping power or opacity of the silver deposits. Hurter and Driffield decided that the most suitable and manageable value to use in their sensitometric studies would be that in the fourth column of the table: the logarithm of the opacity of a silver deposit, which they called its density.

Opacity is preferable to transmittance because its value increases as the deposit of silver grows; the logarithm of opacity is still better because a logarithmic series corresponds closely to the way in which the human eye perceives differences in light intensity.

Having decided upon density as the measure of the light-stopping power of a negative image, Hurter and Driffield

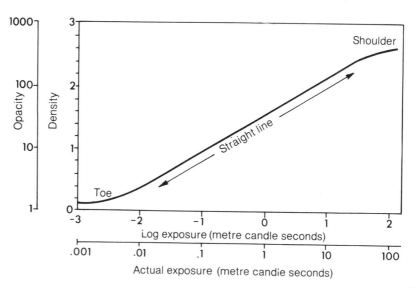

Idealised H and D curve

43

introduced a graphical representation of the rate of change of density with increasing exposure. At first they plotted the densities against the actual exposures (in candle-metre-seconds) that had been given to a particular emulsion, but they soon found that density increases rapidly at first as exposure is increased, and then ever more slowly towards a limit that they did not reach with that method of representation.

By plotting the logarithms of the exposures (instead of the actual exposures) against the density, they created a far more informative representation, and were able to show that if exposure is increased beyond a certain point, densities begin to decrease.

Perhaps without realising the full implications, Hurter and Driffield had shown the way in which the characteristic curve of any photographic material would subsequently be drawn. It is only fitting therefore that some people still speak of the 'H and D' curve of a negative or print emulsion, although others now refer to it as the 'D−log E' curve.

Sensitometers   There are several ways in which precise and reproducible exposures can be imparted to a light-sensitive material, but broadly they can be divided into time-scale and intensity-scale methods. In a time-scale sensitometer, a series of

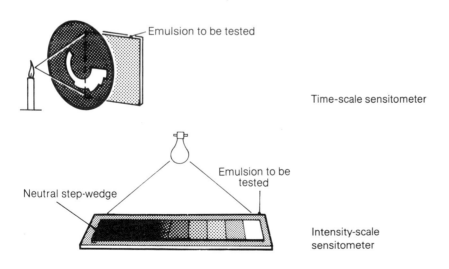

Emulsion to be tested

Time-scale sensitometer

Neutral step-wedge

Emulsion to be tested

Intensity-scale sensitometer

exposures of different duration are given. Hurter and Driffield achieved this by rotating a sector wheel in front of the emulsion to be tested, so that the wheel interrupted light from a candle placed one metre from the surface of the plate.

An intensity-scale instrument, which may simply be a neutral step-wedge, provides a single precisely controlled exposure at a range of different light intensities. This method more closely

44

resembles the way in which most photographic materials are used, but for results to have greater significance the actual time of exposure given to a sensitometric test strip should be similar in duration to the kind of exposure the film or plate will receive in practical use. Generally this means that negative materials are exposed in an intensity-scale sensitometer for between $1/20$ and $1/100$ second.

Densitometers   The densitometer used by Hurter and Driffield was based on a Bunsen grease-spot photometer, with which light from two different sources can be compared and matched as two halves of a circular spot. For many years optical comparison in a matching field was the principle on which densitometers were built and used, but as photo-electric sensing devices became

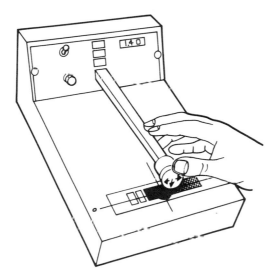

Transmission densitometer
with digital readout

reliable they were adopted in densitometry. Today, photo-electric densitometers are far more sensitive and can cover a much wider range of densities than the earlier optical instruments; furthermore they are consistent, although as with any other measuring instrument a densitometer should be checked against a standard from time to time.

It is now generally accepted that the densities of photographic images are best measured using diffuse rather than specular light. Diffuse density is obtained when all the light transmitted by a sample is collected and evaluated. By comparison, specular density is the result obtained if only the light that emerges at right angles to the sample is measured, and none of the scattered light. In 1890 Hurter and Driffield had lengthy arguments with Sir William Abney about the importance of scattered light in densitometry. In

45

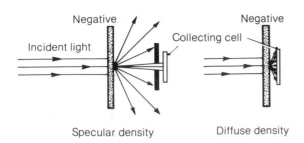

Specular density   Diffuse density

Optical arrangements for measuring specular and diffuse densities

retrospect we can see that Abney was right to argue that light scatter can be significant when measuring the density of a photographic image.

Speed rating methods Perhaps the most important discovery made by Hurter and Driffield was that there is (or was with the plates of that time) a linear relationship between the logarithms of exposure and the resulting densities over a very useful range of exposures. Four separate regions of exposure were recognised: underexposure, correct representation, overexposure and reversal. Today, the first three of these regions of the characteristic curve of an emulsion are more often referred to as the toe, straight-line and shoulder of the curve. Reversal, or solarisation, is rarely met and is not usually considered.

Hurter and Driffield's method of assessing the speed of the plates they examined was simply to extend the straight-line portion of the characteristic curve of the material until it reached the log exposure axis. They called this point the 'inertia point' and noted that it is unaffected by development. To convert the inertia value in metre-candle-seconds to a speed number, it was simply divided into 34; thus a plate with an inertia value of $\frac{1}{5}$ second would be said to have an H and D speed of 170 ($34 \div \frac{1}{5}$).

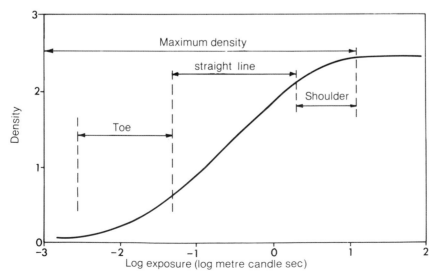

Characteristic curve obtained by plotting density against the logarithm of exposure

46

When manufacturers began to use double-coating techniques, and plates and films became faster, it became difficult to discern a straight line in the characteristic curves of emulsions that have an extended toe. Such a toe is quite important in practical use, but would be ignored by the H and D method of speed rating. It was therefore necessary to devise more precise ways of determining the speed of a negative emulsion. Over the years, many different methods have been proposed and adopted, including the Scheiner, DIN and Weston systems. In 1939, Lloyd A. Jones in the United States proposed that the effective camera speed of an emulsion be expressed in terms of an exposure that is some function of gradient. Jones took this view because: 'Tone reproduction theory indicates that there is only one characteristic of the negative curve that is significant in expressing the capacity of the material to reproduce brightness differences, and it is upon the way in which brightness differences are reproduced that the quality of the final positive must depend.'

Jones and his co-worker Nelson based their recommendations on a great deal of practical work, coupled with the large-scale subjective judgement of prints made from under- and overexposed negatives of typical amateur subjects. Their early proposals led to both the American Standards Association and the British Standards Institution adopting the same methods of speed rating. However, the original DIN system remained in use in Germany, and it was not until the early 1960s that a single international system was agreed. Speed ratings can now be exactly converted between arithmetic (ASA, BS) and logarithmic (DIN) systems; in fact the ISO system gives both the arithmetic and logarithmic ratings (e.g. ISO 400/27°). An ISO speed rating is obtained from

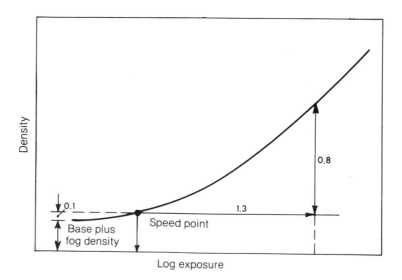

Measurement points for determining ISO speed rating of pictorial negative material (based on 1/20 to 1/80 second exposure)

the characteristic curve of a material after developing samples of it in a specified metol-hydroquinone developer so that a density of 0.8 above the speed point (taken as fog plus base density of 0.1) is obtained at the high-density end of a 1.3 (20:1) log exposure range.

Fog density and base density   In any negative emulsion, some silver halide grains that have not been exposed to light will be reduced by development. These spontaneously developed grains give rise to a level of unwanted density that is known as fog. Since the fog is uniform throughout the whole area of the negative, it has little effect on subsequent image formation, but merely extends printing times and makes a negative look denser that it otherwise would. Fog density increases with development time, and it will go on increasing after all the light-struck grains have been developed. Typically, the fog density for a fast negative material is about 0.1.

The base of a 35 mm film incorporates a neutral density to reduce halation. This base density combined with emulsion fog density often totals a density of 0.2, which can be discounted in sensitometry by quoting density measurements above 'base plus fog'. The subject brightness range of 20:1 that is used in the ANSI standard might be considered very low, but it does include estimated losses due to camera lens flare – one of several variables that serve as a reminder that absolute speed rating is for the sensitometrist and not for the photographer.

Gamma   In any discussion about negative quality the term 'gamma' is likely to crop up, although its meaning is often not understood. Gamma is a measure of the degree or extent of development. There is no guarantee, if a film is developed strictly according to instructions to achieve a gamma of say 0.65, that the resulting negatives will yield good prints. Much will depend upon the subject, its lighting, the negative exposure and, most important, the way in which the negatives are printed.

To be precise, gamma (γ) is the slope of the straight-line portion of the D–log E curve, and is obtained by taking the tangent of the angle formed by extending the straight-line part of a characteristic curve to meet the log E axis. In the simple case of a straight line at 45° to the exposure axis, the negative would have been developed to a gamma value of 1.0 (tan 45 = 1.0).

Modern negative materials, however, do not have such straight-line sections in their characteristic curves as did the emulsions of Hurter and Driffield's day; much more use is made nowadays of the foot or toe part of the curve in order to achieve maximum film speed.

Average gradient   If there is no straight line present in a characteristic curve, gamma cannot be deduced. Instead, an average slope or gradient, called the 'G-bar' ($\bar{G}$), is used. This can be found by drawing a line between the two points on the curve that are considered to mark the limits of useful shadow and highlight recording. When this line is extended to the log E axis, the intersection gives a $\bar{G}$ instead of a gamma value. The term 'contrast index' is also used as a measure of the ratio of subject brightness range to negative density range.

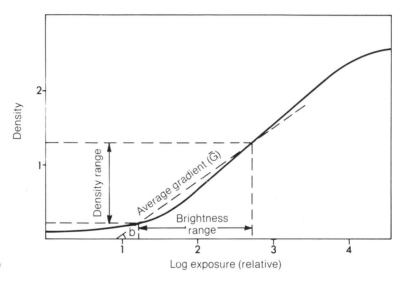

Average gradient = density range/brightness range of subject = tangent of angle b

Ilford Limited publish curves showing how $\bar{G}$ values vary with different development times and with various negative developers. Once a suitable $\bar{G}$ value has been found by experience to suit a particular set of conditions (which will include subject matter as well as lighting and printing conditions), a time/contrast curve facilitates adjustments in development time when any of the conditions is changed.

Gamma infinity   It can be seen from a set of extended time/gamma or time/$\bar{G}$ curves that, beyond a certain time of development, the rate of change in contrast slows down until a point is reached beyond which there is no further change in image density. If development is continued beyond this time, known as gamma-infinity, the continued growth of fog reduces the effective density range of the negative. It is not often necessary to develop continuous-tone negatives to gamma-infinity, but that is what Bert Hardy once did after he had photographed Londoners in Underground air-raid shelters in 1940. Here is his story.

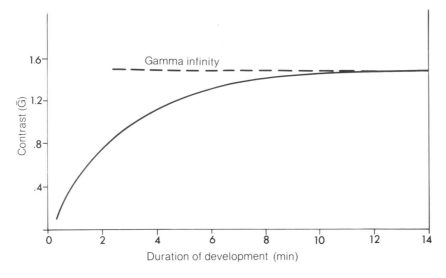

Change in contrast with increasing development time for a negative material

'I'd got four films to develop and I developed in a Correx tank in a developer I made up myself. I called it Super Soup! I used to put two films in the Correx tank, back to back, and the developing time was approximately 15 minutes for Agfa Ultra film. Well, I decided that 15 minutes wouldn't be long enough, so I gave them half-an-hour (this was now round about eleven or twelve o'clock at night) and I looked at the film in the dark green light. Not a bloody sausage on 'em! Not a bloody thing! Well, I felt dreadful. My first commissioned job! So I put them back in again and gave them another half an hour; so they've had an hour! Then I pulled them out and gave them another quick look, and there's the tiniest pinpoint! I popped them back in, shut the office up, and walked over Blackfriars Bridge to my mum's. Then I made myself a cup of tea and sat there in an armchair by the remains of the fire for about an hour and a half or more, after which I walked back to the office, by which time four hours had gone by. I didn't look at the films again, but chucked 'em straight into the hypo. When I fished them out they had something on them, but incredible contrast, fierce blacks and whites: they were like paintings, like Rembrandt's! And where Picture Post only wanted one page of my pictures to make up this ARP issue, they used four pages, and then they were sold to Life Magazine.'

That was development to gamma-infinity, and then some! Today we would call it 'push processing'.

Exposure latitude   The variation in exposure (usually expressed in *f*-stops) that can be made while still producing a printable negative is known as the exposure latitude of that particular material. The great exposure latitude of modern negative films such as FP4, HP5 or XP1 is enhanced by the fact that they have

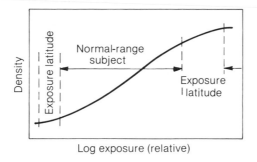

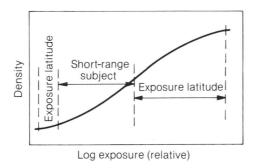

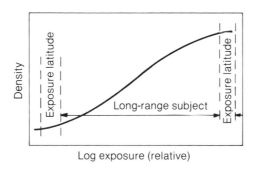

Dependence of exposure latitude on brightness range of subject

two emulsion layers: one has a high sensitivity to deal with minimum exposure, while the other is slower and can absorb excess exposure.

The exposure latitude of any photographic material depends largely upon the brightness range of the subject. However, the image quality of a print made from an overexposed negative is usually inferior, in sharpness and graininess, to a print made from an adequately exposed negative. XP1 film is an exception, in that an exposure up to some four times the 'correct' one does not result in increased grain. An explanation of this surprising fact is given on page 56–57.

Reciprocity effects When Hurter and Driffield carried out their earlier sensitometric work, they maintained that: 'All photo-chemical investigations which have hitherto been made have proved that the amount of chemical action is proportional to the "exposure" (i.e. the product of intensity of light and time).' It is unlikely that this was strictly the case with the plates they examined, and it is certainly not true of the film and paper products we use today.

Unfortunately it cannot be assumed that a photographic emulsion will respond in a strictly proportional way to any combination of intensity and duration of exposure. A very short exposure given at a large lens aperture may not produce the same negative densities as a longer exposure at a calculated equivalent smaller aperture. This inability of some photographic materials to meet theoretical expectations is known as failure to comply with the reciprocity law.

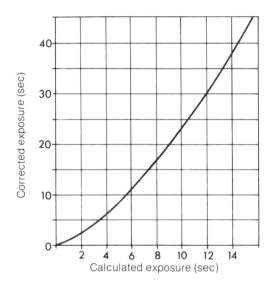

Corrections necessary when exposing HP5 or FP4 film for times longer than one second

There are two forms of reciprocity failure. One results when a sensitive material is exposed to a higher light intensity than would normally be the case, and the other when exposures are made at very low light levels. When an emulsion is designed to be exposed for times between, say, $\frac{1}{10}$ and $\frac{1}{100}$ second, it can happen that the same film would require the equivalent of two or three times as much exposure at very high light intensities, and as much as ten times the calculated exposure at very low intensities. Clearly reciprocity failure can be a nuisance.

Intermittency effect   As an indirect consequence of reciprocity failure in a photographic emulsion, we sometimes have to recognise the intermittency effect, because of which it is not always possible to achieve the same result by giving an emulsion a series of short exposures as it is by using a single longer one of the arithmetically equivalent duration.

Pushed to the limit in development and enlargement, small areas of a 35 mm negative on fast film such as HP5 inevitably yield prints displaying coarse grain. But the spirited action caught by A. Slater of PA Photos overrides such technical considerations

52

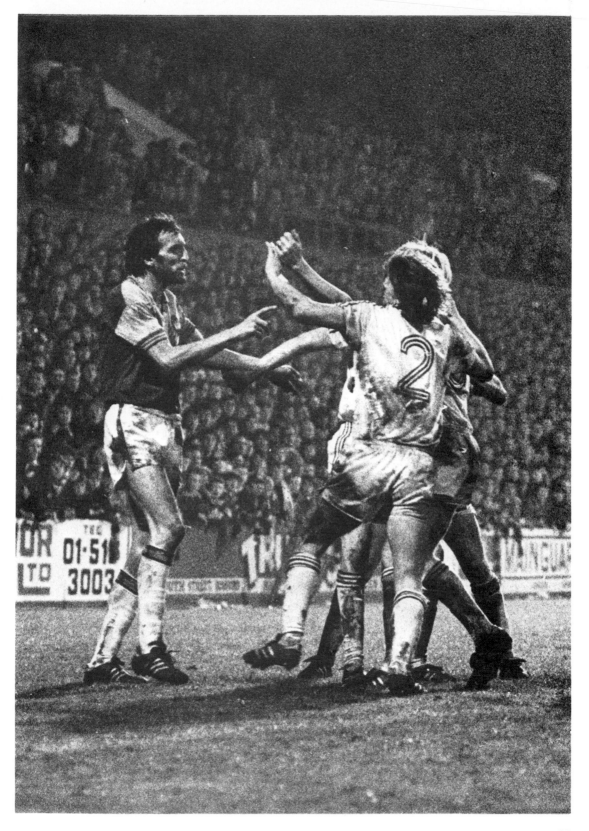

Photographic definition The subjective concept of definition can be said to be that quality of a photograph which determines its rendition of detail. Photographic definition depends upon a number of factors, including graininess, sharpness and resolving power.

Because the negatives used in their time were large, Hurter and Driffield never concerned themselves with a study of the graininess of photographic images. Interest in the subjective effects of granularity became serious with the advent of motion pictures and with the increasing use of ever-smaller image formats in still photography.

In general, the granularity of an emulsion increases as its sensitivity increases, and consequently the photographer's choice of film is usually a compromise between the film speed required for a job and the graininess of the resulting print. Special developers or development techniques can do little to compensate for this compromise. Use of a 'fine-grain' developer usually causes some loss in film speed, while an energetic developer, or extended development time, causes a relatively fine-grain emulsion to yield negatives with a coarser grain than they should have.

In practice, therefore, any photographer who wants to obtain the best possible print quality from a particular negative format should constantly ask himself whether he could use a slower film. Obviously some kinds of photography demand a high-speed emulsion, either because of fast-moving subjects or because the camera must always be loaded with film that can best deal with any eventuality. But the photographer who habitually uses HP5 (ISO 400/27°) with today's wide-aperture, short-focus lenses may find that he could have given adequate exposure in all cases with a slower film like FP4 (ISO 125/22°). Use of an even slower film, such as Pan F (ISO 50/18°), is more problematical. Such a slow emulsion can only suit jobs where light levels will be high or where exposures can be relatively long and perhaps made with the aid of a tripod.

Contrary to popular belief, the grainy or mealy appearance sometimes visible in a print made by ten or more times enlargement from a negative is not due to individual grains of silver being delineated, but to the random grouping or clumping of these grains.

So far as a negative material is concerned, there are two factors determining the sharpness of the recorded image: the size of the emulsion grains themselves, and the degree of light scatter that takes place within the emulsion layer during exposure. One way of minimising light scatter within an emulsion layer is to make the layer as thin as possible, as in high-resolution films such as Pan F.

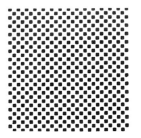

The same number of black squares (grains) uniformly distributed (top) and randomly distributed (bottom)

54

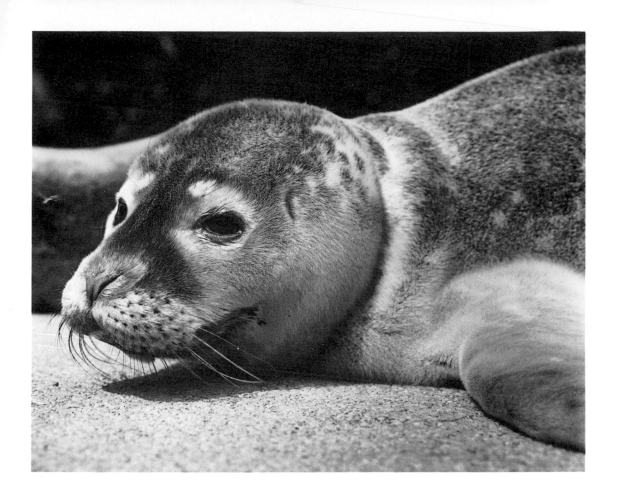

Carefully exposed, processed and printed (by Dave Batt from a 35 mm HP5 negative by Dave Stevens), this shot reminds us what superb resolution can be obtained with what used to be called a 'miniature' camera

Unfortunately, restricting the thickness of an emulsion layer tends to result in a lower coating weight, which necessarily reduces exposure latitude. Again a compromise has to be made. The photographer must decide which property he prefers to have: optimum image quality for a given size of negative, or the flexibility of exposure and the higher speed that comes with double-coated films such as FP4 and HP5.

Now that popular negative formats are so small, the photographer's assessment of the sharpness of a negative usually depends upon visual examination of a print made from it. For practical purposes this method serves quite well, provided that the subject matter includes areas of fine detail or some well-defined line of demarcation between areas of quite different density.

Adjacency effects   The sharpness of an image may sometimes be enhanced by what are known as adjacency effects during development. The mechanism can be more easily understood by reference to the image of a sharp edge. During development, the emulsion layer on the heavily exposed side of the edge will accumulate a high concentration of bromide as a by-product of the development reaction. Some of this soluble bromide will tend to migrate from the high-density side of the edge to the low-density, less exposed side, where it will inhibit development and minimise the resulting density along the border, producing what is known as

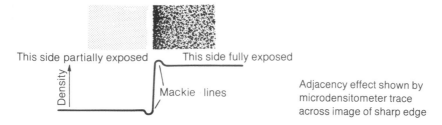

This side partially exposed   This side fully exposed

Density

Mackie lines

Adjacency effect shown by
microdensitometer trace
across image of sharp edge

a 'Mackie line'. Conversely, unused developer will tend to move from the less exposed side of the edge to the fully exposed side, where it will boost the density along the line adjacent to the border. This increase in density along one edge of a border, and the reduction of density along the other, improves the apparent sharpness of a print.

Much the same enhancement of sharpness is obtained by the use of development-inhibitor-release (DIR) couplers in XP1–400 film.

Exceptional properties of XP1–400   Not only does the chromogenic development of XP1–400 film allow the use of DIR couplers to enhance sharpness, but the fact that the final image is comprised of dye, not silver, gives rise to even more significant improvements in the performance of the film. As Geoffrey Crawley, Editor of the *British Journal of Photography*, has said: 'When XP1 was launched, the *Journal* described it as the most important development in black-and-white photography for a century, which remark had in mind the introduction of the gelatino-bromide process in the 1870s. Subsequent, more detailed, testing has only confirmed this statement, and Ilford Limited have succeeded in breaking the grain barrier previously evident at ASA 400. They have done this not by an "if and but" margin but by a degree at once apparent.' Crawley further said: 'At its optimum, it all but equals the best medium-speed film'.

This remarkable improvement in speed/graininess ratio is explained by the man behind XP1, Dr Jim Doyle. 'With opaque silver grains a grey patch can only be produced by leaving a proportion of the area completely uncovered by silver. Local fluctuations in density are high and perceived graininess is high. A grey patch of the same density can be produced from a much larger number of semi-transparent dye clouds with much smaller local fluctuations in density and lower graininess.

'The only method for reducing the graininess of conventional silver-image films is by reducing the area, not the opacity, of the developed grain. This is achieved either by making the silver halide grains smaller or by incompletely developing large grains. Both of these methods reduce speed, but the chromogenic method of reduced opacity does not.

'In XP1–400, development-inhibitor-releasing (DIR) couplers are used to restrict individual dye cloud densities and also enhance sharpness. In areas of high exposure large quantities of inhibitor are released and growth of density of individual grains is restricted. Inhibitor also diffuses to suppress the density of surrounding areas, providing a means of sharpness enhancement which is not available with conventional black-and-white development.'

From this it can be readily understood why, with XP1 film, the effects of development inhibition become greater as exposure is increased. Overexposure therefore leads to lower granularity rather than the increased granularity encountered when silver-image negatives are overexposed. The characteristic curve of XP1–400, with its long 'shoulder', also shows the influence of DIR couplers in that they prevent the build-up of excessive density as exposure increases.

The effective density of these two greatly enlarged and schematic representations of equivalent areas of an HP5 silver image (left) and an XP1 dye image (right) would be equal, but their apparent graininess is very different

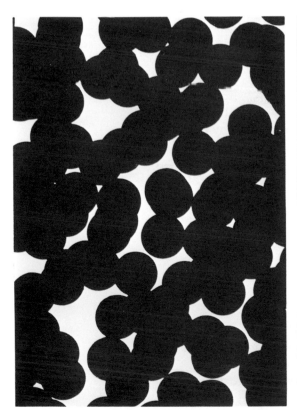 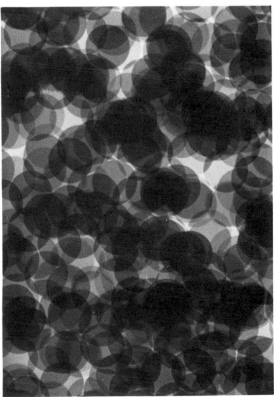

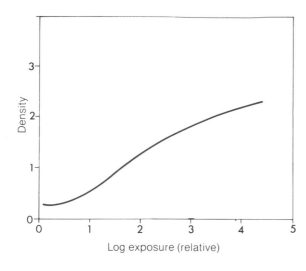

Characteristic curve of XP1-400 film; density readings were made through a tricolour blue filter

After completion of processing, an image on XP1 film is made up of a combination of balanced proportions of a yellow, a magenta and a cyan dye, so that the visual appearance of the negative is neutral and its printing performance is normal. Although not apparent to the eye, the absorption peaks of the three dyes can be detected in a spectral transmission curve of an XP1 negative.

Unlike most black-and-white negative materials, the emulsion side of XP1 film has a rather glossy surface, both before and after processing. This can cause difficulty for someone who is handling XP1 negatives for the first time, since he will not be able to simply place the film 'matt side down' in the negative carrier of the enlarger. Instead, he should merely ensure that the frame numbers along the edge of the film are right-reading when projected.

Because a dye image scatters very little light when it is being printed in an enlarger, there is no significant difference in contrast whether an XP1 negative is printed by means of specular or diffuse illumination. In other words the effective contrast of the negative will remain the same in any enlarger, because its Callier coefficient is about zero.

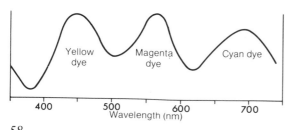

Spectral transmission of exposed and processed XP1-400 film

Characteristics of papers

The obvious difference between photographic film and paper is that the emulsion layers have been coated on quite different supports. Until relatively recently, almost all print materials merely had a layer of baryta between the paper and the emulsion. This meant that during processing a print absorbed something like its own weight of any aqueous solution in which it was immersed. After development and fixing, a protracted period of washing was therefore necessary if the photographic image was to remain stable after being dried. Washing times of 30 minutes for single-weight and 45 minutes for double-weight papers are commonly recommended.

Not only does a print made on unprotected paper base need careful washing, but its size is not the same after processing as it was when the printing exposure was made. The amount of expansion varies, and is not the same along the two dimensions of a print because of the direction of the paper fibres. Typically, a 20 × 25 cm (8 × 10 in) print may expand by 5 mm (0.2 in) along the shorter dimension and 8 mm (0.3 in) along the longer dimension. During drying a print may shrink to some extent, although if it is hot glazed it will retain its expanded size.

Fortunately, precision of image size is not often important in everyday photography, although it is essential for applications such as aerial mapping. For such specialised work, photographic papers with water-resistant coatings of polyethylene on both surfaces are much more suitable because they expand only about one-tenth as much as an unprotected paper: say 0.5 mm (0.02 in) on a 20 × 25 cm print.

Resin-coated (RC) papers also have the great advantage of requiring much shorter washing and drying times than fibre-based papers. (The term 'fibre-based' is often used to distinguish an unprotected paper base from the polyethylene-coated types, but it should be remembered that both materials depend upon paper as the principal component of the support.) One square metre of unprotected black-and-white paper of average base thickness will absorb something like 150 grams of developer or other aqueous processing solution in which it is immersed. The emulsion layer of a paper protected on both sides by polyethylene will take up only about one-tenth as much, thereby permitting washing and drying to be carried out in much shorter times.

When they were first introduced, resin-coated black-and-white papers were expected to prove superior to fibre-based papers in terms of their image stability. It was thought (quite rightly) that less processing solution would be absorbed by the prints; also, because washing the emulsion layers free from residual hypo would be easier when there had been no absorpton of chemicals by the paper base, it was expected that prints made on RC paper would last longer than prints on fibre-based papers.

The prediction that emulsion layers of RC prints would be better washed, and therefore less likely to contain residual thiosulphate, proved correct. However, another problem gradually revealed itself during the first few years in which black-and-white RC papers were used. It was found that, under certain conditions of display, some prints made on paper protected with polyethylene layers began to show signs of small surface cracks, not unlike the cracks or crazing that can be seen on some old oil paintings. This form of deterioration can happen to the surface of fibre-based prints, but not very often. Clearly it was essential to find out why the fault was more likely to occur with water-resistant papers.

Fortunately it did not take the paper manufacturers and Ilford Limited very long to discover that the cause of the crazing was the oxidation of the polyethylene layers by strong light and heat. Polyethylene layers are now stabilised against oxidation, and cracking should no longer occur.

Characteristics of the paper base Photographic printing papers are generally supplied in three base thicknesses, known as single-weight, medium-weight and double-weight. The thinnest has a paper base weight of about $100 \, g/m^2$, medium weight is about $180 \, g/m^2$, while double-weight (used for large prints and for exhibition purposes) is usually about $250 \, g/m^2$.

Since photographic paper is coated with emulsion on one side only, the paper will tend to curl with its emulsion side out when it is wetted. Then, if dried beyond a certain point, it will reverse its curl so that the emulsion side is concave. One of the more obvious ways of minimising curl is to ensure that the thickness of the emulsion layer, in terms of the gelatin coating weight, is held at a minimum. It is also possible to substitute a substance such as latex for a proportion of the gelatin. While behaving like gelatin in some respects, latex has less tendency to swell and shrink under changing humidities. Treatment of the back of the paper base at the time it is manufactured can also reduce its subsequent tendency to curl. Once a printer has used paper which remains flat throughout all the stages of making an enlargement, he will never tolerate the irritation and inconvenience of working with paper that curls, whether in the easel, on the baseboard of the enlarger or in the developing dish.

More black-and-white paper is sold with a glossy surface than any other kind. This is not surprising, because the maximum

60

densities obtainable with a glossy-surfaced paper are higher than can be achieved with a matt surface. Typically the maximum black of a glossy print on Ilfospeed 1M may reach a density of 2.0 or more, while a semi-matt paper such as Ilfospeed 24M may have a maximum density of 1.6 or 1.7. Between the extremes of glossy and matt, many print surfaces are possible. The appreciation and description of these are necessarily subjective, but in the case of Ilford papers they are called semi-matt, velvet-stipple and pearl.

Fifty years ago, Ansel Adams reported his discovery of the merits of glossy paper. 'I have finished, since starting to print on glossy paper, eighty-five prints. All new negatives: that is, those made last year but not printed, and a number of old favourites which have become new favourites, so incomparably finer do they register on glossy paper. It is a joy like unto making a first print, to reprint negatives I was tired of. No other surface is now to be thought of. I can print much deeper than heretofore, with no fear of losing shadows, or muddying half tones by drying down: or I can use a more contrasty grade of paper, resulting in amazingly rich blacks yet retaining brilliant whites.'

The back of a print made on Ilfobrom or Galerie paper has much the same surface properties as any other sheet of paper, and can be used for writing on or backstamping. A paper base that has been coated with polyethylene layers, however, does not accept ink without special treatment. The resin-coated paper base used for Ilfospeed and Multigrade papers has been treated so that the prints accept pencil, most ball-point pens, non-water-soluble felt-tipped pens, and any fast-drying stamp-pad inks.

Characteristics of paper emulsions   One of the principal differences between the emulsions used for black-and-white papers and those used for camera exposure materials is that papers have a restricted colour sensitivity. This insensitivity to yellow, orange and red light permits black-and-white paper to be handled under quite high levels of safe-lighting. This not only allows easy handling during exposure and processing but also enables the printer to exercise judgement of image quality during the course of development. A variable-contrast emulsion, such as Multigrade, has to be sensitive to green as well as blue light, but it can still be handled quite safely in light from a light-brown (Ilford 902) filter in front of a 15-watt lamp.

The ways in which printing papers are used and judged are quite different from the ways in which we expose films and use negatives, so the methods of assessing paper speeds are also different. At one time it was thought that it would be satisfactory to rate paper speeds on the basis of the exposure required to

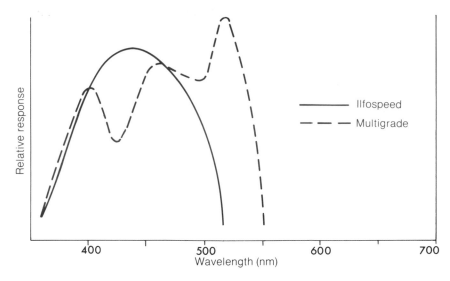

Sensitivities of
Ilfobrom/Ilfospeed and
Multigrade papers

produce a just-measurable density. This method might have been acceptable if there had been only one contrast grade of paper in use, but if two prints are made from the same negative, one on grade 1 paper and the other on grade 3 paper, then, if their highlight densities are matched, the print on grade 3 paper will appear to have been overexposed.

It has been found that the best compromise is to base the estimation of paper speeds on the exposure the paper requires to produce a mid-tone density of 0.6. In 1966 the ANSI standard PH2.2, *Sensitometry of Photographic Papers,* was introduced and has since been adopted by most manufacturers. This standard measures sensitivity with reference to a reflection density of 0.6, and a series of speed numbers is derived from the formula $S = 1000 \div E_{0.6}$, where S is the speed number and $E_{0.6}$ is the exposure (in metre-candle-seconds) required to produce a density of 0.6. The series of speed numbers is: 1, 1.2, 1.6, 2, 2.5, 3, 4, 5, 6, 8, 10, 12, 16, 20, 25, 32, 40, 50, 64, 80, 100, 125, 160, 200, 250, 320, 400, 500, 650, 800 and 1000. If a speed number is doubled, exposure of the paper is halved, in the same way as with the ASA method of film rating. Papers such as Ilfobrom and Ilfospeed have ratings of around 320, and Multigrade is still higher.

Because printing papers almost always fail to follow the reciprocity law, it is essential to use an intensity-scale sensitometer when studying their behaviour. Widely different exposure times could yield quite different results from those obtained in practical use of the paper. The duration of exposure recommended in the ANSI standard is within the range 0.1 to 10 seconds.

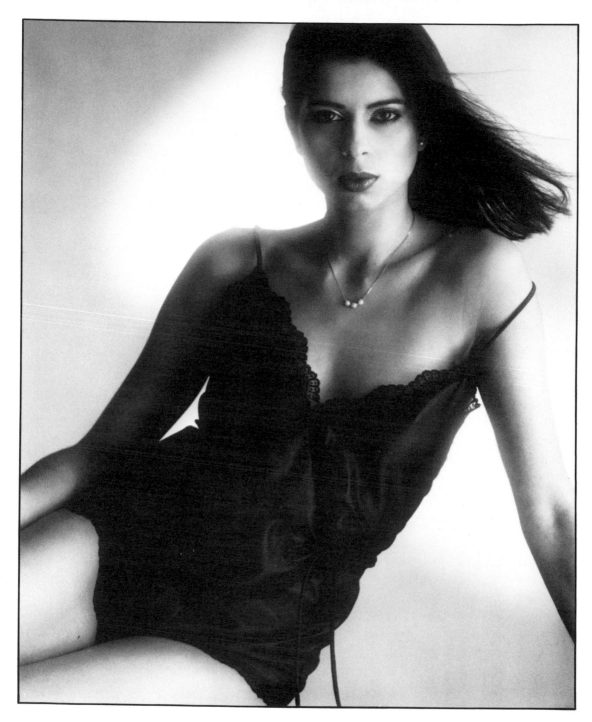

Retaining both the delicate
flesh tones and detail in the
black lingerie required
good teamwork between
Kevin Smith, the
photographer, and Mike
Campbell, who printed the
Pan F negative

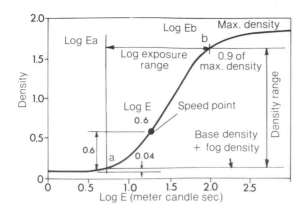

Measurement points for determining paper speed (ANSI)

In order for any system of speed rating to be useful, it is necessary to stipulate that the material being tested must be processed in a particular developer and in some specified way. This is just as important for papers as for films.

Development latitude   The development latitude of a paper can refer to one of two quite different characteristics. On the one hand, it can represent the extent to which prints can be successfully under- or overdeveloped in order to compensate for some departure from optimum exposure; conversely, it can refer to the extent by which development time or activity can be allowed to vary without significantly affecting print density.

Paper contrast   The contrast of a paper should not be thought of in the same way as the contrast of a negative material. In fact the term is something of a misnomer, since all 'contrast' grades of paper produce about the same density scale between the white of an unexposed area and the maximum black that the paper can give. The contrast of a printing paper can best be thought of as a measure of the rate of change in density with exposure. The more rapidly density increases as exposure increases, the more 'contrasty' the emulsion is said to be. In other words, printing exposure becomes more critical as the contrast of the paper increases. Ilfobrom and Ilfospeed papers are both made in six grades, rated from 0 to 5 in increasing contrast.

For a long time it was universally accepted that papers having different contrast characteristics would necessarily have different speeds. In other words, when a print was made on a grade 2 paper and found to be too soft, a second print from the same negative made on grade 4 paper would require a considerably longer exposure if it was to have the same mid-tone density and therefore look satisfactory.

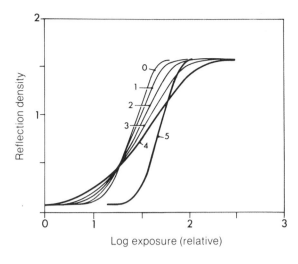

Characteristic curves of Ilfospeed paper, showing equality of effective speed for grades 0 to 4, lower speed for grade 5

The inconvenience of having to alter exposure when changing from one grade of paper to another was removed by the introduction of Ilfobrom papers in 1968. The only contrast grade in the Ilfobrom series that requires any adjustment of exposure is the extra-hard grade 5, which needs just twice as much exposure as any of grades 0 to 4.

The principal reason why printing papers are produced in a variety of contrast grades is that the brightness range of subjects, and thus the density scale of negatives, varies widely. An average negative, if there is such a thing, might have a density scale of 20:1, that is to say the lightest areas of the negative (the shadow areas of the image) would transmit twenty times as much light as the densest (highlight) area. Such a negative might be expected to print satisfactorily on a 'normal' or grade 2 paper because its density scale will just about fit the exposure scale of that paper. A negative with a greater scale of densities (either because of the subject, which can often display brightness differences of 1000:1, or because of the way it was developed) would need a paper with a longer exposure scale, i.e. a softer grade. Conversely, a negative exposed on a foggy or hazy day may require a more contrasty paper if there is to be sufficient distinction between the features in the printed image. If plates or cut sheet films are used to record each subject, it is feasible to develop each negative in such a way as to produce images that can all be printed on the same grade of paper; this is the proposition on which the Zone System is based. But since more and more photography is done on roll and 35 mm films (often bearing images of several different subjects on the same length) this is not generally practicable.

There are two further reasons why a variety of paper grades is useful. First, the optical conditions of projection printing

65

equipment vary so much that different grades of paper are necessary to obtain matching prints from the same negative when using different enlargers. Second, a variety of grades gives the monochrome photographer/printer the opportunity to create an effective picture without attempting to comply with the theoretical requirements of the 'perfect' print.

The alternative to having five boxes of different paper available is to use a variable-contrast paper such as Ilfospeed Multigrade, with which prints can be made to match those that would be obtained by using any paper grade between 0 and 5. For a long time the equivalent of grade 5 has been unobtainable with variable-contrast papers, but Multigrade Mk 2 will make it obtainable; it will therefore be unnecessary to use more than one box of paper for all requirements.

Image colour   The image colour or tone of the silver image in a print is usually described in such broad subjective terms as 'warm' or 'cold'. The colour of a monochrome image formed by the reduction of silver largely depends upon the grain size of the emulsion that was used. To some extent, the colour also depends on the thickness of the gelatin layer in which the silver image is held, and is also affected by processing conditions, particularly by the choice of developer. When processed in the developers recommended for them, Ilfobrom, Galerie, Ilfospeed and Multigrade papers produce images that the majority of users describe as neutral to slightly warm.

Permanence   Historical evidence shows that when processing, particularly washing, has been carried out carefully and when prints have been stored well, a silver image on good-quality paper base will resist change for more than a hundred years. If the silver image is protected with a shell of gold or selenium, the life of a print can be extended still further.

In the light of recent improvements in the stability of the protective layers used to render photographic papers water-resistant, monochrome prints on RC papers are likely to resist change for as long as any other type of photographic printing material.

2 Principles of photographic processing

Because few photographers now make up their own developers and fixers, a knowledge of the principles of development and fixation of photographic materials is less important than it once was. However, there remain many ways in which the quality of negatives or prints can be adversely influenced in processing. The photographer or printer who understands something of the principles involved is less likely to make or repeat mistakes than one who does not.

The development process

The first and most important step in processing a negative or a print is development. Fox Talbot's development process has already been described. At the time, 1840, Sir John Herschel picturesquely described the phenomenon as 'the awakening of the sleeping picture'. The chemical agent that made it possible was gallic acid, which distinguished between the exposed and the unexposed parts of the sensitised sheets of paper Fox Talbot used in his camera, so that only the light-struck grains of silver chloride were converted into metallic silver. The chemical reaction involved in such a conversion is known as reduction; it must not be confused with the other common use of the term in photography, when it relates to the removal of silver to decrease the density of an image by what is more likely to be a process of oxidation.

Developing agents   Since the days of gallic acid, hundreds of other developing agents have been discovered and used. But now the list of those in common use is quite short, for as Dr C. E. K. Mees once said, 'the abundance of developing agents only increases the number of ways in which identical results can be obtained'. The most frequently used agents are metol (N-methyl-4-aminophenol sulphate), hydroquinone (p-dihydroxybenzene) and Phenidone (1-phenyl-3-pyrazolidone).

Most of the developers regularly used in black-and-white processing today include combinations of metol and hydroquinone (MQ) or Phenidone and hydroquinone (PQ). There are good reasons for using two developing agents instead of one.

When Phenidone is added to hydroquinone, their combined activity is greater than could be achieved with either agent alone. This useful effect is known as superadditivity. It occurs to a greater extent when hydroquinone is used with Phenidone than with metol; in fact, so much less Phenidone is needed to activate a given amount of hydroquinone that it has greatly helped in the formulation of liquid developer concentrates.

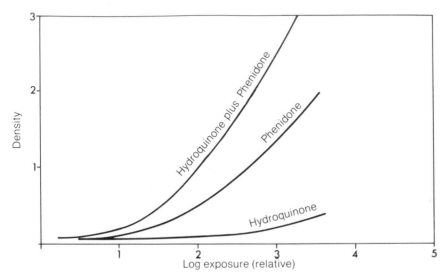

Relative energy of hydroquinone and Phenidone used separately, and the superadditive effect of using them together

Another advantage of combining metol or Phenidone with hydroquinone is that the hydroquinone regenerates the metol or Phenidone as it becomes oxidised. This means that not only is the developer active when freshly made, but it remains active over a longer period. Phenidone has the further advantage that it does not cause dermatitis, unlike metol.

A solution of a developing agent alone does not make a practical developer. In addition there usually must be an activator (or accelerator), a restrainer (or anti-foggant) and a preservative.

The accelerator   The accelerator is necessary because most developing agents become active only when in alkaline solution. An exception is amidol, which will work in a neutral or slightly acid solution, although it is not much used today. According to the degree of developer activity required, the accelerator can be chosen from a range of alkalis of different strengths. The alkalinity of a solution is measured in terms of its pH, over a range from pH7 (neutral) to pH14 (very strongly alkaline).

In order of increasing alkalinity, some of the commonly used developer accelerators are borax, sodium carbonate, potassium

68

carbonate and sodium hydroxide. Typically, a negative developer such as Ilfords's ID11 has a pH of 9, while Ilfospeed print developer works at pH11.

The restrainer Although a developing agent distinguishes between exposed and unexposed halide grains, there is a tendency for some unexposed grains to be reduced to silver. This gives rise to fog, which is only tolerable if kept below a certain level. To control the amount of unwanted density arising in unexposed areas, an anti-foggant or restrainer must be added to the developer. The best-known and most used restrainer is potassium bromide, although it causes some loss of emulsion speed. There are also some organic anti-foggants, such as benzotriazole, which are particularly effective with Phenidone and cause little loss of emulsion speed.

Sometimes potassium bromide and an organic restrainer are used together in a developer; this is because soluble bromide finds its way into the developer as a by-product of development, and would change the activity of the developer more rapidly than if a certain level of bromide were present in the first place.

The preservative A freshly mixed solution containing developing agent, alkali and restrainer can be used immediately to develop an exposed negative or print, but the developing agent quite quickly begins to take up oxygen from the water and the air, turns brown and rapidly loses activity. To prevent this happening, one further and very important ingredient is needed: an anti-oxidant or preservative. Sodium sulphite is almost always used to delay the formation of coloured oxidation products, which cause stains and destroy the developer.

In formulae such as ID11, the high concentration of sulphite has a further purpose: it acts as a mild solvent of silver. The silver that is dissolved from the halides first of all goes into solution in the developer and is then 'plated' back on to the silver image.

Other additions Sometimes additional ingredients are included in a developer to offset undesirable side-effects rather than to affect the nature of the developed image itself. For example, when a developer is made up with hard water containing a higher content of calcium salts than average, the calcium and the carbonate may react to cause an insoluble precipitate. Some of this may settle and dry on the surface of a negative, forming chalky marks that will certainly show up on finished prints. To prevent this kind of precipitate forming, it is often necessary to include a small amount of a calcium-sequestering agent such as sodium tripolyphosphate.

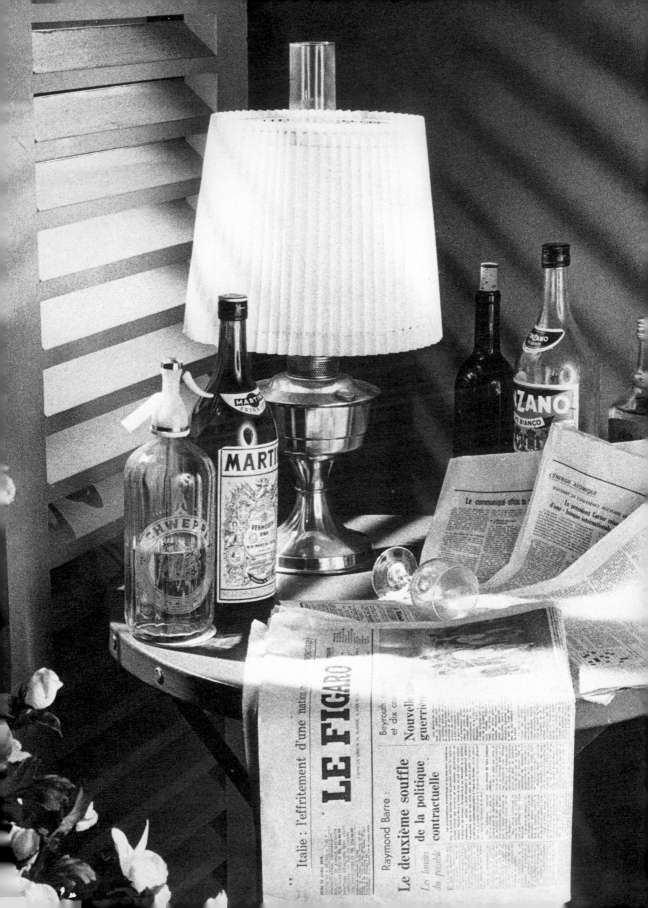

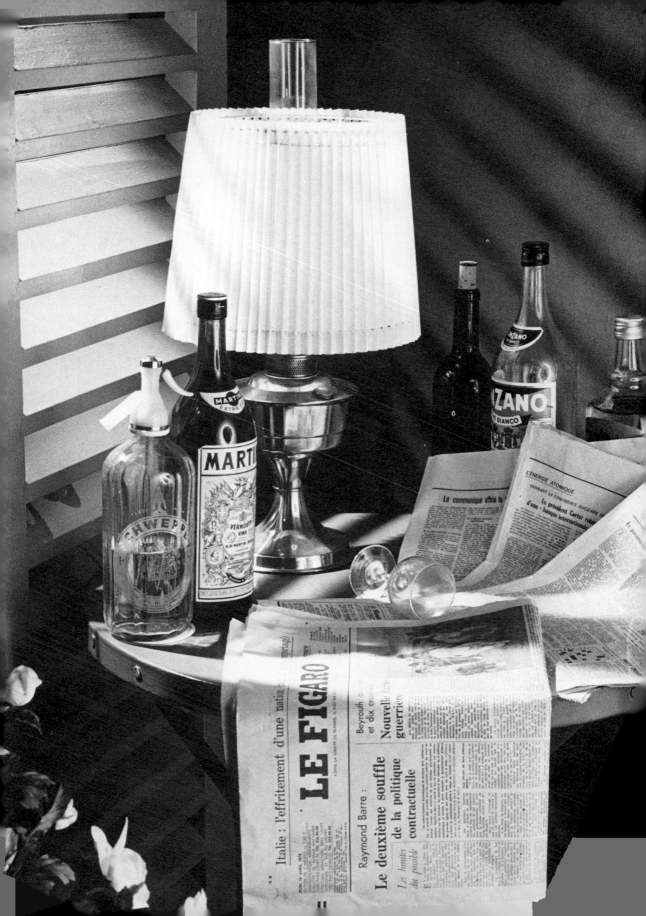

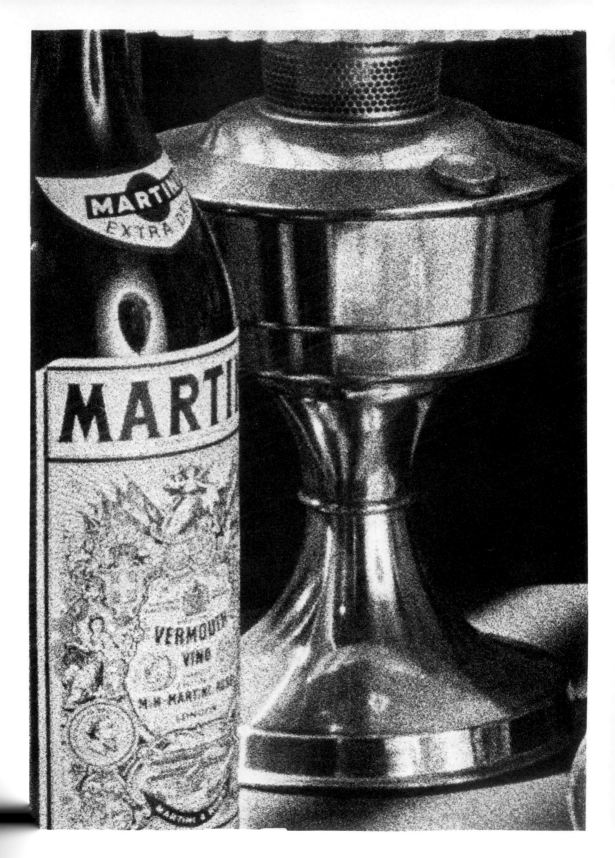

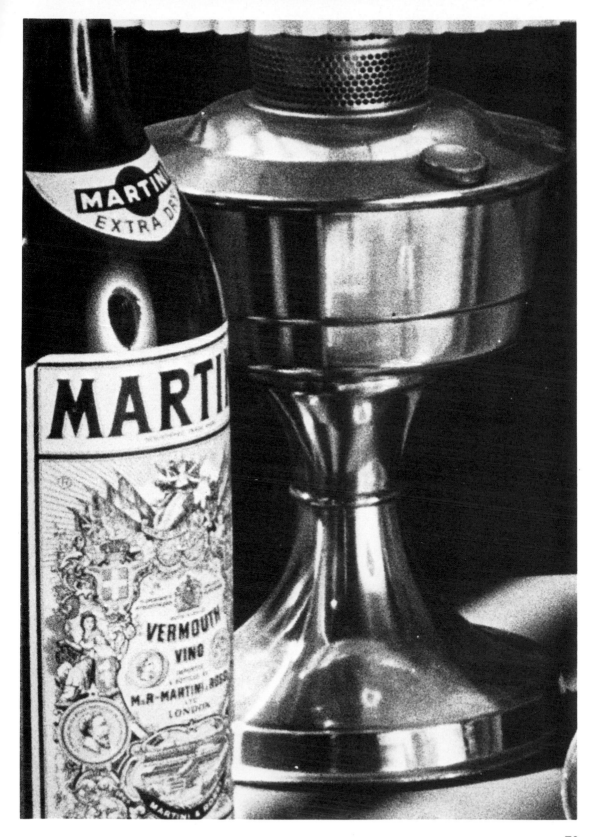

Developer categories   The major factor governing the activity of a developing solution is its alkalinity. Black-and-white developers tend to fall into three broad categories based on their alkalinity.

1 So-called 'fine-grain' developers use metol or Phenidone, hydroquinone, and borax as a 'mild' activator, giving pH9. This kind of developer is typified by Kodak's D76 and Ilford's ID11, which are widely used by both photographers and photo-finishers. The formula given by Ilford for ID11 is:

metol	2 g
sodium sulphite	100 g
hydroquinone	5 g
borax	2 g
water to	1000 ml

2 General-purpose MQ or PQ developers use sodium carbonate as the alkali and work at pH10 to 10.5.
3 High-contrast developers (for line work and other special requirements) use hydroquinone alone at high alkalinity. The accelerator is usually sodium or potassium hydroxide, so that the developer works at pH11 or higher.

Chromogenic development   One other type of developer is now being used in monochrome photography to process films such as XP1–400. These so-called chromogenic (colour-forming) films still depend upon silver halides for the formation of the initial

Pages 70 and 71: the two negatives from which these prints were made, one on HP5 (left) and the other on XP1, received exactly the same exposure

Pages 72 and 73: these prints are 25× enlargements from corresponding areas of the two original negatives

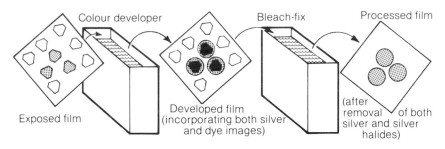

Colour developer   Bleach-fix   Processed film

Exposed film   Developed film (incorporating both silver and dye images)   (after removal of both silver and silver halides)

XP1-400 processing sequence

negative image, but during the course of processing, and after the necessary dye image has been created, all the reduced silver and unused halides are removed together in a combined bleach/fix or 'blix' solution.

A colour developing agent differs from those developers that are used simply to produce silver images from black-and-white emulsions, in that the by-products produced during the reduction of the latent image to metallic silver combine with other organic substances in the emulsion to produce a dye image alongside the silver one. The colour-coupling substances included in the emulsion can be chosen to yield any one of a wide range of colours. In a colour negative film or a colour paper, a yellow, a magenta and a green coupler are used, one in each of the three layers. When a single monochrome negative image is required from which to make black-and-white prints, as with XP1–400, a mixture of colour couplers can be incorporated in the same emulsion layer so as to produce a visually neutral, composite dye image that will print in very much the same way as a silver image.

Although XP1–400 film can be processed in a standard colour negative developer such as C41, the quality of the resulting negatives, while being perfectly serviceable and usually superior to any ISO 400/27° silver-image film, will not yield the very best results obtainable from the product. The developer designed by Ilford for use with XP1, when used in the recommended way with intermittent agitation, produces sharper images than can be obtained by any other processing method.

Development controls

The rate at which development can proceed and the limit it can reach are governed to a large extent by the composition of the developing solution itself. There are, however, several other variables that have a significant effect on results.

Adequate control of the variables in black-and-white processing is not difficult to achieve. In general, the limits within which the variables need to be held are much wider than they are for colour photography, partly because of the several ways in which adjustments or corrections can be made when producing a black-and-white print. Nevertheless, the work is made easier and quality is more consistent if reasonable care is taken to ensure that once good negative quality has been established, it is maintained. To do this there are four things to be considered when using the same developer formulation with the same type of film: duration of development; temperature of the developer; agitation; and activity of the developer (if it is being used repeatedly).

Duration of development   When other things remain constant, increasing the development time increases both the density and the contrast of a negative image, and at the same time tends to increase speed, granularity and fog. For a given film and developer combination, therefore, an optimum development time must be found.

The most that any film or developer manufacturer can do is to indicate likely periods of development, to be used as starting points when processing film of a particular type. Ilford provides guidelines that give a choice of contrast levels: one that may be considered 'normal' and one 'high'. Each level suits particular combinations of subject brightness range and enlargement conditions. Development-time curves are available for the Ilford black-and-white films HP5, FP4 and Pan F when used with a range of different developers.

If the development time for a photographic material is to be accurately controlled, development must be stopped abruptly and not allowed to continue at a reduced rate after the allotted time. It would be possible to arrest the development process by transferring the film or plate to very cold water, but risk of reticulation of the gelatin layer precludes this. Instead, transferring the film to an acid stop-bath, such as Ilford IN1, serves to terminate development promptly. In practice, an acid fixing-bath is often used to stop development and start fixation simultaneously.

Temperature of developer Like most other chemical reactions, the reduction of light-struck silver halides to metallic silver proceeds faster as the temperature of the developer is increased. Roughly, if the working temperature of a developer is raised from 15 to 25°C, the time required to reach a given contrast will be halved. However, there are limits beyond which the temperature of a developer should not be raised, simply because thereafter the gelatin emulsion layer becomes softer, more swollen and more prone to damage. Furthermore, fog often increases at a disproportionate rate as the temperature of a developer is increased. Finally, the very short development times necessary at higher temperatures are difficult to control, except in machine processing.

Nevertheless, processing temperatures tended to increase with the advent of colour materials, for which inconveniently long times of development were at first required. This change is now spreading to black-and-white processing with products such as Ilford's XP1–400, for which the recommended temperature for development is 38°C.

Although modern emulsions are well hardened during manufacture, high developer temperatures do bring a greater risk of reticulation if any of the other solutions in the processing cycle are significantly lower in temperature. Reticulation is not always easily recognisable; it can be subtle enough to be mistaken for coarse grain. As a rough guide, the temperature of each successive solution should not differ from the preceding one by more than 5 or 6°C.

Agitation If an exposed film is immersed in a developer and neither the film nor the solution is moved, the resulting negative will display quite different characteristics from those of a similarly

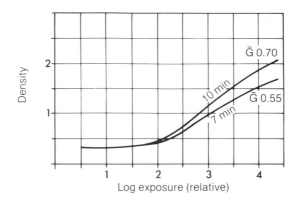

Characteristic curves of
FP4 developed to two
values of $\bar{G}$ in ID11
developer at 20°C with
intermittent agitation

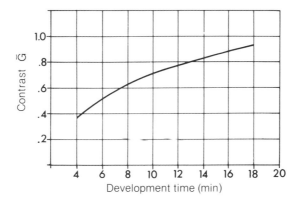

Contrast-time curve for FP4
35 mm film in ID11
developer with intermittent
agitation

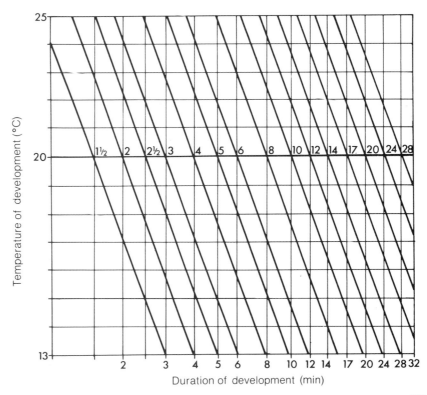

Time-temperature chart for
typical PQ and MQ
developers

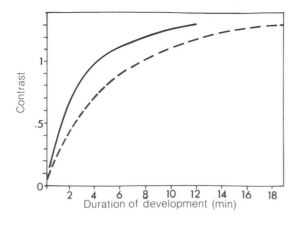

Solid curve: rate of growth of contrast when continuous agitation is used during development. Broken curve: much slower increase when there is no agitation

treated film that has been moved frequently relative to the solution. This relative movement between the surface of an exposed emulsion and a developer is loosely called agitation, and can be achieved in several different ways.

If nothing is done to effect movement of a developer across the surface of an emulsion being processed, a layer of exhausted developer and by-products accumulates at points of exposure; the greater the exposure, the more concentrated the by-products. When this happens, excessive concentrations of bromide occur locally and restrain development, thereby reducing the potential density and contrast of the negative image. Furthermore, if the negative being processed is held vertically in a tank of developer (perhaps in a rack or suspended from clips) then the bromide released in high-density areas, being heavier than the surrounding solution, slowly sinks and in doing so restrains development in those parts of the negative immediately beneath the areas of high density. When this happens, streaks or 'streamers' of reduced density are formed. The effect is known as 'bromide drag'. Phenidone-hydroquinone combinations in a developer are less sensitive to bromide concentration than when metol is used.

Efficient agitation, in the form of film or solution movement or both, increases the rate of development and improves its uniformity, although above a certain amount of movement development is no longer affected.

Decline in activity of developer   When films or prints are developed, the two principal changes that take place in the developer are loss of activity due to the consumption of developing agents and loss of activity due to the release of bromide ions from the processed emulsion. For these reasons alone, a developer that is to be used continuously needs to be replenished if its activity is to be maintained at a uniform level.

To compensate for loss of developer activity, increase development time for each successive film by 10 per cent after the first when using 600 ml of developer

Films developed (y-axis)

Minutes development in fresh stock solution (x-axis)

An alternative way of offsetting the gradually declining activity of a developer is to extend the development time for successive films. This method is simple and effective in the short run, but when large number of films are to be developed, perhaps in a processing machine that does not easily allow development time to be altered, activity of the developer must be maintained by replenishment. A developer replenisher for small-scale tank processing maintains activity by a simple topping-up process. In this way, the volume of developer removed in and on the films when they are transferred to the stop bath or fixing bath is replaced at intervals by an equal volume of replenisher. Topping-up can be continued successfully over a period of weeks but should not be carried beyond the point when the volume of replenisher used equals the initial volume of developer. One characteristic of a developer replenisher is that it contains little or no restrainer, since the build-up of soluble bromide in the working bath makes any addition unnecessary.

For the amateur or other small-scale processer, it is probably best to avoid all replenishment problems by employing the 'one-shot' or 'total-loss' method of development. In other words, use fresh developer for each film.

'Push' processing   It sometimes happens that a film is known to have been underexposed, either because conditions did not allow any more exposure or because of a mistake. It is then tempting to believe that there must be some way of increasing the effective speed of the film by using a different developer or development technique, in other works to 'push' the film. In reality, all that can be done (and often it is useful) is to choose an active developer such as Microphen, and then develop at a high temperature or for

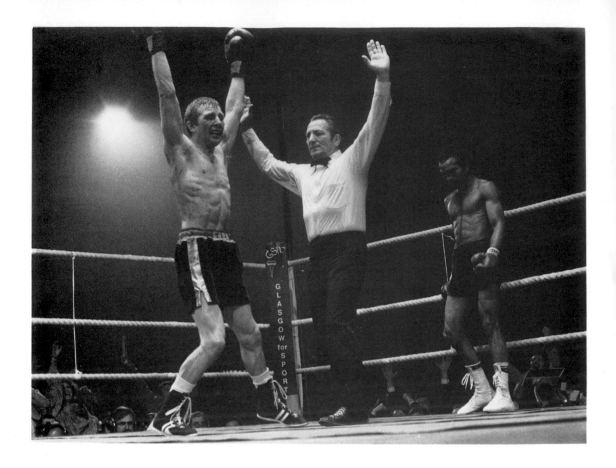

a longer time than normal; every bit of shadow exposure is then utilised to the full, even at the cost of excessive contrast and grain. The true speed of the film, as measured sensitometrically, will remain unchanged, but more useful prints may result.

When XP1–400 film has been inadvertently underexposed in poor lighting conditions, slightly more information may sometimes be obtained from the negatives if development time is extended. Although the emulsion speed cannot strictly be re-rated simply because of the longer development time, its foot speed can in effect be considered to reach 'ISO 800/30°' with 6½ minutes development or even 'ISO 1600/33°' if development is extended to 7½ minutes at 38°C.

The fixing process
The term 'fixing' is really another misnomer that has been adopted by photographers. In fact, we do not fix the image but dispose of the residual emulsion that would otherwise spoil our negatives and prints.

At one time sodium thiosulphate (the most common silver halide solvent) was incorrectly known as sodium hyposulphate,

Above: without 'push' processing his HP5 negative, Arthur Kinloch of the *Glasgow Herald* might not have managed to separate the vanquished boxer from the background

Right: XP1 negatives can be 'pushed' when the nature of the subject or the lighting justifies doing so. Keith Davidson estimates that the effective speed he obtained in this case was about 800 ASA

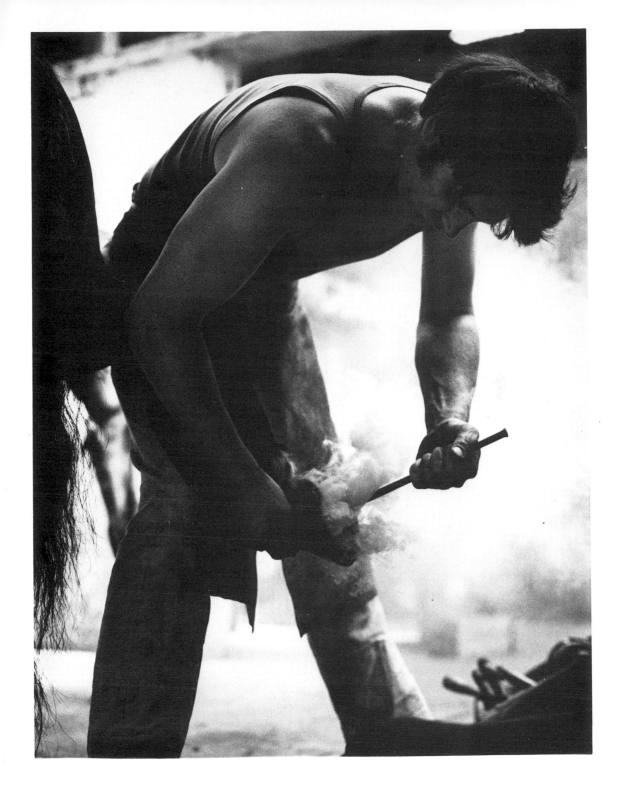

hence the term hypo. Sodium or ammonium thiosulphate removes residual silver halides from a developed emulsion layer by converting them to complex silver thiosulphates, which can be washed out of the gelatin layer. Unless a fine-grain negative or a print is left in a fixing bath for a long time, the thiosulphates do not significantly affect a reduced silver image.

A plain solution of sodium thiosulphate would dissolve the unused halides in a film or paper emulsion, but it is better to use an acidified fixing solution so that any alkaline developer carried over with negatives or prints will not make the fixing bath alkaline and thereby allow staining to occur. An acid fixing bath such as IF23 will stop development immediately a negative or print is immersed in it.

Fixing solutions are generally made acid by the addition of potassium metabisulphite, or acetic acid and sodium sulphite. The sodium sulphite prevents decomposition of the thiosulphate by the acid, and also prevents oxidation turning traces of developer brown, with consequent staining of negatives or prints.

Sodium thiosulphate can be replaced by ammonium thiosulphate when a faster-acting fixer is necessary, or when fixing has to be done at a low working temperature. Two strips of negative film held in solutions of each fixer at the same temperature display quite different clearing times; ammonium thiosulphate is up to five times faster-acting than sodium thiosulphate.

The clearing time can be used as a simple indication of the activity of a fixer, the old rule being to 'fix for twice the clearing time'. This may not be entirely safe with a fast negative emulsion such as HP5, which contains some silver iodide, the least soluble of the silver halides. *Three* times the clearing time would be safer.

For the 18th Hurter and Driffield Memorial Lecture in 1954, Dr H. Baines chose as his subject 'Fixation – the chemistry of the hypo bath'. Among several concepts he questioned was that fixing time decreases beyond a thiosulphate concentration of 40 per cent. He pointed out that if wet film is used (as is the case in practice) fixing times continue to decrease until a thiosulphate concentration of at least 70 per cent is reached. All the earlier experiments had been carried out with dry film!

As with developers, the activity of a fixing bath increases as its temperature is raised. Fixing is also speeded up by agitation. The time required to fix a film at 10°C is twice as long as at 20°C. As an approximation, a medium-speed negative film should be properly fixed in a freshly made ammonium thiosulphate fixer such as Ilford Hypam (diluted 1:4) after 3 or 4 minutes at 20°C. A print would be fixed in Hypam (diluted 1:9) in 60 seconds or so, provided that it was not sandwiched between a lot of other prints in the same tray.

Hardening fixers By the time an emulsion layer has reached the fixing bath, having been through a developer, and perhaps a stop bath or a rinse, it has swollen and softened considerably. If it is not hardened while in the fixer, it will continue to swell and soften still more while being washed. To guard against damage to the

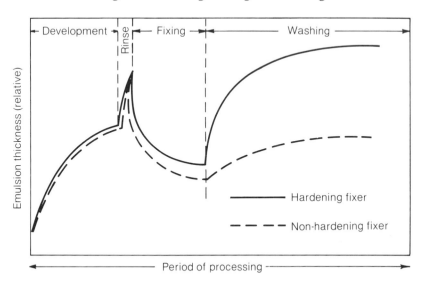

Typical swelling history of emulsion layer during processing

softened emulsion layers, it is common practice (particularly in negative processing) to use a fixing bath that incorporates a hardener.

Potassium alum is commonly used as a hardening agent in fixers. In addition, a buffer is usually added to maintain the solution between pH4 and pH6, the range within which the alum will work well and be unlikely either to sulphurise or to form an aluminium sludge. A liquid acid hardener is supplied by Ilford for use with their IF23 fixer, but it can be used with any other non-hardening fixer.

Although hardening the gelatin layer during the course of fixing can safeguard negatives from accidental damage, there are some disadvantages in using a hardener-fixer for paper prints. It is more difficult to remove residual chemicals from a hardened gelatin layer than from one that remains swollen. For this reason, prints that are required to remain stable for the longest possible period of time should not be treated in a hardener-fixer.

Replenishment of fixers In small-scale tray or tank processing it is not usual to replenish a fixing solution. Instead, baths are simply replaced when fixing times (usually judged by comparison with the clearing time) become noticeably extended.

A fixing bath becomes exhausted for two main reasons: it is continually diluted by solution carried into it with the negatives or prints that are being processed, and the silver content of the bath rises steadily with use. The extent of dilution can be gauged by measuring the specific gravity of the fixer, although this is only done in large-scale processing where replenishment is worthwhile.

Fortunately, the silver content of a fixer can easily be determined by using test papers. This method is especially useful when fixing prints, where there is no visible evidence of 'clearing

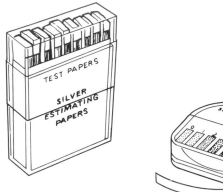
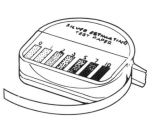
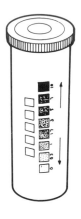

Test papers for assessing silver content of fixing baths

time'. As a safeguard, two separate fixing baths are often used; the first is discarded when its silver content reaches 2 grams per litre, after which it is replaced by the second bath while a fresh solution is made.

When continuous film or paper processing machines are used, the inconvenience and expense of discarding and replacing the large volumes of solution make it essential to replenish continually both developer and fixer. Unlike the developer, the fixing solution in a processing sequence does not lose volume (except by evaporation), because as much solution is carried into the tank on and in the film or paper as is removed from it and transferred to the washing section. The fixer is therefore continually diluted. At the same time, as material is processed soluble silver salts accumulate in the fixing bath, so satisfactory regeneration cannot be achieved by topping-up. Instead, a certain amount of used solution must be discarded to permit the addition of replenisher, and the silver content of the bath must be kept down by electrolytic silver recovery. If the silver is not extracted the only way of keeping a fixer in continuous use is to over-replenish, so that the build-up of silver does not reach a level at which it significantly interferes with fixing. This, of course, wastes both fixing chemicals and silver.

On average, negative materials are coated with emulsions containing some 5 to 7 grams of silver per square metre, while printing papers usually carry about 1.5 to 2.0 grams for the same area. Although the proportion of silver halide used to form the negative or positive image will vary according to subject matter and exposure, it is safe to say that a good deal less than half the available silver is used to form negative images, while rather less than half is required when making prints. This means that a great deal of silver finds its way into fixing baths.

Silver recovery Whenever the price of silver rises dramatically, there is a renewed interest in the recovery of silver from used photographic fixing and bleaching solutions. The problem with most small-scale photographic processing is that the volume of spent fixer is seldom sufficient to justify investment in a modern electrolytic silver-recovery unit of the kind now used in conjunction with film and paper processing machines. Nonetheless, if solutions are collected in a treatment vessel there are a number of ways in which useful quantities of silver can be saved from the drain. The approximate amounts of silver that could theoretically be recovered from different black-and-white materials are given in the table, as a guide when determining whether an attempt should be made to collect some of it.

Black-and-white material	Silver potentially recoverable, per 1000 units
Film unit	
35 mm (20 exposure)	2 to 3 grams
35 mm (36 exposure)	3 to 5 grams
120 rollfilm	3 to 5 grams
4 × 5 inch sheet	1 to 1.5 grams
5 × 7 inch sheet	2 to 3 grams
8 × 10 inch sheet	3 to 5 grams
Paper unit	
5 × 7 inch sheet	0.75 to 1 gram
8 × 10 inch sheet	2 to 2.5 grams
5 inch × 500 feet roll	700 to 900 grams
8 inch × 500 feet roll	1000 to 1500 grams
10 inch × 500 feet roll	1400 to 1800 grams

Broadly, there are three different methods of extracting silver from a used fixing solution: electrolytic recovery, metallic replacement (often by steel wool), and precipitation.

Electrolytic silver recovery units can be grouped into two categories: those that operate at low currents and those (usually the larger and always the more expensive machines) that can use high currents to remove more silver more quickly. All electrolytic units are operated by passing a direct current between an anode (usually carbon) and a cathode (often stainless steel) while both are immersed in the used fixing solution. Silver is deposited on the cathode in an almost pure (98 per cent) form. High-current units can only be used when there is high concentration of silver in the bath being treated or when there is rapid movement between the cathode and the solution. If neither of these conditions is observed, silver sulphide is formed in the fixing solution, which must then be discarded. Because the rate of recovery with a low-current unit is necessarily slow, the surface area of the cathode must be as large as possible, which tends to limit the application of this type of

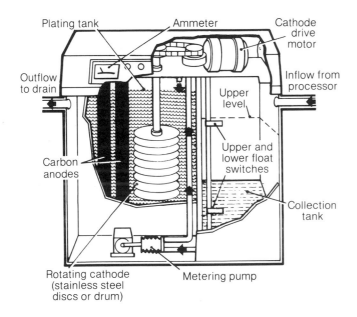

'Meterflow' system of electrolytic silver recovery. Used fixer from processing machine flows into collection tank; when level reaches upper float switch, metering pump is energised and begins to transfer fixer to plating tank at predetermined rate depending on silver concentration in fixer and current (amps) passing between cell electrodes

unit. Apart from the fact that the amount of silver deposited on the cathode of an electolytic recovery unit can be accurately estimated, the method also offers the possibility of reusing the fixer after suitable regeneration.

The only advantage of the metallic-replacement method of extracting silver from a fixing solution is the low cost of the equipment required. In effect, all that is needed is a large container (plastic dustbins have been used) filled with steel wool (rotary floor-cleaner pads, for example) through which the spent hypo is passed *en route* to the drain. For the method to work well the flow of the fixer must not exceed a predetermined rate, and there must be no blockage or 'channelling' to prevent the incoming solution from reaching any part of the steel wool.

Commercially available steel-wool canisters are designed so that the silver-bearing hypo is fed into the bottom of the container and then flows upwards through the steel wool to an outlet that is connected to a drain. There is usually a by-pass to prevent overflowing should the unit become blocked. When a container has been used to treat a predetermined volume of fixer, it should

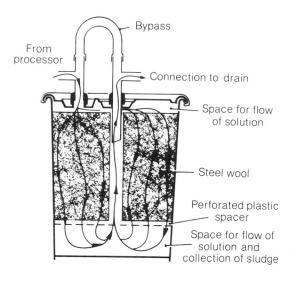

Solution flow through typical steel-wool silver-recovery canister

be returned to the supplier, who extracts the silver from the sludge that has formed at the bottom of the canister. The outcome of the refining process is unpredictable, and is the most unsatisfactory aspect of recovering silver in this way.

One of the earliest methods of getting silver out of used fixer was to collect it in a large container and precipitate the silver as silver sulphide. The reaction between sodium or potassium sulphide and fixer produces a very unpleasant smell; this, together with the nuisance of collecting and drying the sludge-like precipitate of silver sulphide, caused the method to fall into disuse. However, there has been some renewal of interest in the precipitation method: if reducing agents such as sodium dithionite or sodium borohydride are used in a strongly alkaline solution, there is no smell and the yield of silver can be very high.

Washing

Washing a gelatin layer, and sometimes an associated paper support, until they are sufficiently free from processing chemicals is the last stage in any 'wet' processing cycle. Once again, temperature and agitation influence the process and largely determine the time it will take. The thoroughness of a washing procedure can be judged by estimating the amount of thiosulphate remaining in the gelatin layer or, in the case of unprotected paper-based prints, in the total gelatin, baryta and paper assembly.

One fairly simple way of checking the amount of thiosulphate that is left in a paper print is to apply one drop of an acid solution of silver nitrate to the margin of a print. A straw-coloured stain of varying density will appear if significant amounts of thiosulphate remain. For films and prints that must be stored unchanged for very long periods a more complicated analytical procedure is required. Expertly used, the 'methylene-blue' method can detect less than 0.01 microgram of thiosulphate in one square centimetre of material.

Because film base is for practical purposes non-absorbent, it is much easier to wash a negative to some required low level of residual hypo than a print on an unprotected paper base. Resin-coated or water-resistant papers, on the other hand, can be considered to behave in much the same way as film-based negatives. The hardness or extent of swelling of a gelatin layer also has a significant effect on the rate of washing. A negative image layer that has been hardened during fixing can take up to four times longer to wash than an unhardened film of the same type.

It is often mistakenly assumed that efficient washing can only be achieved by using large volumes of water for long periods of time. But, as G. I. P. Levenson has pointed out, it would be possible to wash 1000 feet of motion picture positive film to archival standard in one litre of water, provided that the water was used efficiently. He has also reported that: 'Excellent washing of a processed roll-film was achieved in a spiral tank by giving just three half-minute changes of cold water and agitating well during each period. The tank was just emptied after each wash with no attempt to drain thoroughly. After the third wash, the film was wiped before hanging it up to dry.'

It has been proposed that there should be two 'safe' levels of thiosulphate in photographic materials, one for archival storage and the other for ordinary commercial use. As his target for adequate commercial washing of film, Levenson aimed at diluting one hundredfold the concentration of thiosulphate solution in the image layer when it left the fixer.

Washing prints is not so straightforward, particularly when they are treated in trays. There is a tendency in busy print rooms for large numbers of prints to be immersed in the same tray, so many of them are in contact with layers of stagnant water. Practical steps can be taken to ensure that each print in a batch is adequately washed. One way is to use a series of two or three trays so that transfer of the prints, one by one, from one tray to the next ensures movement between the prints and the water. Another way is to use an automatic syphon in the water supply line, so that at regular intervals all the hypo-laden water is drained from the tray or tank, which is then refilled with fresh water. Rotary print-washers can also be used to keep a batch of prints constantly on the move and well separated. Smaller numbers of prints can be washed to archival standards in specially designed washers that

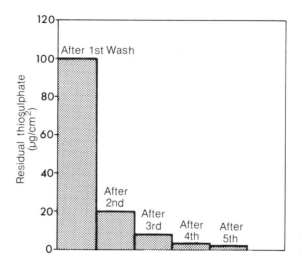

Effectiveness of washing with five changes of water

hold the prints vertically to ensure complete separation and ready access of the wash water.

If prints are required in a hurry and yet must be relied upon to remain unchanged for as long as possible, the period required for washing can be considerably shortened by treating each print in a two per cent solution of sodium sulphite for about ten minutes before washing it in water for no more than five minutes. The idea of using a washing aid of this kind came from the observation that prints are washed more quickly in salt water than in fresh water.

When a continuous-processing machine is used for film or paper materials, it is not practical to discard the whole of the washing water periodically. Instead, water is fed into one point of the washing section of the machine at some controlled rate and then overflows to waste from another point. The principal source of water movement is the transport of the material being processed through the washing tank or tanks. When more than one washing tank is incorporated in a processor, best use will be made of the water if it is fed through a flowmeter into the last tank first, and then into the preceding tank via an interconnecting pipe at the bottom of the tank, until it runs away to waste from the top of the first wash tank. This method of passing water through the washing section of a processor is known as 'counterflow' washing.

Drying

Except that the medium used is air and not water, much the same physical conditions determine the efficiency of drying as those that govern development, fixing or washing. Raising the temperature and increasing the velocity of the air used for drying will speed up the process. Obviously there is a limit beyond which the air temperature must not be raised if a wet gelatin layer is not to be melted, and the velocity of drying air must not be so high as to cause negatives to flap about while they are drying.

Films and prints often have to be dried without the aid of any kind of machine or cabinet; they are then usually left, often overnight, to dry slowly in whatever ambient conditions exist in the available room. Provided that the drying process is allowed to continue undisturbed by movement that stirs up dust, this simple procedure works quite well, although it may not be very practical for a large batch of prints. One of the greatest advantages of resin-coated papers is that they dry very quickly, either in a dryer such as the Ilford 5250 or 'naturally' while hanging from clips or laid out on racks.

Glazing

Before resin-coated papers came into widespread use, most black-and-white prints on glossy paper were dried on flat-bed or rotary glazers. This method of drying can impart a very highly glazed surface to prints, but it takes time and may cause 'oyster-shell' markings due to the spasmodic release of the print from the stainless-steel surface of the plate or drum; the prints may even stick to the drum and have to be torn off. It now seems likely that, as resin-coated papers become more widely accepted, drying prints by glazing will be unusual.

Short cuts in processing

There are ways in which negatives and prints can be processed without carrying out all the steps described so far. A film, for instance, can be developed and fixed in the same solution, known as a monobath. The idea of having only one solution instead of two seems attractive, but as might be expected there are some snags, not the least being a loss of emulsion speed. For results to be satisfactory, the rate at which development proceeds ahead of fixation also has to be balanced precisely, and this really means that a separate formulation is required for each type of film. The use of Phenidone, with its super-additivity effect on hydroquinone, has allowed some improvement in the performance of monobaths.

In activation/stabilisation processing, black-and-white prints can be made without involving the processes of fixing, washing and drying. If a silver halide emulsion contains a developing agent such as hydroquinone, it can be activated after exposure by contact with an alkaline aqueous solution. The residual silver halides need not then be removed by thiosulphate, but can instead be 'stabilised' by treatment with a solution containing a thiocyanate, which forms relatively stable complexes with them.

The advantages of activation/stabilisation are that the two-step process takes only about twenty seconds, is not very temperature sensitive and can be carried out in a small, relatively inexpensive machine that requires no plumbing. Some disadvantages come from not removing unused halides from an image layer and from not washing stabilisation chemicals out of that layer. First, stabilised prints usually feel damp to the touch. Second, and more important, they are not stable. In time, particularly in humid conditions, a stabilised print will deteriorate, although it can be safeguarded by fixing and washing in the orthodox way. Washing a stabilised print without fixing it will make it even less stable than if it had been left alone. Some photographers activate and temporarily stabilise their prints and then transfer them to a bath of hypo for fixing prior to washing and drying. This speeds up the first part of the process while ensuring image permanence.

Black-and-white emulsions on resin-coated paper base cannot undergo activation/stabilisation processing because the water-resistant base would not serve as a 'sink' to receive the chemicals that must remain in the print and that would quickly crystallise out on the surface.

Preparing solutions

No matter whether dry chemicals or liquid concentrates are chosen, some preparation is always necessary before photographic solutions are ready for use, and suitable means of measuring, dispensing and storing them are necessary.

Before deciding upon the size, shape and material to choose for graduates, beakers and bottles, it is wise to consider which system of measurement to adopt. There is much to be said for using the metric system when measuring weights, volumes and temperatures in photographic processing. It really is more convenient to work in grams and kilograms when weighing solid chemicals, or millilitres (ccs) and litres when measuring liquids, than it is to use ounces, quarts and gallons, which are not even equivalent in the UK and the US.

In these days of proprietary processing chemistry, it is not often necessary to weigh out quantities of solid chemicals, since even when a formula is supplied partly or wholly in dry form the ingredients have already been dispensed into separate packets. A precision chemical balance is therefore hardly justified, but simple, low-cost alternatives are available, which will weigh liquids or solids accurately enough between one gram and 100 grams. Most measuring cylinders or graduates are calibrated in both millilitres and ounces, although before long the latter may be omitted. Transparent plastics have largely replaced fragile glass for almost all purposes in photographic processing. The use of polypropylene rather than glass has enabled a new type of storage bottle to be introduced, one with concertina or bellows-like sides.

There has always been a problem of deterioration when part of the initial contents of a bottle, particularly a developer, remains in contact with air that would quickly oxidise it. With a collapsible concertina bottle, the air can be expelled by compressing the bottle before screwing back the cap, so that the bottle retains its reduced size and shape. This usually works until about half the initial content of the bottle has been used.

Liquid concentrates

Undoubtedly the easiest way of preparing a working-strength developer is to make it up from a liquid concentrate by diluting a suitable volume of the concentrate with the correct volume of water at the right temperature. This enables the working-strength solution to be used immediately.

PQ Universal developer   Liquid-concentrate developers such as Ilford PQ Universal also have the advantage that they can be used for both negative and print processing, although different dilutions are required for each purpose. However, no compromise of this kind can give the best of both worlds. The technical information leaflet on PQ Universal says: 'it is suitable for general-purpose sheet film when a fast-working, high-contrast dish developer is required and a high degree of enlargement is not necessary'. In other words this is no fine-grain developer, and it will result in a loss of speed. The formula for PQ Universal developer is:

sodium sulphite (anyhydrous)	50 g
sodium carbonate (anyhydrous)	60 g
hydroquinone	12 g
Phenidone	0.5 g
potassium bromide	2 g
benzotriazole (1% solution)	20 ml
water to	1000 ml

Complete development of prints takes between 1½ and 2 minutes at 20°C (68°F) at a dilution of 1+9, but can be speeded up to about one minute if dilution is reduced to 1+4. If diluted to 1+19, controllable development times can be obtained with film emulsions; for example, 10 minutes at 20°C is suitable for FP4 roll film.

Ilfosol 2 Ilfosol 2 is also a Phenidone-hydroquinone developer in liquid concentrate form, but unlike PQ Universal it gives fine-grain images, and does so without loss of emulsion speed. Ilfosol 2 (supplied in 250 ml bottles) is intended for one-shot use, although the concentrate itself has very good keeping qualities, so it is well suited to the hobbyist who wants to process films occasionally. As an example, if a single 35 mm film is to be processed in a 300 ml daylight tank, 30 ml of Ilfosol 2 is diluted to make a total volume of 300 ml of working-strength solution. The dilution should be carried out immediately prior to using the developer, which should not be stored in the diluted form. Since 90 per cent of the working bath is added as water, it is not difficult to ensure that the developer is at the required temperature and ready for use as soon as it has been thoroughly mixed. To make life even easier, the cap of the Ilfosol 2 bottle is graduated so that small volumes of concentrate can be accurately dispensed without the need for a separate graduate.

While the normal dilution factor for Ilfosol is 1+9, the developer can be used at greater dilution (for example 1+14) if high ambient temperatures, or films such as Pan F, mean that the duration of development would be uncomfortably short. Table 1

Table 1 Dilutions of Ilfosol 2

Tank capacity	Dilution 1+9		Dilution 1+14	
	Ilfosol 2 concentrate	Water	Ilfosol 2 concentrate	Water
300 ml	30 ml	270 ml	20 ml	280 ml
450 ml	45 ml	405 ml	30 ml	420 ml
600 ml	60 ml	540 ml	40 ml	560 ml

Table 2 Recommended development times for Ilfosol 2 at 20°C

		Normal contrast			High contrast	
	ISO	1+9	1+14	ISO	1+9	1+14
Pan F rollfilm and 35 mm	50/18°	3½ min	6 min	64/19°	5 min	8 min
FP4 rollfilm and 35 mm	125/21°	4 min	7½ min	160/23°	6½ min	11½ min
HP5 35 mm	400/27°	7 min	12½ min	500/28°	13 min	20 min
HP5 rollfilm	400/27°	8 min	13 min	500/28°	16 min	22 min

indicates the volumes of concentrate required to suit different tank capacities at two dilutions.

Table 2 gives suggested development times at 20°C to achieve two levels of contrast: one represents a $\overline{G}$ value of 0.55 and likely to suit condenser enlargers; the other is intended to produce negatives having somewhat higher contrast ($\overline{G} = 0.70$) and therefore more likely to suit diffusion enlargers, such as colour heads when used for black-and-white printing. The times given in this table assume effective agitation, either by inversion of the tank every 15 seconds or, if the tank does not permit this, vigorous agitation of some other kind for 10 seconds of each minute during development.

Hypam   The companion to Ilfosol is Ilford's concentrated liquid fixer, Hypam, which can be used for both negatives and prints. Since it is based on ammonium thiosulphate it is fast-acting, particularly when used at the same temperature as the developer, say 20°C. As with almost any chemical reaction, fixing proceeds faster if the temperature is raised as much as is reasonably possible, bearing in mind the problem of maintaining the higher temperature and the risk of softening the emulsion layer too much. For example, the clearing time for HP5 film in Hypam is reduced from about one minute at 10°C (50°F) to about 40 seconds in the same solution at 20°C (68°F). The recommended dilution ratios for Hypam are 1:4 for films and 1:9 for papers, although the higher concentration can be used for prints if they must be fixed as quickly as possible.

Hardener fixer   In order to reduce the risk of damaging the emulsion surfaces of negatives during processing and drying, a hardener can be added to the fixer. Ilford Rapid Hardener is a liquid concentrate that can be used as a two per cent addition to working-strength Hypam in order to reduce greatly the swelling and softening of any gelatin layers. Hardening inevitably slows the reaction of the thiosulphate, and fixing times need to be extended (see Table 3).

Table 3   Fixing times at 20°C

	Dilution	Fixing time without hardener	Fixing time with hardener
General-purpose film	1+4	2 min	4 min
Paper	1+4	½ min	4 min
	1+9	1 min	4 min

Useful life of fixer   There is an easy way of checking the activity of a fixing bath that is being used for films or plates. First remember to find the clearing time required by a freshly mixed solution when fixing film of the kind normally used. Then, when one litre of the bath has been used to fix about twenty-five 36-exposure 35 mm films or the same number of 120 rollfilms, check the clearing time again. If it takes more than twice as long to clear a sample of the same kind of film as you used for the initial test, the fixer should be replaced. Table 4 is a guide to the capacity of a Hypam fixing bath.

Table 4   Unreplenished capacity of working-strength Hypam fixer

Film or paper unit	Capacity (units per litre)	Dilution of Hypam
120 rollfilm	25	1+4
35 mm film (36 exposure)	25	1+4
Sheet film, 4 × 5 in	100	1+4
Sheet film, 8 × 10 in	25	1+4
Ilfobrom paper, 8 × 10 in	50	1+9
Ilfospeed paper, 8 × 10 in	100	1+9

Instead of periodically discarding a fixing bath and making up a fresh one, the same bath can be kept in use by replenishment. A suitable rate of replenishment can be estimated from Table 5.

Table 5   Replenishment rate for Hypam fixer

Film or paper unit	Number of units	Dilution of Hypam	Working-strength solution to be added
120 rollfilm	10	1+4	400 ml
35 mm film (36 exposure)	10	1+4	400 ml
Sheet film, 4 × 5 in	40	1+4	400 ml
Sheet film, 8 × 10 in	10	1+4	400 ml
Ilfobrom paper, 8 × 10 in	10	1+9	250 ml
Ilfospeed paper, 8 × 10 in	10	1+9	125 ml

Two other simple tests can be made to determine the condition of a fixing bath; both require the use of indicator papers, a large range of which is now available. The pH of a fixer should be between 4.5 and 5.5, but may rise above this if no acid stop-bath is used after development and too little care is taken to avoid carry-over of developer into the fixer. A few drops of acetic acid can be added to adjust the pH of a bath as determined by an indicator paper with a range of, say, 2.5 to 10.0. Silver concentration can also be estimated reasonably accurately by means of test papers; in fact, those made by Merck indicate both silver content in grams per litre and pH between 4 and 8.

Although there are no hard-and-fast rules, it is generally accepted that the silver content of a fixer used for films should not be more than four or five grams of silver per litre; the silver content of a paper fixing bath should be held below two grams per litre when it is being used with unprotected fibre-based papers such as Ilfobrom, although it can be allowed to go higher with Ilfospeed papers because they are easier to wash.

IF23 fixer   The slower-working but cheaper liquid-concentrate fixer, IF23, is based on sodium thiosulphate and therefore requires appreciably more time to fix either films or papers, particularly if it is used with a hardener.

Powdered chemicals

Unfortunately, processing solutions made by diluting liquid concentrates are nearly always more expensive than formulations supplied wholly or partly in powder form. The principal reason is the greater bulk of liquid concentrates, and therefore their higher packaging and transport costs. The extra cost may be acceptable for the small-scale user who is willing to pay for the convenience of concentrates, but the medium- and large-scale processer must carefully balance convenience against cost. As a result, powdered chemicals are still used extensively.

When composite packs of chemicals are supplied in powder form to be made up to a given volume, no attempt should be made to prepare smaller quantities of solution by taking fractional parts of the dry chemicals. The powdered ingredients may have been dispensed in succession so that they will not be mixed until they are dissolved together in water.

ID11 developer   Perhaps the best-known powdered developer in the Ilford range is ID11. Its widespread use is reflected by the range of units in which it is supplied, from 600 ml for the hobbyist to 35 litres for the photo-finisher. Although not quite as simple to prepare for use as Ilfosol 2, mixing 600 ml of ID11 stock solution from two packets is not difficult: 'Dissolve the contents of the small bag in about 450 ml of warm water (about 40°C). When all the chemicals have dissolved, add gradually the contents of the larger bag and stir until completely dissolved. Add cold water to make up the total volume.' When used undiluted at 20°C (68°F), the suggested development times for ID11 are as shown in Table 6.

Table 6 Development times for ID11, undiluted at 20°C

	Negatives to be used in condenser enlargers	Negatives to be used in diffusion enlargers
Pan F 35 mm and rollfilm	6 min	8½ min
FP4 35 mm and rollfilm	6½ min	10 min
HP5 35 mm	7½ min	10 min
HP5 rollfilm	8½ min	12½ min
FP4 sheet film	7½ min	10½ min
HP5 sheet film	7 min	10 min

For those who, for reasons of interest or economy, want to prepare ID11 from the basic components, Ilford provide the following formula:

metol	3 g
sodium sulphite (anyhydrous)	100 g
hydroquinone	5 g
borax	2 g
water to	1000 ml

Note that the ingredients are listed in the order in which they should be dissolved in about 750 ml of warm water. Metol will not dissolve readily in a sulphite solution. The additional water to make one litre can be used to adjust the temperature of the solution, if it is required for immediate use.

Six 35 mm or 120 rollfilms can be developed satisfactorily in 600 ml of undiluted ID11 used repeatedly, although the development time must be extended by about 10 per cent for each successive film if uniform contrast and density are to be maintained. The extent of the compensation that should be made for the gradual exhaustion of the working bath can be found from the diagram on page 79.

If ID11 stock solution is diluted with an equal volume of water, the resulting image displays better sharpness. The longer development time for any given film is usually worthwhile for subjects having a long brightness range. Further dilution improves grain and apparent sharpness even more, although development times become inconveniently long if more than three parts of water are added to one part of stock solution. See Table 7.

ID11 replenisher   Diluted ID11 developer should not be re-used, but must be discarded after each film or batch of films has been developed. Because of the dilution (particularly if it is 1+3) the cost of 'one-shot' processing is low; in addition, uniformity of results is assured if the developer is thrown away each time.

Table 7 Development times for ID11, diluted 1+1 and 1+3 at 20°C

	Dilution	Negatives to be used in condenser enlargers	Negatives to be used in diffusion enlargers
Pan F 35mm and rollfilm	1+1	8½ min	12 min
	1+3	12½ min	18 min
FP4 35mm and rollfilm	1+1	9 min	14 min
	1+3	15 min	22 min
HP5 35mm	1+1	12 min	18 min
	1+3	21 min	28 min
HP5 rollfilm	1+1	14 min	20 min
	1+3	22 min	30 min

However, ID11 can be used as a replenishable developer. The necessary powdered chemicals are available in packaged form, or can be made up to this formula:

metol	3 g
sodium sulphite (anyhydrous)	7.5 g
borax	20 g
water to	1000 ml

ID11 replenisher is used undiluted. When the volume of working solution is small, 10 ml of replenisher should be added to the developer after each 35 mm (36-exposure) film or 120 rollfilm has been processed. The easiest way of doing this is to add the 10 ml to the residue of developer in the storage bottle, so that when the used solution is poured from the developing tank back into the bottle, some of it is surplus and can be discarded.

When dealing with larger volumes of working solution, the developer tank should be topped up with replenisher when it is estimated that about five per cent of its initial volume has been removed by being carried over with films. This method is rather crude, and should not be depended upon for too long without evidence that negative quality is being satisfactorily maintained. If under-replenishment is detected, it is necessary to discard some of the working bath to make room for additional replenisher.

Ilfofix This is a general-purpose sodium thiosulphate hardener-fixer in powder form. It is supplied in a single pack, the contents of which simply need to be dissolved in three-quarters of the final volume of water. The initial amount of water should be warm; after all the powder has been dissolved, the additional water can usually be added at a temperature that ensures the fixer is ready for use if required.

98

Ilfofix solution is used undiluted for fixing films or plates, and diluted with two parts of water for fixing papers. At 20°C (68°F) a 'safe' fixing time for films is 10 minutes; prints can be fixed in half this time.

IF2   IF2 is the simplest and cheapest fixer in the Ilford range. It contains sodium thiosulphate and potassium metabisulphite, without any hardener. Ilford liquid hardener can be added to IF2 if it is used regularly for fixing negatives. The formula, using hypo crystals instead of the anyhydrous powder, is:

sodium thiosulphate (crystals)	200 g
potassium metabisulphite	12 g
water to	1000 ml

(Dissolving the crystals lowers the temperature of the water, so warm water should be used to offset this effect.) A somewhat faster working bath can be made by doubling the quantities of hypo and metabisulphite in the formula. The difference in performance should be checked by a clearing test.

Other negative developers
Besides the tried and trusted ID11, there are several other negative developers available to suit different aims and requirements. Perceptol, for example, is a metol-based developer recommended by Ilford for the finest grain and highest resolution with FP4 or HP5. The cost of these improvements in image quality is some loss of speed, the extent depending on the degree of development required to suit any particular enlarging optics. See Table 8.

Table 8   Development times and effective speeds using Perceptol at 20°C

35 mm and rollfilms	Negatives to be used in condenser enlargers	ISO rating (effective)	Negatives to be used in diffusion enlargers	ISO rating (effective)
Pan F	11 min	25/15°	16 min	32/16°
FP4	10 min	64/19°	13 min	100/21°
HP5	11 min	200/24°	16 min	320/26°

When loss of speed cannot be accepted, but high-quality enlarged prints are essential, Microphen is probably the best choice. This is a Phenidone developer that works at a relatively low pH, but is capable of enhancing the rated speed of most emulsions to a significant extent. As can be seen from Table 9, the

Table 9 Development times and effective speeds using Microphen at 20°C

35 mm and rollfilms	Negatives to be used in condenser enlargers	ISO rating (effective)	Negatives to be used in diffusion enlargers	ISO rating (effective)
Pan F	4½ min	64/19°	7 min	100/21°
FP4	5 min	200/24°	7½ min	320/26°
HP5 (35 mm)	6 min	500/28°	8½ min	640/29°
HP5 (roll)	6½ min	500/28°	9 min	640/29°

rated speed of FP4 can be doubled, and HP5 film 'lifted' to ISO 500/28°, without raising developer temperature or extending development time.

By extending development of an underexposed film beyond the time required for adequately exposed negatives, an increase in contrast and density can be obtained. This can lead to a print bearing more information than could have been obtained if the negative had been developed any less. This form of 'push' processing is sometimes thought to increase the effective speed of an emulsion, and in one sense it does, although not in terms of the accepted ISO method of assessing film speed. What really happens is that additional development applied to an underexposed negative ensures that what little image was recorded on the foot of the curve of the emulsion is emphasised as much as possible. As a consequence, higher-density areas of the negative, particularly highlights, are inevitably overdeveloped and tend to be difficult or impossible to print through. However, there are many occasions, under difficult available light conditions, when 'pushing' a negative in development is the only way to get a useful print, and Microphen is an excellent developer with which to do it. Table 10 indicates the meter settings that can be used, and some would say the 'effective speeds' of HP5, for development times between 8½ and 16 minutes. The table also shows that ID11 can be used for 'push' processing in the same way, but not to the same extent.

Developer for machine processing The requirements for a developer to be used in a 'dipping', roller-transport or continuous helical-path processor are special in several respects. First, the working bath must be replenishable, since the volume of solution in use is too large to be discarded. Second, the formula should include a hardener so that no damage occurs to the emulsion surface of the film during the early stages of processing, particularly in roller processors. Ilfoneg developer fulfils these

Table 10 Recommended meter settings for HP5 films when developed for extended times in Microphen or ID11

Developer	Meter setting	Development time for HP5 (35 mm)	Development time for HP5 (rollfilm)
Microphen (stock solution)	800/30°	8½ min	9 min
	1600/33°	11 min	12 min
	3200/36°	16 min	18 min
ID11	800/30°	12 min	14 min
	1600/33°	18 min	20 min

requirements. The recommended rate of replenishment is 18 ml for each 35 mm film or rollfilm that is developed, which works out at approximately 350 ml per square metre of film area. Development times with Ilfoneg at 30°C are short enough to be measured in seconds rather than minutes (Table 11).

Table 11 Development times for Ilfoneg developer at 30°C

	Negatives to be used in condenser enlargers	Negatives to be used in diffusion enlargers
Pan F 35 mm	25 seconds	50 seconds
FP4 35 mm	30 seconds	55 seconds
HP5 35 mm	45 seconds	75 seconds
Pan F rollfilm	25 seconds	50 seconds
FP4 rollfilm	35 seconds	60 seconds
HP5 rollfilm	50 seconds	90 seconds
FP4 sheet film	40 seconds	75 seconds
HP4 sheet film	60 seconds	110 seconds

Print developers

When the Ilfospeed system of black-and-white printing and processing was introduced in 1972, one of its less obvious but very important features was the performance of the new Ilfospeed print developer. Ilford had realised that an enormous amount of time was wasted by print processers throughout the world when they developed prints by inspection. These printers had become accustomed to waiting 20 or 30 seconds before seeing any sign of image on a correctly exposed print, and then taking another minute or even a minute and a half to achieve complete development of the print. What they really wanted was a paper/developer combination that would produce the first signs of an image on a correctly exposed print as soon as possible after the print had entered the developer, followed by a steady growth of image up to the completion of development in about 60 seconds.

Ilfospeed developer does just this. At 20°C, a correctly exposed image on Ilfospeed paper begins to appear in about six seconds and reaches complete development in about one minute. Ilfospeed developer is a liquid concentrate based on the versatile combination of Phenidone and hydroquinone, and is normally used after dilution with nine parts of water.

There are several good reasons for using Phenidone as a developing agent in a print developer. First, its oxidation products are colourless, so used developer does not turn brown and will not stain prints or fingers. Second, Phenidone is unlikely to cause dermatitis. (During development a printer should only handle prints with tongs or when wearing gloves, of course, but there are those who sometimes break the rules.) Finally, because Phenidone is not as sensitive to bromide and variations in bromide concentration as metol/hydroquinone developer, a working-strength solution of Ilfospeed developer will retain constant activity over a much longer period of use. As an example of the economy that results, some sixty 20 × 25 cm (8 × 10 in) Ilfospeed prints can be processed in one litre of Ilfospeed developer.

Ilfospeed 2000 developer   Now that more and more black-and-white prints are developed in roller-transport processors such as the Ilfospeed 2001 machine, another kind of developer is required, one that will work quickly and economically and yet remain stable over long periods. Ilfospeed 2000 chemistry comprises a developer/replenisher concentrate and a fixer/replenisher concentrate. To start up a new or overhauled processor, a five-litre unit of developer/replenisher concentrate is diluted with four parts of water, but 10 ml of Ilfospeed starter concentrate must be added to every litre of the resulting developer. This brings the bromide concentration of the new developer to about the level it would otherwise attain only after being in use for some time, during which period the effective speed of the Ilfospeed paper being used would have continually changed. The fixing bath is made up by diluting the concentrate with four parts of water, and this solution is also used for replenishment.

As a guide to replenishment rates, about 8 ml of developer replenisher and 12 ml of fixer replenisher are required to compensate for processing every 20 × 25 cm (8 × 10 in) print. Put another way, if 20 × 25 cm prints are continually fed side by side into the machine, the developer needs to be replenished at the rate of 45 ml per minute and the fixer at 75 ml per minute. The recommended processing temperature for an Ilfospeed 2001 machine is 30°C for a development time of about 25 seconds.

Bromophen   Like Ilfospeed developer, Bromophen is a Phenidone/hydroquinone formulation, but in powder form. Its performance is not quite as striking as that of Ilfospeed, since both induction time and development time are a little longer. However, its capacity is quite high, even when diluted 1+3, so that some forty-five 20 × 25 cm prints can be developed in one litre of the working bath.

Print fixers   All the fixers mentioned previously can be used to fix prints as well as negatives, but Ilfospeed fixer was specifically designed as part of the Ilfospeed printing and processing system. Like Hypam, it contains ammonium thiosulphate and is therefore rapid-acting. It is supplied as a liquid concentrate for dilution 1+3 to give a fixing time of no more than 30 seconds at 20°C. A hardener is not recommended for fixing Ilfospeed papers, because ammonium thiosulphate is more difficult to wash out of an emulsion layer when the gelatin has been hardened. A longer washing time would defeat the aim of the Ilfospeed system, which is to make it possible to produce high-quality black-and-white prints in four minutes.

3 Processing the negative

Photographers able to process their films in a darkroom designed and equipped for that purpose alone are fortunate. Millions of hobbyists and freelance photographers must be content with a temporary conversion of a bathroom, or even a cupboard under the stairs. The equipment for processing negatives varies from the single-film daylight-development tank to the automatic film processors employed in photo-finishing and the roller-transport machines used by newspapers and press agencies. Let us consider the simple methods first.

Daylight-loading film tanks

The daylight-loading film processing tank enables film to be developed without the use of a darkroom of any kind. The first daylight-loading tank for rollfilms was introduced by Eastman Kodak in 1903. The film was first wound up spiral fashion with a spacer between the turns, and then the usual sequence of developer, fixer and wash water was introduced and drained out through a light-tight inlet and outlet. When 35 mm, or miniature photography as it was then known, began to gain popularity in the late twenties and the thirties, Leitz produced their Correx daylight-loading tank with its edge-embossed celluloid spacing apron.

Modern versions of daylight-loading processing tanks are made by both Agfa and Jobo. There are two Agfa Rondinax tanks, one for 35 mm and the other for 120 film. The Jobo 2400 tank is intended only for 35 mm film.

Dark-loading film tanks

Possibly because they are rather expensive, daylight-loading tanks are not as much used as their convenience suggests they should be. Instead, tanks that can be used in the light after they have been loaded in darkness are used by most amateurs and many professionals throughout the world. There are two basic types of film-processing reel; both utilise a spiral groove configuration, but one loads from the centre outwards and the other from the outside inwards. Whichever type is used, when loading a 35 mm film the protruding tongue of the film should first be removed by cutting

104

between an opposing pair of perforations, and the resulting two sharp corners snipped off.

The reels and most of the tanks made by Nikor and Kindermann are constructed from stainless steel and cannot be adjusted to take more than one film width. These reels are always loaded by attaching one end of the film to a clip in the centre spindle of the reel and then winding the film into the space between the two facing wire spirals. To do this, it is necessary to squeeze the edges of the film slightly between finger and thumb as the reel is rotated. In other words, the film is sprung into the grooves in a continuous rotating movement. One or two trials in daylight soon enable a beginner to achieve this, first with eyes closed and then in a darkroom or with a changing bag. To make it easier to load stainless-steel spirals, reel-loaders are available. They are mounted on a simple base and back-plate, and impart the right amount of transverse curl to the film as it enters the reel.

Because they are metal, wire-type reels can be quickly dried by heating, which gives them an advantage over plastic spools.

The Paterson tank and reel are both made from plastic. The reel incorporates an ingenious rachet, using two tiny steel balls working in oppositely inclined planes to ensure that the film only moves in towards the centre of the reel. All that it is necessary to

Dark-loading plastic tank and reel; cam action feeds film into spiral as spool is rotated back and forth

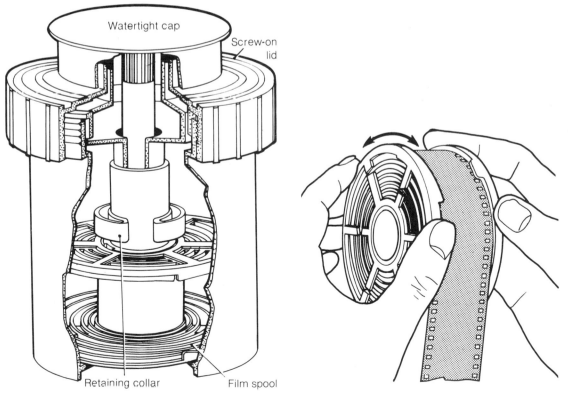

Watertight cap

Screw-on lid

Retaining collar

Film spool

do, once the end of the film has begun to enter the grooves, is to rotate one half of the reel back and forth through about 20 degrees until the whole length of the film has been drawn into the reel.

Any plastic film-processing reel must be absolutely dry before an attempt is made to load it. A single drop of water left on a reel will wet the emulsion, making it sticky and preventing the film from sliding into the grooves of the spiral.

The flanges of some of the Paterson reels can be easily adjusted to suit any standard film width between 35 mm and 120 rollfilm. Before loading a 120, 127 or 126 film into a reel, the backing paper must separated from the film itself. After the outer turns of paper have been unwound, one end of the film is reached; since this end is unattached to the backing paper, it can be allowed to coil up separately until the attachment tape is found. Then, after the film and paper have been pulled apart, the paper can be discarded. The film should next be carefully rewound so that its other end can be fed first into the reel. Rewinding avoids the risk that some of the tape adhesive might prevent the film from freely entering the reel, but is not necessary when using a centre-loading stainless-steel spool. Black-and-white 126 Instamatic films are not much used, but when they are the combined roll of exposed film and backing paper can only be removed from the plastic cartridge after it has been broken open.

Obviously it is more difficult to load a 72-exposure film into a processing reel than a shorter length, but Ilford supplies a reel-loader for use in conjunction with their stainless-steel (11.5 cm diameter) spiral reel. In order to have sufficient film emerging from the cassette while the loading end is being attached to the centre of the reel, three frames rather than two should be wound on before the first good exposure is made in the camera. A

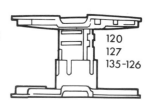

Separation of flanges on some plastic reels is adjustable to suit various film widths

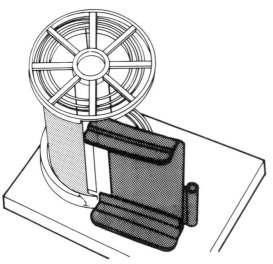

Sheets of cut film can also be loaded into special spools with the aid of a loading jig

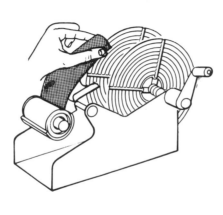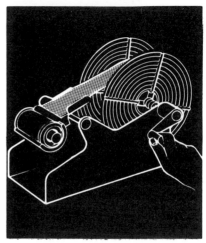

A 72-exposure length of Autowinder film loaded into a stainless-steel spiral by means of a jig; loading can be started in white light

lower-cost plastic spool is also available for use with HP5 Autowinder film. The plastic spiral is also centre-loading and is small enough to fit into any tank that will accommodate a stainless-steel reel. Loading the thin polyester-base film into either type of reel needs to be practised in the light with a scrap film, and again in the dark, before the first 'good' film is processed.

Charles Ley of the *Daily Mirror* captured this feat by using HP5 Autowinder film in a rapid-fire camera

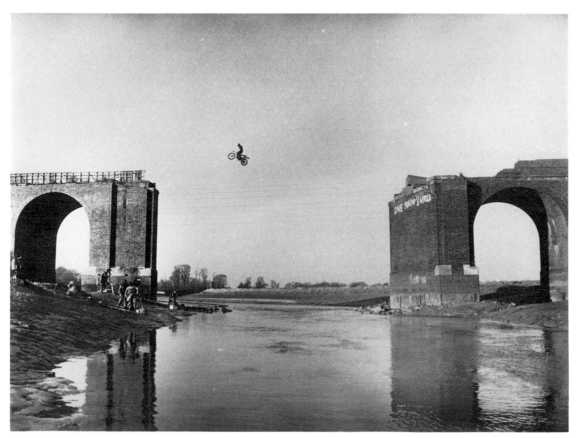

From time to time a film proves difficult to load into a reel. In that case it is best to remove the film carefully from the reel in order to start afresh. If the film is handled roughly it will be kinked or stressed, and the negatives will bear the evidence. Any film or plate, at any time, must be handled by its edges only.

Changing bags   Even a tank that must be loaded in darkness does not necessarily require a darkroom. A changing bag or box can be used instead. Changing bags have been used since the earliest days of photography. The device can be described as a black shirt with two sleeves but no hole for the neck. In use, the bag is zipped open in order to put in the reel, tank and lid as well as the film to be processed. The protruding tongue of the film, if it is 35 mm, should be removed first. Then, after closing the zipper securely, arms are inserted through the elasticised sleeves so that the film can be removed from its cassette, wound into the reel and placed in the tank, which is then closed with its lid. All of this may sound fairly easy until one tries it for the first time, using a scrap length of film. As with any other task carried out entirely by touch, a good deal of practice is essential.

Although they may look very much alike, there are some important differences between the types of cassette used for 35 mm films. With Ilford films, for example, the end-cap can be removed simply by tapping the protruding end of the spool on a firm surface. Other cassettes have their end-caps 'staked' on mechanically so they cannot be removed without using a tool of some kind, for example a bottle opener. It is important to know what type of cassette you are dealing with before you start work in a changing bag.

Darkroom   The next step forward from using a daylight-loading tank, or a dark-loading tank loaded in a changing bag, is to do the job in an improvised darkroom or closet. But no dark space should be considered dark enough to allow fast film to be handled unless you can see absolutely nothing after waiting in the room or cupboard for at least 20 minutes with no internal light.

The eyes adapt to darkness slowly during the first ten minutes after exclusion of light, and more rapidly during the next twenty or thirty minutes. This can mean that you start off thinking your 'dark' room is safe, but by the time you have the film in the reel you are beginning to see what you are doing! If the room or space you plan to use has a blacked-out window, be sure to check its safety when the sun is on that side of the building; some black polythene sheeting is not as opaque as it might seem. Draught-proofing strips can be used around doors to keep out light as well as draughts.

Once every crevice has been blocked up to exclude light, there may be no way for fresh air to enter. While this may not be too serious if you intend to stay in the room just long enough to load a film into a tank, a longer stay would become first unpleasant and later even dangerous. An extractor fan is unnecessary for a small room or closet that is to be used only occasionally for loading films into reels and tanks, but a light-tight static ventilator of the double-louvre type should be fitted in a door or window.

Safelighting

There was a time, before fast panchromatic emulsions became commonplace, when negatives were developed by inspection, using some colour of illumination to which the emulsion was either insensitive or only slightly sensitive. As W. Eugene Smith used to say: 'In the early days it was easy to develop by inspection. You had these blind films you could hold up to a bright safelight and just look through. Now you turn on the dim green safelight a couple of minutes beforehand so your eyes get used to the light. Then, at eight minutes or so, you take the film out of the developer, hold it a foot and a half or so from the light, and turn it until the light reflects off the surface of the film for just a few seconds. It's a question of being able to evaluate the blacks and greys. Usually a certain tone of charcoal comes out being satisfactory to me. A black man standing against a black background is a more difficult inspection problem than if he were standing against a white wall.' Eugene Smith was an old hand at the game, but clearly such a procedure would not help anyone who had no previous experience of assessing negative quality under such adverse conditions.

Another reason why it is now much more difficult to develop films by inspection is that 35 mm films and rollfilms are usually wound on to spiral reels, and certainly cannot be removed and replaced periodically during the course of development. Furthermore, it has been found that much more predictable results can be obtained by developing a film for a specific time at a given temperature, rather than by attempting to assess the quality of negative images by fleeting glances under an extremely dim light.

With orthochromatic or merely blue-sensitive materials, there is every reason to take advantage of the useful level of safelighting they permit. Follow the guidance given by the manufacturer of the film or plate. Any safelight intended for use with negatives (or, for that matter, positives on a transparent base) should be installed on the wall immediately over the position from which the developing films will be inspected. A safelight for this particular purpose is no use positioned overhead so that dripping negatives have to be held up high for examination.

Processing

Once a film has been wound into a spiral reel and the lid is safely on the tank, the wet part of the processing job can be carried out anywhere that allows the use of solutions. Amateurs often carry out this stage in the bathroom or the kitchen. Of the two, the bathroom is probably the better, since its temporary use for photographic processing is likely to cause less domestic disruption.

More than one film can be processed at the same time by housing a number of reels with the same cross-section in a deeper cylindrical tank. As many as eight 35 mm or five 120 films can be accommodated in separate spirals in the same tank. Some allowance should be made for the longer times required to fill and empty these longer tanks, but provided that the same routine is followed every time they are used there need be no inconsistency in negative quality.

Controlling temperature   When using any developer, there are three variables to consider: temperature, time and agitation. Although there is nothing magic about it, the working temperature often recommended for a developer is 20°C (68°F), and for many parts of the world this is probably the value that causes least difficulty throughout the year. Unless the room temperature is 20°C, it is necessary to warm the developer or extend the development period. There is a good case for working at a lower ambient temperature, provided that the necessary increase in development time does not become inconvenient. As an example, if the room temperature is only 16°C (61°F), more predictable and reproducible results will probably come from developing for 15 minutes instead of the 10 minutes required at 20°C. Working at room temperature also reduces the chance of development commencing at one temperature and ending at another.

Altering development time to suit the temperature cannot be taken far without introducing other problems, however. Some developing agents begin to lose activity at a disproportionate rate when they are used at too low a temperature. Similarly, while any developer becomes more active at higher temperatures, this activity does not necessarily increase at a constant rate. Furthermore, as developer temperature is raised, development time eventually becomes so short as to make reproducibility impossible with manual processing.

When it is not possible or it is inconvenient to use solutions at room temperature, some other means must be found to bring the working solutions to the required temperature, and to hold them at that temperature while in the tank.

If the working-strength developer is made up by diluting a concentrated stock solution, the temperature of the added water

110

can be adjusted to bring the working-strength solution to the right temperature. After that, provided there is not too much difference between the developer temperature and the room temperature, there should be no problem. If, on the other hand, the ambient temperature is significantly lower than the proposed working temperature, an attempt can be made to split the difference by starting with the developer at a slightly higher temperature than the aim, in the expectation that by the end of the period the temperature of the developer will have dropped slightly below the aim point. Alternatively, an adjustment in time can be made to offset a fall or rise in temperature during development. As a rough guide, a departure of 2°C up or down from a nominal 20°C necessitates an extension or reduction of development time of about 15%. This is no more than an approximation, since different developing agents respond in different ways to changes in working temperature.

These measures are no more than expedients, however. If processing results are to be as predictable as possible, a predetermined and constant temperature for the whole period of development must be ensured. One fairly simple way of doing this is to improvise a water-bath in a wash-basin or the kitchen sink. The developing tank can then be stood in water that has been brought to the right temperature. Provided that the volume of the water-bath is large, the temperature changes only slowly and maintains the temperature of the tank and its contents throughout any normal time of development.

Stainless-steel tanks adjust to the surrounding temperature more quickly than those made from plastic material, but with either type the actual temperature of the working solution should be checked, not just the temperature of the surrounding water.

Developer temperature need not be measured in absolute terms, but it is important to know that you are working at the same temperature each time you process a film. There is some advantage, therefore, in using one of the stainless-steel rotary dial thermometers that are made with useful ranges for photographic purposes, since they can be read easily and are unlikely to be broken.

Controlling development time   Having ensured that the necessary solutions are ready in their required volumes and at the correct temperature, the next thing to measure is the duration of development. Any watch or clock could be used for this, but a timer that sounds a warning at the end of a pre-set period can prevent mistakes happening because the precise starting time is forgotten or some distraction causes delay in termination of development.

Largely as a result of the more numerous steps involved in colour film processing, programmed timers with many facilities and digital read-out indicators have become available. These are really unnecessary for black-and-white processing, where development time is usually the only step that need be precisely controlled. In practice, a large-dial timer with a range of one second to 60 minutes and an audible alarm signal is suitable for black-and-white processing and printing.

It is almost as important to be consistent in the way each processing step is carried out as it is to carry them out in the correct order. If you start your timer at the same moment as you begin pouring developer into the tank, always do so. On the other hand, if you pour developer into the tank before starting to time the development period, always do it that way.

Sometimes bubbles are formed while developer is being poured into a tank, and some may become attached to the emulsion surface of the film. If they are not disturbed quickly, the bubbles can remain in position long enough to delay local development and cause light spots on the negative. Rapid rotation of the reel is one way of removing bubbles that may have lodged on the film, but a sharp rap of the tank on the table or bench top is more likely to jolt bubbles off the emulsion. Either of these precautions must be taken at the commencement of development.

Sometimes a film is given a short pre-soak in water before development. This is intended to wet the film so that the developer will immediately cover the emulsion and also to adjust the temperature of the film, the reel and the tank itself to the required working temperature. It also provides the opportunity to remove any air-bubbles before development commences. A pre-wet is recommended when processing XP1–400 film (see below).

Agitation   If a stirring rod or spindle is provided with the developing tank, agitation can be created in the developer by vigorously rotating the film in its reel. This may not prove sufficient for uniform development, however, The unidirectional movement, plus the fact that the outside turns of film move faster and further than the inner turns, can result in irregularities that may be noticeable in large uniform areas of the prints. To overcome these limitations, some photographers choose to work in the dark without a lid on the developing tank so that the film can be 'pumped' up and down in the developer as well as being rotated periodically.

If the tank has a sealing cap to fit over the central filling hole and a gasket in a screw-fitting lid to make it leakproof, the whole tank can be inverted to provide thorough movement of developer relative to the film. Before using the 'inversion' method of agitation during development, make sure (with water and no film) that your particular tank does not leak when turned upside down.

Opinions differ on the frequency at which the film should be rotated or the tank inverted. Strictly speaking, the frequency should be increased as development time is shortened. For a treatment period of between five and ten minutes, ten seconds of vigorous agitation at the commencement of development and ten seconds agitation during each subsequent minute should result in uniform development.

XP1–400 The processing temperature that is recommended for Ilford XP1–400 film is high by comparison with that required for other black-and-white films. There are two reasons for the difference: the colour developer used is less active than a normal black-and-white developer, and the bleach/fix time would be too long at a lower temperature. Development and bleach/fix times are five minutes each at 38°C, but if the film is processed at 30°C these two steps must be extended to nine minutes each.

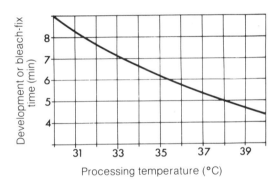

Development and bleach-fix times for XP1-400 film processed at different temperatures

The frequency and form of agitation given to XP1–400 film during development is important, since limited agitation is necessary to preserve the edge effects that enhance sharpness in the negatives. It is recommended that the tank containing the film and developer be inverted four times during the first 10 seconds of development and four times at the commencement of each minute of subsequent development and bleach/fix.

XP1–400 processing steps are as follows:

1 Pre-wet, 1 minute at 40°C (2°C above developer temperature).
2 Develop, 5 minutes at 38°C.
3 Bleach/fix, 5 minutes at 38°C. Resist any temptation to curtail the bleach/fix time or to use the solution at a lower temperature, since residual silver in the final image not only causes a deterioration in quality but also greatly extends printing time.
4 Wash, 3 minutes (or six changes) at 35–40°C.

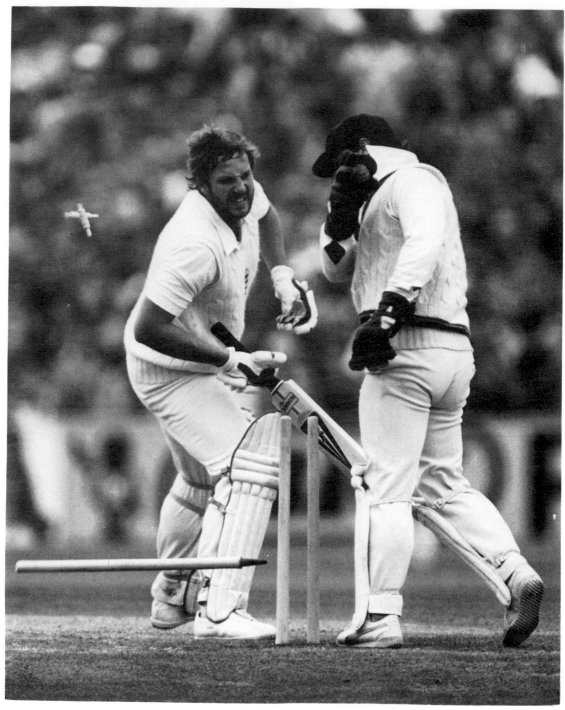

Very short exposures and
very long lenses call for a
fast film like XP1, with its
relative freedom from grain.
Adrian Murrell got this fine
shot of Ian Botham, which
Mike Campbell printed for
him

5 Final rinse in Ilfotol wetting agent diluted 1:40.
6 Squeegee or wipe with sponge, then dry in air up to 50°C. The processed film has an opalescent appearance until it is dry.

Termination of development

When processing ordinary silver-image films, pour the developer away ten or fifteen seconds before the end of the development period, according to the time it takes to empty your tank. If it will not be used again, pour the solution down the drain; otherwise use a funnel to put it into a storage bottle. Once the tank is empty, refill it with an acid stop-bath and vigorously agitate for 15 seconds or so. Then, after returning the stop bath to its bottle, refill the tank with fixing solution. Agitate the fixer for the first ten seconds and occasionally thereafter until the chosen fixing period has elapsed.

Provided that a fixing bath has not been exhausted by too much previous use and is at a reasonable temperature (say, not less than 20°C), almost any negative emulsion should be adequately fixed within five minutes. A rough test of the efficiency of a fixing bath can be made by observing the time it takes for a sample of the film to become clear when immersed in the fixer. For the clearing test to be reliable, the scrap of film used must be of the same emulsion type as the one being processed, and it should be immersed in developer and stop bath before being placed in the fixer for timing. The old rule was to fix a plate or film for twice as long as its clearing time, and this is still good advice. Fast emulsions such as HP5 often contain small quantities of silver iodide; since this halide is difficult to dissolve in thiosulphate solutions, fast films generally take longer to fix.

Removal of the fixer from the tank and its storage for future use mark the completion of the reaction stages of black-and-white processing. The film is now ready to be washed and dried. At this point there is often a great temptation to take a look at the negatives and to remove some or all of the film from the spiral in order to do so. The temptation should be resisted, because it is always difficult to get the film back into a reel and damage can easily occur while you are trying to do so.

Washing

Although it may seem almost too easy, a film can be quite adequately washed while still in its reel if it is subjected to four or five half-minute changes of water at about 20°C (68°F). Levenson has explained the fact in these terms: 'Only a small dilution factor, of the order of a hundred-fold, is needed to bring the thiosulphate content of the emulsion down to a satisfactory level. This condition can be achieved comfortably in a three-stage wash, and the wash-water flow can be cut down until the washing proceeds not in the water but, in effect, in a series of dilute fixer solutions.'

Washing a film with a sequence of changes of prepared water is a particularly sound way of processing whenever the temperature of the water from the mains supply is very low, as it frequently is in winter in many countries. The time taken to prepare a few litres of water at around 20°C is worthwhile, because the alternative of washing the film in cold water has to continue for a long but uncertain time, and its effectiveness cannot be assured.

When running water is used to wash a film while it remains in a reel, the flow of water should cover all parts of the film. This will certainly not happen if water merely runs into the top of a tank and out again over its sides. A better way is to connect a flexible pipe to the water tap and insert the other end into the centre hole of the reel; the water then enters the tank at the bottom and has to pass upwards through the turns of film before flowing to waste. The Jobo Cascade film-washing device connects the tank to a water outlet and injects a mixture of water and air into the tank, providing intensive washing from the bottom of the tank. The injected air bubbles improve washing efficiency by 'scouring' the film surface.

Yet another way of washing a film in running water is to sacrifice a spare film tank (which can usually be purchased separately) by perforating its base. With a reel and film inside, it can then stand in a wash-basin or sink and allow water to flow downwards past the film before reaching the drain. This method has the advantage of encouraging the heavier, hypo-containing water to move downwards.

A slightly more elaborate way of washing films in spiral reels is to use a 'turbine' washer. This is simply a cylinder that can take two or three films in their reels. Mains water is introduced tangentially into the base of the cylinder, thereby inducing a strong swirling motion to the water as it spirals to the top to overflow.

There is not much to be done about the quality of the public water supply, except to filter it if it is dirty. For the amateur, Paterson have a simple 20 micrometer stainless-steel filter for fitting directly to an outlet with a rubber connection. When a larger supply of clean water is required, Cuno filters are often used because they are easily fitted and can be obtained in a wide range of particle filtration sizes.

The hardness of water is measured in terms of its calcium carbonate content, which can vary from 40 (soft) to 200 (hard) parts per million. In the case of a hard water supply, great care should be taken when wiping or sponging down negatives, to see that no droplets of water remain to dry out and leave whitish marks on the film. With very hard water, it may be necessary to rinse films in a final bath of distilled water.

Drying

A negative cannot be considered completely processed until it has been safely dried. This last step must be carried out just as carefully as earlier treatments if damaging marks are to be avoided. Next to dust and hairs, drying marks are probably the most frequent cause of spotting on prints made from 35 mm negatives.

There is little agreement about the best way of removing surface water from a washed film, although it is generally accepted that it should be done. A trace of wetting agent such as Ilfotol added to the last tank of wash water reduces surface tension so that the water spreads uniformly over both sides of the film, but this treatment alone is really not enough. It is better, particularly if the negatives are needed quickly, to remove all the surface water from the film by wiping or squeegeeing both sides before it is hung up to dry. With a hanger clip attached to one end of the film and the clip held up by a rod, a two-bladed squeegee can be used to wipe all the water from both surfaces of a film. The rubber blades of a squeegee must be soft and should be wetted in water before they contact the film. (Those who have the confidence to use the method swear that there is no better way than to use the 'squeegee' formed by the first and second fingers of one hand.) When both surfaces of the hanging film have been wiped, a weighted clip is attached to the lower end of the film so that it cannot flap about while wet or curl up when dried. The simplest, but slowest, way to dry a film is to hang it up in a room where it can be left undisturbed until drying is complete. For the amateur, this means that drying often proceeds overnight.

Remember that there is a short period during the process of drying when a film is as tacky as fly-paper, and this is when any dust or hairs that come into contact with it will stick. So, once a film has been hung up to dry, leave it undisturbed by any movement in the room.

If it is essential to make prints from a negative as soon as possible after it has been processed, as a temporary measure the briefly fixed and washed film can be immersed for a minute or so in a saturated solution (about 150 grams per 100 ml) of potassium carbonate, which will displace most of the water from the gelatin layer so that it is dry enough for printing. When the urgent prints have been made, the negative should be re-fixed and washed thoroughly in the usual way.

If a fixed and washed film is immersed for a short time in ethyl or isopropyl alcohol to which about 10 per cent of water has been added, it will dry very quickly after removal. Methyl alcohol is not recommended since it can attack the film base.

There are other ways of shortening the time taken to dry films and of making the period more predictable. Provided that the film has been processed in a stainless-steel spiral, it can be dried while still in the reel by means of a rapid flow of filtered air from a fan or turbine dryer. With the Kindermann rapid dryer, for example, either a single 120 rollfilm or two 35 mm films can be dried at one time. If the surrounding air is known to be clean and the negatives are required urgently, the drying time can be further reduced by removing the air filter.

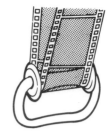

Weighted roller for long lengths of 35 mm film touches the film only at its extreme edges

When more than a few films have to be dried at the same time, a purpose-made film-drying cabinet becomes necessary. These cabinets are usually made of well-protected sheet steel and are provided with a fan or blower linked to a thermostatically controlled heater. A thermal cut-out guards against excessive heat spoiling films by some accident, and sometimes a time switch is incorporated. Film-drying cabinets can be used to dry a wide variety of films and plates because several different hanger and shelf positions are provided.

A drying cabinet for fully extended 36-exposure lengths of 35 mm film needs to be about seven feet (2.1 metres) high. Alternatively, a full 36-exposure length can be looped back over a weighted bottom roller to halve the effective length. The emulsion surface should of course be on the outside of the loop, and the roller should be recessed so that it touches the film at its edges, not within the image area.

A full 72-exposure length of HP5 Autowinder film is almost nine feet (2.75 metres) long, and once it has been removed from a processing reel it can pose some problems. Obviously, if the film can be cut into two roughly equal lengths it immediately becomes more manageable. The outer turns of the processed film should be carefully drawn out of the reel until about half the length has emerged. The starting end should be fastened to a clip and the clip attached to a hanger of some kind. The cut should be made carefully between two frames unless a waste frame was exposed for the purpose. A bottom clip should then be attached to the end of the removed film, which is then ready for wiping down and drying. The second half of the film can then be dealt with in the same way. When it is inconvenient to cut the film into two pieces, a weighted bottom roller clip should be used so that the film can be looped 'emulsion out' round the roller and then be suspended by its two ends.

118

Small portable or 'flexible' film-drying chambers are available for drying a few films at a time while protecting them from dust in the surrounding air. These chambers comprise a thermostatically controlled fan heater located above, and connected directly to, a zippered plastic compartment in which films can be suspended until they are dry. A very simple film dryer can be made from a suitably sized wooden or hardboard cabinet fitted with a 60 W incandescent lamp in its base. The slight convection current of warm air significantly reduces drying times, and the cabinet protects films from dust and hairs.

Tray or dish processing

When rollfilms and film-packs were commonly used by amateurs, they were often developed in trays or dishes. A rollfilm could be 'see-sawed' up and down so that every part of its emulsion was passed repeatedly through the developer, first in one direction and then in the other. The separate sheets of film from a film-pack were developed either singly or several at a time by continually moving the bottom film to the top of the stack throughout the development period. Film-packs are no longer made, and better ways have been found to process roll films, but sometimes it is still convenient to be able to process sheet films in a tray.

Good agitation can be achieved simply by rocking a tray containing developer, but the pattern of movement should be irregular to avoid creating any areas of greater or lesser density. Temperature can be maintained by surrouding the tray with water at the required temperature in a larger and deeper tray.

With practice, several sheets of film can be developed in the same tray at the same time, provided always that sufficient solution is used. To avoid the possibility of sheets sticking together when first immersed in the developer, they can be briefly wetted in a separate tray of water before development. After they have been wetted, the films should be transferred in rapid sequence and emulsion side up into the developer. Their relative positions must be changed regularly throughout the whole period of development, so that the bottom film of the stack is removed and placed at the top. This procedure should be repeated when the films are transferred to the stop bath and then to the fixer. Pre-wetting a plate or film so that the emulsion layer contains water when it enters the developer has a delaying effect on development, and some allowance should be made for this by slightly extending the development time.

The chances of damaging films while they are being 'shuffled' in a dish or tray are obviously rather high. Two simple measures that minimise this risk are to have short finger nails, and to work at low rather than high temperatures to restrict swelling and softening of the emulsion layers.

Since the volumes are small, it is best to discard developer after it has been used for processing negatives in a tray. Fixer may be re-used once or twice, but even this is hardly worthwhile.

Larger-scale processing

All the processing methods described so far are suitable for the occasional development of a few films. When the number of films increases and the frequency of processing is higher, investment in special equipment usually becomes viable and more efficient methods of working become possible.

One of the most versatile methods of processing is by means of a permanent hand-tank line installed in a darkroom fitted with a sink in which the tanks can stand. However small the darkroom, it must have a dry bench or shelf on which exposed films can be loaded into reels. If this dry area has to be close to the 'wet' side, it may be necessary to erect some kind of shield to prevent any accidental splashes from reaching the loading bench.

The standard size of tank for a hand-operated line used to be three gallons. The nearest equivalent now is 15 litres, although there is also a narrow 7.5 litre tank available. Tanks were once made of hard rubber, but now they are more likely to be constructed from rigid PVC or moulded polypropylene. Light-tight lids are provided for developer, stop and fixing tanks. A floating lid covers the developer when it is not in use, so that oxidation and loss of activity are delayed.

When processing several 35 mm, 120 or 220 rolls at the same time in a tank-line, the film spirals are best handled in racks or baskets, usually constructed of stainless-steel wire. A 15 litre tank normally takes a rack containing up to thirty reels loaded with 35 mm films or up to eighteen reels containing 120 rollfilms. A 7.5 litre tank usually takes fifteen reels of 35 mm film or nine containing 120 rolls.

A hand tank-line can also be used to process plates and sheet films. The separate negatives must be held in special frames or hangers so that they can be suspended in the tanks. Plates are held in stainless-steel frames with grooved sides, while sheet films can be held in wire frames fitted with clips to grip the films at each corner. It is risky to try to process films or plates spaced too closely, for some may be damaged by the repeated lifting and reimmersion that is necessary; furthermore, agitation becomes inadequate when films are so close together that the developer cannot flow freely over the emulsion. This limitation applies even when gas-burst agitation is used (see below).

Brian Tremain, working for the National Maritime Museum, used an 8 × 10 in sheet of FP4 film to record this beautiful composition of the Tulip Staircase in the Queen's House, Greenwich

120

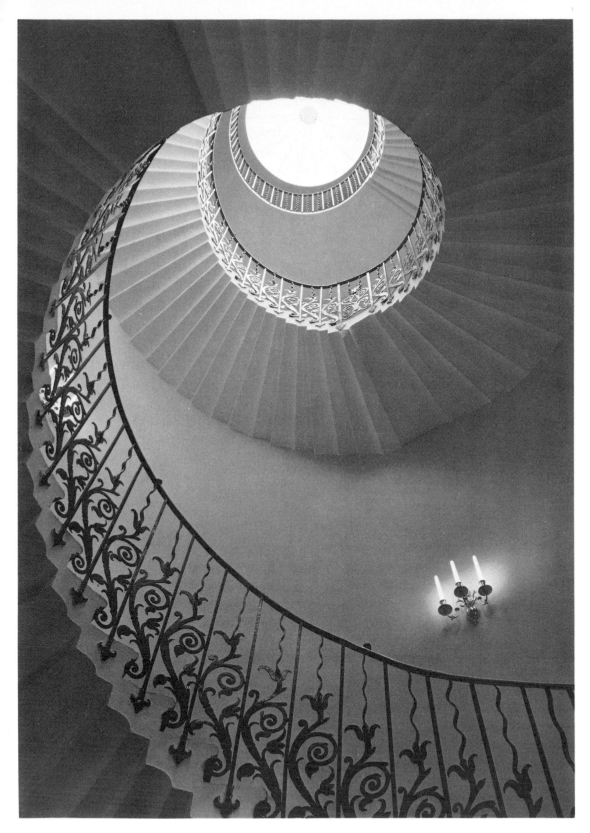

Although the method demands constant attention throughout the processing cycle, uniform development can be assured if film or plate hangers or racks are moved manually to ensure the initial removal of air-bells and subsequent dispersion of the layer of used developer adjacent to the emulsion layers. For example, the procedure might be as follows:

1 Immerse film hangers or rack in developer in one smooth movement.
2 Immediately bump hangers or rack on inside of tank to dislodge any air-bells.
3 Lift hangers or rack out of developer after one minute and then drain, tilting the hangers first one way and then at an opposite angle.
4 Repeat the lifting and draining operation at one-minute intervals.
5 Remove hangers or rack from developer 10 or 15 seconds before completion of development, and drain them over the developer tank before transferring them to the stop bath.

As with so many other operations in photography, the exact sequence and manner of handling films or plates in a hand tank-line are not as important as doing the same thing every time.

Gas-burst agitation   Because of the stricter requirements of colour film and paper processing when three emulsion layers have to reach the required degree of development simultaneously, gas-burst agitation is now commonly included as part of any new installation. What is good for colour processing can also be used to advantage for processing black-and-white materials, even if it is not quite so necessary.

Two forms of solution movement result from the intermittent release of a distributed burst of gas into the bottom of a tank. First the whole bulk of solution is lifted slightly with a sort of piston action, and then a myriad of bubbles rises to the surface past the surfaces of any suspended films or plates. The frequency and direction of the bursts of gas can usually be controlled independently by means of an adjustable regulator.

Generally it is possible to achieve an adequate level of agitation by increasing the frequency of short bursts rather than by extending the length of the bursts, which is a wasteful way of using the gas. Because it is inert, relatively cheap and easily obtained, nitrogen is usually chosen for use in developers, although compressed air is sometimes used for other solutions and in wash tanks in larger processing installations.

Temperature of solutions   The simplest way of raising the temperature of solutions in a tank-line is to heat them by inserting an immersion heater or a tubular stainless-steel heating coil. This method has the advantage of giving quick results, but it cannot maintain the required temperature during processing, so that if more than one batch of films have to be developed, reheating is usually necessary between batches. It is also very easy to overshoot the required temperature when using a portable immersion heater. Whenever solutions need cooling rather than heating, ice cubes contained in plastic bags can be immersed in the developer or fixer.

A far more satisfactory way of reaching and maintaining a given temperature for all the solutions in a hand tank-line is to use a water bath or to surround the tanks with air at the right temperature, in effect an air bath. If necessary, a time switch can be used to switch on the heater early enough for the line to be ready for use at some predetermined time of day. The necessary components in a thermostatically controlled water bath are a heating element, a temperature control device and a circulating pump. A combination of these things can now be obtained as a unit; this need only be connected to the sink containing the processing tanks by two flexible pipes.

Washing Washing tanks for negatives are usually larger than the developer, stop and fixing tanks, to allow several batches of negatives to be washed at the same time. Satisfactory washing will not result from simply letting water into the tank at one position and out at another. Either water distributor pipes should be arranged in the bottom of the tank or compressed air should be supplied through distributor pipes. In the Kindermann Rapid Washing tank, both water and air are distributed from the base of the tank, which also incorporates rapid overflow and drainage devices.

A washing tank or section is often built into an integrated tank-line. Water is supplied through bottom-entry spray pipes, with a counter-flow cascade arrangement if there is more than one wash section. The temperature of the washing water can be maintained at a predetermined level by a thermostatically controlled water-mixing valve, provided that there are supplies of both hot and cold water at about the same pressure.

Deep tanks

Before the days of spiral film reels, rollfilms and some 35 mm films were processed by suspending them in deep tanks. There are still some merits in the method, which is still used by newspapers in Fleet Street. It is possible to handle a batch of several films at the same time in a darkroom with quite a small floor area, provided that the height of the room is sufficient to allow the films to be

123

lifted clear of each tank while they are being transferred to the next one. The tanks must stand clear of the floor to allow periodic draining, so the ceiling must be at least 2.6 m (8 ft 6 in) from the floor even if 36-exposure 35 mm films are looped back to halve their effective length.

The disadvantages of a hand-operated deep-tank line are the risk of damage to the films and the difficulty of manipulating a hanger full of dripping films in the dark. Nevertheless, the method is both effective and cheap.

Although the manual transfer of films from one solution to the next in a deep-tank line may be satisfactory for a relatively small-scale operation, such as in the photographic department of a newspaper, it is a laborious method of working and the quality of resulting negatives depends very much on the operator. Long ago, photo-finishers found ways of mechanising their rollfilm processing by using a machine to dip films automatically into the sequence of solutions.

'Dipping' machines
As the name implies, a dipping (or 'dunking') machine immerses films into first a tank of developer and then into other tanks for whatever times are required by the process. The films are usually

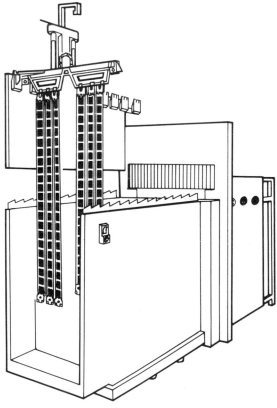

Typical machine for automatically dipping films into required sequence of processing solutions

suspended from rods in groups of five or six, with weighted bottom clips to keep them hanging vertically. Lifting arms, driven by an arragement of endless chains, transfer the films from tank to tank; another mechanism shunts the film hangers from one end of each tank to the other in a series of uniform steps. When a rack and its films have been moved stepwise from the front to the back of a tank, it is automatically picked up by the lifting arms and put either into the next tank or, at the end of the wet sequence, into a drying section. In this final stage, the rack again moves along a track until the films are dry and can be removed from the machine.

Strictly, the lower parts of the films processed by dipping receive more development than the upper parts, since the bottom of a film enters the developer first and leaves it last. To minimise this difference, some machines transfer hangers as rapidly as possible without making the suspended films swing about too much.

Usually the volume of developer removed with the films being processed leaves room in the developing tank for replenishment to be carried out by a simple topping-up procedure. A recirculating pump is usually connected to the developer tank of an automatic dipping machine so that the added replenisher is dispersed quickly in the body of the solution. With a hand tank-line, a stirrer or mixing paddle should be used to ensure that the replenisher poured into the top of the tank is properly dispersed throughout the developer before the next film is processed.

Roller transport processors

There is another way in which all forms of film-based negative materials can be processed automatically and with great convenience. In 1957, Russell of Eastman Kodak patented a roller transport processor for use with X-ray films, but it is unlikely that he could have foreseen how widespread the use of similar machines would become for processing almost every kind of photographic material. In his patent, Russell described the merits of a roller transport film processing machine in these simple terms: 'The transport of sheets of material by rollers is preferable to hangers because it is less bulky, reduces the floor space requirements of the overall processing machine, and provides a faster transport, thereby greatly reducing the time required to process a film.'

Something else that has made roller processors popular throughout the world is their extreme convenience. No photographic processing technician, whether in a hospital, a graphic arts department or an industrial or commercial laboratory, would choose to move wet films around in a darkroom if he can simply 'post' them into one end of a machine and have them emerge properly processed and dried at the other end of the machine only minutes later. To a certain extent this also applies to print processing as will be seen later.

There are several different ways of using rollers to move a sheet or length of film through a series of adjacent but separate solution tanks. Russell's original X-Omat processor and the subsequent Kodak machines such as the Versamat all use a staggered configuration of rollers so that film is moved in a slightly sinusoidal manner down one and up the other side of each tank. In his patent Russell described this, as well as the way in which the film is made to change direction at the bottom of each rack: 'The roller transport mechanism comprises a pair of spaced-apart plates for supporting two parallel rows of rollers arranged in staggered relation to transport the film downwardly, two parallel rows of rollers arranged in staggered relation to transport the film upwardly, and a central roller of large diameter having a plurality of rollers of smaller diameter disposed around a portion of its periphery to transport the film from one of said two parallel rows or rollers to the other of said two parallel rows of rollers.'

The rollers are disposed differently in a Hope processor and there are more of them, so that they comprise an almost unbroken sequence of opposing pairs throughout the whole of the film path. Hope processors are described as 'leaderless'. Other machines, such as the Versamat, require a short length of stiff film to be attached to the leading edge of any roll or 35 mm film to be processed. Roll or 35 mm films for processing in a Hope machine merely receive a crimping treatment along their leading edges to stiffen them and remove any tendency to curl. All the rollers in a Versamat or Hope machine are hard-surfaced, but in a Kreonite processor a 'soft and hard' roller combination is used. It is claimed that this arrangement of rollers handles a wide variety of film thicknesses, ensures contact right across the width of transport, and provides a continuous roller-cleaning action. Only the film loading or feeding end of a roller processor need be in the dark. The rest of the machine including the take-off or receiving bin can be, and usually is, located in white light.

Roller processors were rejected when first offered to some users of roll and 35 mm films, particularly newspapers and press agencies; there was a fear that film fed into a roller processor might never emerge at the other end, or if it did, it might be so badly marked after contact with dozens of rollers that it would be useless. Gradually these fears have been dispelled as it was learned that, provided a roller processor is properly cleaned and maintained, there are fewer reasons for films being damaged than by any other system of processing.

126

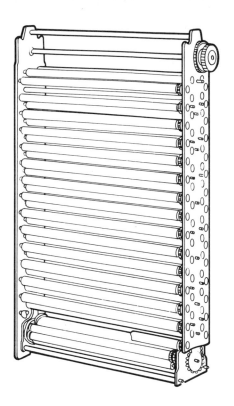

Film drive rack from Kodak
processor, showing
staggered arrangements of
guide rollers

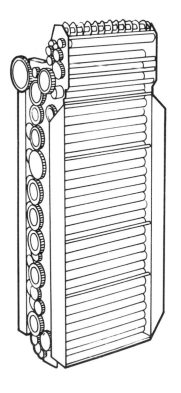

Film drive rack from Hope
processor, showing closely
spaced pairs of guide
rollers

The Versamat Model 5A–N can process 35 mm, roll and sheet films up to five inches (12.5 cm) wide and of any length. The speed of transport through the machine can be varied between 12 inches (30 cm) and 10 feet (3 metres) per minute, and this is the variable that can be used to achieve a particular development time. At the maximum machine speed of 10 feet per minute, and running two films side by side, more than a hundred 35 mm films (36-exposure) can be processed in an hour. The Versamat 11C–L handles films up to 11 inches (28 cm) wide and can run at twice the speed of the 5A–N. Working temperature, which is usually quite high, can be adjusted to any setting between 21°C (70°F) and 40°C (105°F). Replenishment is automatically determined by area of film processed, and wash water is supplied at the required temperature and rate through a thermostatic mixing valve and a rate-of-flow meter.

The Hope 'zero-torque' Model 134 black-and-white film processor requires very little effort to rotate all the rollers in the machine because of its novel bearing design. The machine accepts films up to 11 inches (28 cm) wide or combinations of other sizes. For example: five strands of 35 mm film, three strands of 120 film

Versamat 5A-N film processor. Left, fitted with spools for taking off long lengths. Right, opened to show roller assembly and hot-air ducts

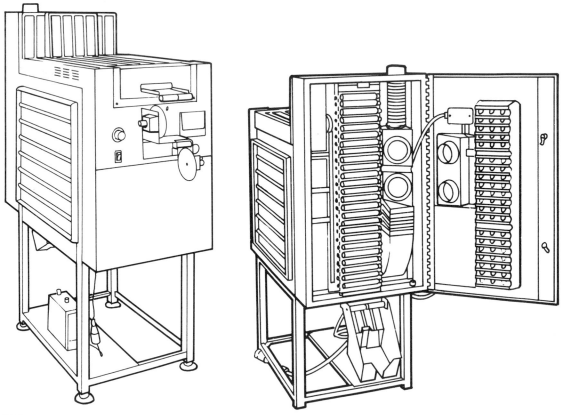

or two 12.5 × 10 cm (5 × 4 in) sheet films side by side. At three feet (90 cm) per minute, treatment times are approximately:

Develop	30 seconds
Fix 1	20 seconds
Fix 2	20 seconds
Wash 1	20 seconds
Wash 2	20 seconds
Dry	18 seconds

Solution replenishment on a Hope processor is governed by sensing rollers that measure both the length and width of any film passing into the machine. This information is used to calculate the volume of replenisher to be automatically added, through metering pumps, to developer and fixer.

The Versamat as well as most other roller processors can be fitted with take-off and take-up spindles so that rolls of 16 mm, 35 mm, 46 mm or 70 mm film up to 300 feet (90 metres) long can be processed without attention once the leading end of the roll emerges from the dryer and has been attached to a take-up spool. The relatively long 72-exposure lengths of Ilford HP5 Autowinder film can easily be processed in a roller transport machine.

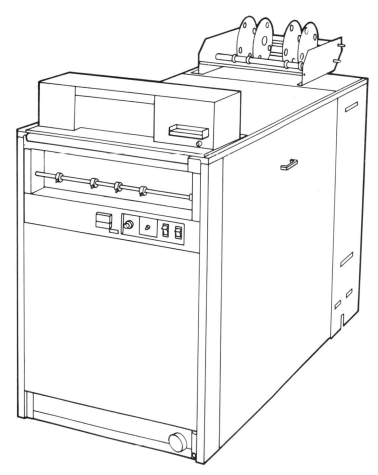

Hope 134 leaderless
black-and-white film
processor

Drum or tube processors

Because of their versatility and the fact that they achieve consistency by using 'total loss' or 'discard' processing with small volumes of solutions, rotary drum or tube processors have become popular when relatively small numbers of a variety of different films and prints have to be processed.

A tube machine requires the exposed material to be loaded into the tube in the dark, but white light can be used after the tube has been placed in the machine. Prints lie safely against the inner surface of a tube, but films must be loaded into reels. The

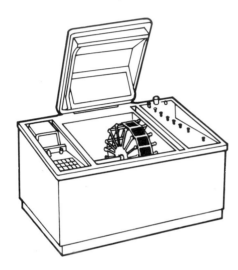

Programmed rotary processor can be used for roll or cut sheet films

necessary sequence of solutions is introduced into the tube, either by manual or automatic controls, from the outside of the machine. After each stage of the process, all the used solution is expelled from the tube by tilting it. Processed films have to be removed from the tube for drying.

In a drum machine, films or prints are attached to the outside of the drum, which may be solid or open. Long films are wound round the drum in a helical path. Solutions are fed sequentially into and out of a trough in which the drum is rotated; because a drain can be located in the trough, there is no need to tilt the drum. When lengths of 35 mm or roll film are being processed in a drum machine, smaller volumes of solution are required than when the films are loaded in spiral reels to fit inside a tube.

Continuous film processors

When the total length of film to be processed at one time adds up to thousands of feet, it is necessary to use the kind of continuous film processor developed by the motion-picture industry and often described as a cine film processor. The distinctive features of these machines are that they usually run at high speeds, and thus the

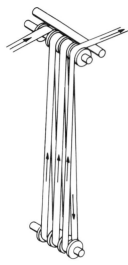

Helical-path continuous
film processor

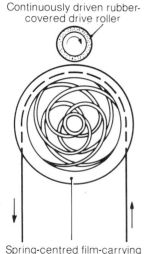

Continuously driven rubber-
covered drive roller

Spring-centred film-carrying
roller

Principle of film transport
using spring-centred rollers
(see text)

film is driven through a helical path over a multitude of rollers
supported on racks that are submerged in the processing solutions.
Generally a continuous cine processor is designed to handle one
width of film only, either 35 mm (including 126 cartridge films) or
16 mm (including 110 cartridge films). But before short lengths of
film can be handled by a fast-running continuous machine, they
must be joined end to end into much longer rolls of several
hundred feet.

Film joining can only be mechanised to a certain extent.
Whatever method of joining is used, the made-up roll must be
checked manually before it is put in the machine. Although heat
splicing is sometimes used, a wrap-around tape joint is more usual.
The perforations of the films can be covered by the tape, since
sprockets are no longer used to drive the film through the
machine. Instead, some form of 'tendency' drive is employed to
prevent undue slackness or tension building up along the machine
as the film first expands in the developer and then shrinks in the
drying section.

There are a number of ways of controlling the tension
throughout the length of a machine that may contain many
thousands of feet of film; basically they all depend on the use of a
'pacer' roller, driven positively at a required speed, at the outgoing
end of the drying cabinet. All the preceding rollers, or at least
those in association with either the top or the bottom shafts of
each film rack, according to which is providing the drive, become
idler rollers whenever local tension in the film exceeds some preset
limit. Forward drive is not transmitted to the rollers until the loops
of film slacken again in that area. This on-off motion is not a
coarse one, but operates at quite a high frequency so that the film
is moving most of the time and is therefore uniformly treated in all
the solutions.

Many different and ingenious ways of providing a 'tendency'
drive have been devised and used in processing machines running
at several hundred feet a minute, but the most elegant solution is
to use spring-centred film rollers. The top row of film-carrying
rollers in a film rack are spring-centred so that they can be pulled
down individually by extra film tension; this downward
movement disengages the rims of the roller from contact with a
rubber-covered rotating driveshaft located immediately above the
row of film rollers. In this simple way, the tension in every film
loop is 'averaged' by a continuous series of 'on-off' motions.

Quality control or monitoring
When large-output machines are used for processing, the value of
processed work and of the solutions in use is large enough for any

serious mistake to be very costly. For this reason alone it is necessary to institute some form of monitoring system. At its simplest, all that is required is a supply of sensitometric control strips, made on a material that is the same as or similar to the films that are normally being processed, and a processed reference strip for comparison. Obviously the reference strip must have been processed in a manner known to be satisfactory, usually but not necessarily by the film manufacturer.

The frequency at which control strips should be put through a machine depends on the volume of work being processed, on the number of occasions when the machine is idle, and above all on the quality aspirations of the company or department. At least once a day, preferably at the commencement of work, a control strip should be processed and *immediately* compared with the reference strip. It is also particularly important to check that the process is in order after a weekend or longer holiday shutdown, or when some major change to the machines or the solutions has taken place.

Visual comparison of a processed control strip alongside a standard or reference has limited value and can only be used to detect any gross change that may have taken place. If a trend is to be detected before results have deteriorated too much to be acceptable, control strips must be measured on a densitometer and plotted regularly on a graph.

To minimise the effects of 'bromide drag', all control strips must be processed the same way round: low-density end leading in a continuous processor, or uppermost in any kind of dipping system. The low-density end of the strip is usually indicated by a notch.

Routine monitoring of a black-and-white process does not require that all the steps of a control strip be measured and plotted in the form of an H and D curve; this is necessary only if something quite unusual seems to be happening to the process. Instead, one high-density step (HD) and one low-density step (LD) are usually indicated by an arrow or a ring on the step wedge, and these are the only two steps that need to be measured. Reference values must be established for each of the marked steps: this will have been done by the supplier of the reference strip. For example, the LD step may have a density of 0.40, while the HD step might measure 1.20. By subtracting the lower reading from the high one, a density difference (DD) of 0.80 results. This can be taken as a reasonable indication of the degree of development the control strip had when it was processed. Limits must then be set for permissible density differences, which might be between 0.70 and 0.90.

132

The values plotted on a running graph can be either in terms of the actual density differences or in terms of the amounts by which they depart from the aim as represented by the reference strip. In the example illustrated, the former method has been used.

Whenever measurements show that the density difference represented by a strip falls outside the limits of tolerance, another strip should be processed before any action is taken. Should the

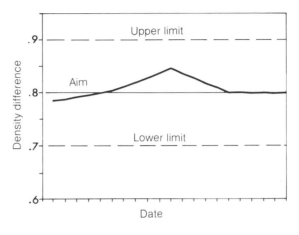

Process control chart based on daily measurement of density differences between two chosen steps of a processed control wedge

second strip confirm the previous result, an attempt must be made to find the cause of the change. If, on reference to the graph, there is evidence that a gradual change has culminated in the out-of-tolerance result, the cause could simply be over-replenishment (if the density difference exceeded the aim) or under-replenishment (if the density difference was too little). If on the other hand the out-of-tolerance result came suddenly and the density difference was low, replenishment may have failed, perhaps because the replenisher tank was empty!

Sometimes the cause of a processing difficulty can prove elusive and the only option may seem to be a complete change of one or more of the processing solutions, but several 'obvious' factors should be checked first. Is the temperature indicated by the remote-control thermometer really the same as the temperature of the developer in the tank on the machine? Is the duration of development really what it is thought to be? Is the developer being circulated at the correct rate of flow? If nitrogen agitation is being used, are the holes in the gas distributors all clear? These and similar matters should not be taken for granted, but should be checked by direct observation on the machine.

After-treatment of negatives
During the early years of photography, when the speed of plates was unpredictable and the only guide to exposure was likely to be some simple form of actinometer (itself depending upon exposure

133

of a strip of print-out paper), errors in exposure were frequent and the density of negatives varied greatly. Consequently it was common practice to attempt to correct unsatisfactory negatives by intensifying or reducing them by some kind of after-treatment.

Auguste Lumière, before the turn of the century, was so anxious not to end up with dense and unprintable negatives that he habitually developed his plates for less time then they might be expected to require; then, after examining the fixed and washed results, he intensified them progressively by successive chemical treatments until they looked satisfactory. This rather roundabout procedure required a treatment that was both controllable and proportional, and Lumière used an intensifier that partially converted the silver image to one of mercury. The overriding advantage of the method was that it could be carried out in daylight.

Today, with the remarkable consistency of modern emulsions and the assistance of exposure meters and controls, there are no longer the same reasons for modifying negative images after they have been processed. Furthermore, while negatives made on sheet film or plates can be dealt with separately, negatives along a length of 35 mm film cannot be treated separately without cutting the film into inconveniently tiny pieces. Another reason for the less frequent dependence on after-treatment of negatives is the availability of a wide range of paper contrasts, either as separate grades or in a single variable-contrast paper such as Ilfospeed Multigrade.

Nevertheless, mistakes do happen. Complete rolls of film can be developed for the wrong time or at the wrong temperature, or the film you have just developed can turn out to be slower or faster than the one you thought you were processing. You might even forget to reset the speed rating on an automatic camera after changing film type. Any of these mishaps could lead you to consider correcting all the images on a film by some form of intensification or reduction. However, before deciding on any form of after-treatment, make quite sure that the negatives cannot be printed satisfactorily on a very hard or very soft grade of paper. Even if no really satisfactory print results from your attempts at printing, it is still advisable to keep the best prints as an insurance against the possibility of irreparable damage occurring to the negatives during any subsequent attempt to improve them.

Having decided to apply some form of after-treatment, take a little time to decide just what must be done to improve the negatives. Are they excessively dense because of gross overexposure or because they were developed for too long or at too high a temperature? Are the negatives thin because they were

134

So far as is possible by means of printing, these nine negative images represent different combinations of exposure and development

1 Underexposed and underdeveloped
2 Underexposed but correctly developed
3 Underexposed and overdeveloped
4 Correctly exposed but underdeveloped
5 Correctly exposed and correctly developed
6 Correctly exposed but overdeveloped
7 Overexposed and underdeveloped
8 Overexposed but correctly developed
9 Overexposed and overdeveloped

1	4	7
2	5	8
3	6	9

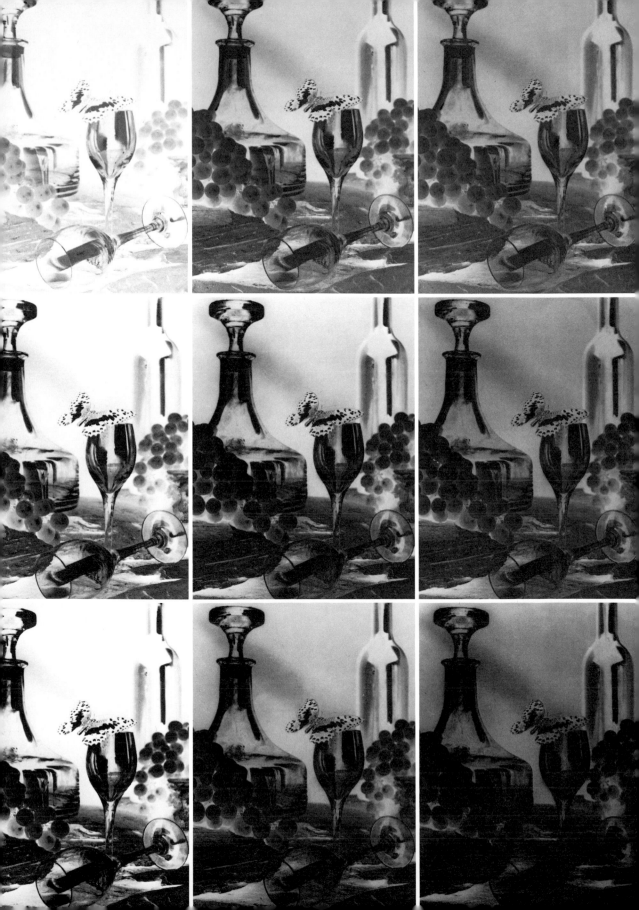

underexposed or because they were underdeveloped? These questions are rather difficult to answer without some experience, but the signs to look for are illustrated on page 135. The nine negatives illustrated were originally made on FP4 35 mm film; when considering any of them, a comparison should be made with the central reference, which was exposed and processed correctly.

There would be little point in trying to improve negatives 1, 2 and 3, since there is too little density in the shadow areas of the images, and no form of after-treatment could put this right. The overdevelopment suffered by negative 6 has resulted in excessive contrast, so if reduction is to be effective it will have to react most in the high density areas; in other words a super-proportional reducer should be chosen. Because its excessive density is largely due to exposure and not development, negative 8 lacks contrast, which might be partially restored by using a 'cutting' reducer, although careful choice of paper grade might do just as well. Negative 9 may prove too dense to print conveniently unless it is reduced in a proportional reducer. It should be possible to obtain satisfactory results from all the other negatives by printing them on paper of appropriate contrast: negatives 4 and 7 on grade 3 or 4, and negative 5 on grade 2 (normal) paper.

Chromium intensifier   An intensifier converts all or part of an initial silver image into a substance (usually another metal, but sometimes a dye) that is more opaque in printing density than silver. Most mercury intensifiers enhance the contrast of a negative by losing shadow detail, and they have largely been replaced by formulae containing chromium.

A hundred years ago, Eder was first to use a chromium intensifier. A silver image is bleached in an acid solution of potassium dichromate before being washed and redeveloped in a rapid-acting developer. A suitable bleach can be made up from two solutions:

A	potassium dichromate	25 g
	water to	500 ml
B	hydrochloric acid	50 ml
	water to	500 ml

The degree of intensification can be controlled in two ways: by altering the ratio of solution A to solution B and by the number of times the process of intensification is repeated. The more acid the working bath, the less the intensification and the slower the bleaching reaction. For a start, mix three parts of solution A and one part of solution B in four parts of water. Use this solution to bleach the silver image thoroughly, and then wash the yellow

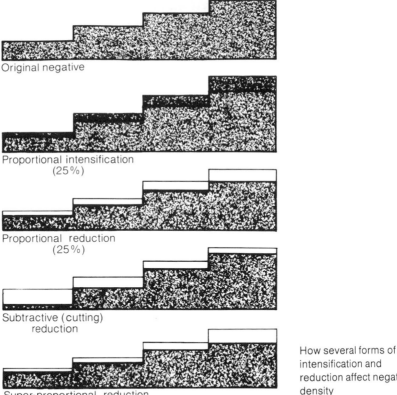

Original negative

Proportional intensification
(25%)

Proportional reduction
(25%)

Subtractive (cutting)
reduction

Super-proportional reduction

How several forms of
intensification and
reduction affect negative
density

dichromate stain out of the negative. Redevelop the image in any
MQ or PQ developer. A final wash for a few minutes completes
the treatment, which can be repeated if the change is judged to be
insufficient.

Farmer's reducer   Now that many amateur photographers load
their cameras with ISO 400/27° films, overexposed negatives are
commonplace, since conditions out of doors in the summer make
it difficult to shorten exposure enough to avoid overexposure. In
an overexposed negative there is more density in the shadows than
really necessary; provided that it has been properly processed,
there is a case for treating it in the best-known of reducers, the one
using ferricyanide and hypo and named after Howard Farmer,
who devised it.

Because the working bath does not keep for more than a few
minutes, Farmer's reducer is made up from two solutions and used
immediately:

A	sodium thiosulphate (crystals)	100 g
	water to	500 ml
B	potassium ferricyanide	50 g
	water to	500 ml

Farmer's reducer works by converting the silver of an image to silver ferrocyanide, which is immediately dissolved by the hypo and washed out of the gelatin layer. The speed of the reaction is dependent upon the concentration of ferricyanide in the working bath. Although 'old timers' judge a reducer's activity by the depth of its colour, those without experience should be more careful: dilute 100 ml of solution A with an equal volume of water and then add 5 ml of the ferricyanide solution. This mixture is pale yellow and must be used immediately.

A 35 mm film or rollfilm cannot be treated conveniently in a spiral developing reel, because the progress of reduction cannot then be observed. It is better to cut the long length into more manageable strips that can be immersed in a tray or dish, preferably a white one. If sufficient reduction of density has not taken place after two or three minutes treatment in Farmer's reducer, the bath should be discarded and replaced by a freshly made one. The new solution must be watched carefully, as it is relatively energetic at first. When reduction is judged to have gone far enough, transfer the negative to water, and thoroughly wash and dry it.

At the concentration of ferricyanide suggested above, the action is reasonably slow and does not affect shadow densities uncontrollably; as the concentration of ferricyanide is increased, however, the reducer not only becomes more active but quickly removes silver from low-density areas, producing a more contrasty image. Negative 8 is therefore a good candidate for treatment in a relatively strong solution of Farmer's reducer, known as a 'cutting' reducer.

Super-proportional reducer Negative 9, overexposed and overdeveloped, is difficult to print because of the long exposure required. Because the highlight areas of the image are excessively dense, they need to be reduced more than other densities, which would certainly not happen when using Farmer's reducer. A reducer that will attack high densities preferentially is known as super-proportional, and one of the best known of these depends upon ammonium persulphate. But there are problems associated with this type of reducer; for example the solution must be slightly acid, and the reduction is highly susceptible to small amounts of impurities, such as iron, chlorides, bromides, etc.

Bleach and redevelop In view of all the problems with super-proportional reducer, it is probably safer to bleach and redevelop a negative that is too contrasty and too dense. To do this, the original silver image is converted to silver bromide or chloride and redeveloped in a low-energy developer until enough

138

silver has been reformed. All this can be done in white light. A suitable bleach comprises an acidified solution of copper sulphate and sodium chloride (note that the acid must be added to the water):

water	1000 ml
copper sulphate	100 g
sodium chloride	100 g
sulphuric acid (concentrated)	25 ml

Bleaching must be continued until no trace of the black silver image can be seen through the film or glass support, but this usually takes only a minute or so. After washing the negative, redevelop it in a low-energy developer such as ID11. Watch the progress of development, again through the base, to make sure that all the silver chloride has been converted back to silver.

Using undiluted ID11 usually results in a negative that requires half the exposure it previously needed on a paper that is at least one grade softer. A really fine-grain developer, based perhaps on a paraphenylene diamine formula, produces an image that is very much thinner and less contrasty than the original negative, and may sometimes make the difference between getting a reasonable print on grade 0 paper and not getting a usable print at all.

Photographic masking   The forms of after-treatment discussed so far depend on chemical conversion to change the characteristics of the original negative. There are ways in which this can be achieved without changing the original image itself.

The printing characteristics of a negative can be altered by the superimposition of a positive image (mask) that has been generated photographically from the original itself. Clearly, if a positive image of the right density and contrast were combined with the negative from which it was printed, the two images could cancel each other so effectively that there would be nothing to print. A positive having less contrast than the negative would reduce the effective contrast of the original, however. Conversely, if a supplementary negative image were combined with the original negative, the effective contrast of the 'sandwich' would be greater than the original alone.

The choice of a material with which to make a mask, the developer in which to process it and the development time to use are matters for experiment. Although it is not necessary to use a panchromatic emulsion, photographers are more likely to have camera-speed films on hand than any other kind; if the inconvenience of working in complete darkness is acceptable, a film such as FP4 can be used quite satisfactorily. With such a fast emulsion, exposure must be restricted in some special way, possibly by the introduction of one or more neutral density filters in the optical system of an enlarger. Development is also a matter for trial and error, although either the normal dilution factor or the development time (or both) must be changed in order to obtain a significantly lower contrast than on the original negative.

For the hobbyist there are two practical disadvantages to the use of photographically produced masks as a means of reducing negative contrast. The business of producing the mask is obviously time-consuming, since it involves experimentation, and the combined 'sandwich' of original negative and mask tends to require a long printing exposure. However, if a number of identical prints are required from the same difficult original, masking is the only satisfactory solution.

Locally applied masking   Some of the disadvantages of photographic masking can be circumvented by local masking provided that the part of the image requiring correction is not too intricate.

When negatives were larger than they usually are now, it was common practice to effect local corrections by applying a red or neutral dye to the film or glass negative. The dye is applied directly to the image layer with a brush, the density being built up gradually with repeated applications. In the case of roll or sheet film negatives, dye can also be applied to the gelatin backing layer. The most popular and easiest dye used to be known as 'neo-coccine'. Similar dyes are still available with names such as Crocein Scarlet. Neutral dyes such as Dyene Black can be used instead of red ones, but it is more difficult to see the effect of the brushwork. For most people the difficulty is to be able to apply the dye accurately, in terms of density and location, when dealing with small areas of 35 mm negatives. Because of this, direct treatment of a negative with dye cannot really be recommended to anyone who is not prepared to spend many hours gaining the necessary skill.

If, after applying dye directly to a negative, the result is judged to be unsatisfactory, the dye can be removed, either by washing it out in water (which may take some time) or by treating the negative in a bleach made up in a two per cent solution of sodium hypochlorite.

Retouching an overlay   Fortunately there is an alternative way of using dyes which, while still requiring skill, does not endanger the negative. A piece of gelatin-coated, clear-base, fixed-out film can be used as an overlay to receive the retouching dye. Black-and-white motion-picture positive film serves this purpose well. The negative and the superimposed piece of clear film must be held together along one or more edges, and the sandwich will need to be placed, gelatin side up, on a diffusely iluminated viewer of some kind. A head-band magnifier makes the retouching easier by allowing one hand to orient the negative while the other uses the brush. The brush must be small and of high quality. When relatively high densities of dye are necessary, successive applications are usually more successful than trying to reach the required density with one application.

Blocking out   Sometimes it is necessary to isolate a subject from its background as completely as possible. This can be done either by using a suitably shaped opaque mask or by applying opaque paint directly to the negative. Opaque paints are generally water soluble, and can be obtained as a liquid or a paste. For black-and-white work they are usually red in colour, which makes them more visible. The work should be done with a good-quality brush on the back of the negative. If large areas have to be blacked out, it is often quicker, having painted round the outline of the subject, to use opaque adhesive tape to block out the rest of the unwanted image area.

This shot is called 'Rockers', and Gene Nocon printed it from an FP4 negative by Jeremy King. Notice how the slight shadow beneath the rocking horse has been left to provide a link with the ground

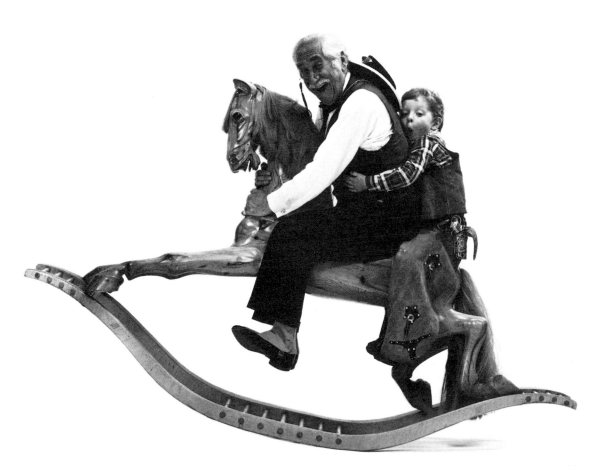

Knifing   When image formats were larger, a great deal of work used to be carried out directly on negatives by knifing to reduce density and pencilling to increase it. Knifing involves physically cutting away silver and gelatin from the surface of a negative with a very sharp knife or scalpel. Clearly this kind of corrective work on a negative, even a large one, calls for a very high level of skill, and retouchers who are capable of it are paid accordingly. Few professional photographers and fewer hobbyists will aspire to working on their negatives with a knife.

Pencilling   The application of pencil to a reasonably large negative, perhaps to lessen or remove wrinkles in a portrait image, is not beyond the capability of anyone prepared to put in a little practice. As negative sizes become smaller, the difficulty becomes greater, so 35 mm negatives should be duplicated and enlarged if the importance of the print order warrants the additional work involved.

Although a small amount of pencil retouching can be done on the untreated surface of a negative image, it is usual to produce a more receptive surface by applying a retouching fluid or lacquer, which dries with a better 'tooth' to hold the lead from a retouching pencil. Retouching leads are usually interchangeable and can be obtained in different grades or hardness; Koh-i-noor leads, for example, are available in a range from 3B to 6H. The softer grades are used where considerable additional density is required. Leads are sharpened to long thin points by rubbing gently on very fine emery paper. The progress of pencilling, like any other work done directly on a negative, is observed by light transmitted through the negative from a diffusely illuminated retouching easel.

Dust and damage   So far, it has been assumed that there is something unsatisfactory about the photographic image itself that needs correction, but there are times when negatives require treatment because of some damage or defect that occurred before exposure or while the film was being processed or printed, or even while it was stored.

As negatives have become smaller, the importance of cleanliness and careful handling has become greater. The tendency for every speck of dust or slight scratch to be faithfully recorded on prints can be minimised by using an enlarger with a diffuse light source, but this should not provide an excuse for careless or dirty work.

Keeping dust off film before it is exposed and before it is processed is really more important than preventing it from getting on a negative before it is printed. Any dust that settles on the emulsion surface of a film while it is in the camera is likely to result in tiny transparent spots on the resulting negative image, while

142

anything, including finger marks, that clings to the emulsion throughout development will also cause transparent areas on the negative. All these transparent areas, whether unexposed or undeveloped, must lead to corresponding black marks on every print made from the negative, and it is much more difficult to remove black marks from a print than it is to fill in white spots.

Convenient canisters of compressed air now make it easy for a photographer to keep his camera and enlarging equipment free from dust. A jet of air directed on to a negative will do a better job than a brush, which can even make matters worse by inducing a static charge on the film.

Scratches on the back or on the emulsion side of a negative, once printed, often prove impossible to remove by spotting or scraping, particularly with polyethylene-coated papers. The time-honoured dodge of transferring a trace of grease from the side of one's nose to the surface of the negative will sometimes help, but a more certain cure is the application of a lacquer such as Repolisan. Great care must be taken to provide clean and undisturbed surroundings while the lacquer is drying, otherwise the scratches may be removed at the cost of a crop of dust and hairs.

4 Exposing the print

Fifty years ago it was quite easy for amateurs to make their own prints with the simplest of equipment and solutions and the help of the sun. The relatively large negatives of those days were contact printed in a spring-backed frame on to printing-out paper, known as P.O.P.

Today, while films can be processed in tanks that may be used (and sometimes loaded) in daylight, it is no longer practical to make prints in ordinary room light because the small negatives now generally used need to be enlarged. Nevertheless, contact printing is still important for proofing groups of negatives made on 35 mm film or 120 rollfilm and for commercial and industrial printing from large-format sheet-film negatives.

Contact-printing from small negatives

Proofing a group of 35 mm or 120 negatives on to a single large sheet of paper is a common editing step preceding the production of large prints. Proof or contact sheets are usually made on 20 × 25 cm (8 × 10 in) paper, which conveniently allows 36 exposures on 35 mm film to be printed together in six strips of six frames, or twelve exposures on 120 film in four strips of three frames.

At its simplest, all that is required to expose a proof sheet is a controllable light source and a sheet of clear glass. The glass should be fairly thick, say 6 mm (¼ in), and free from defects; it is used to hold the negatives in contact with the printing paper. The emulsion side of the film strips must face the emulsion surface of the paper for the prints to be the right way round. If the glass has to be cut specially, it should be a little larger than 20 × 25 cm, with all its edges slightly ground for safer handling.

Strips of negatives cut from a processed roll of film can be inserted into special transparent sleeves, so that positioning the negatives on the printing paper is easier and involves less handling. After the contact sheet has been made, the negatives can remain in the sleeves until required for enlargement. The size of these transparent printing/storage sleeves is often A4, and printing paper can also be obtained in this format.

There are a number of special frames available to ease the task of proof printing. The Paterson contact proof printer is typical. It

The upper section of a contact proof sheet was printed normally. The one below was 'normalised' by being printed on a Milligan masking printer.

144

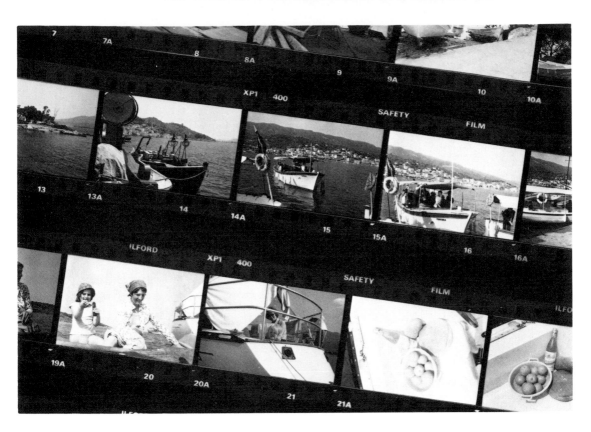

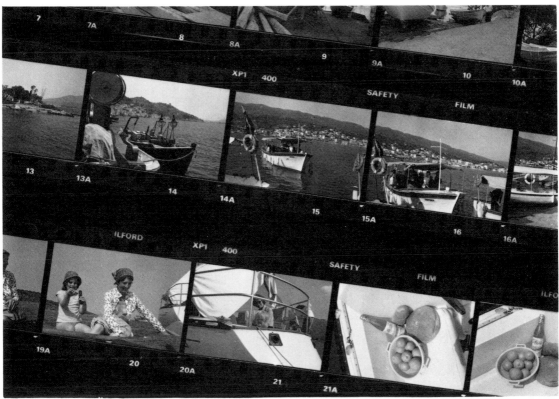

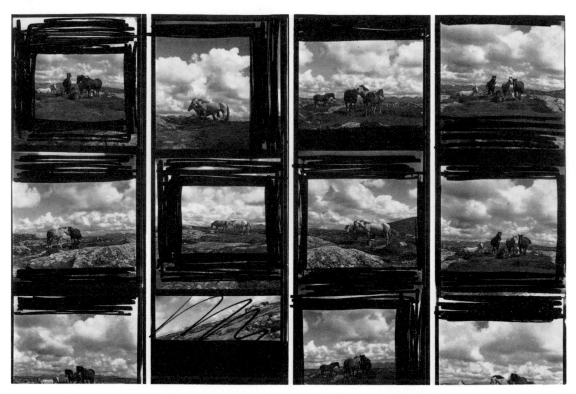

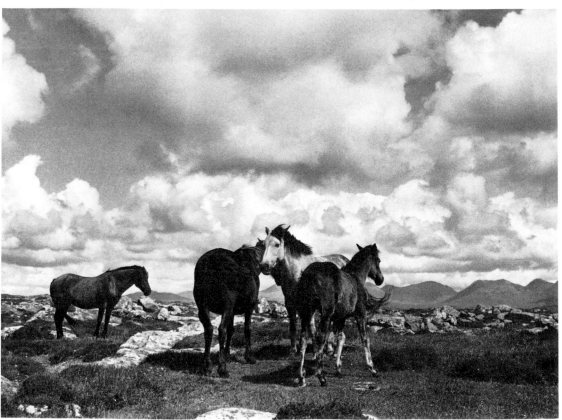

146

consists of a glass plate, hinged to a rigid base that is covered with a sheet of sponge material to ensure good contact between the negatives and the printing paper. The most important feature of the printer is the opaque mask attached to the underside of the glass. This mask serves to retain and align the negative strips so that they are uniformly positioned during exposure. A clip at one end of the frame clamps the glass and the negatives tightly into contact with the paper. After processing, the print not only carries the positive images of all the negatives but also bears their frame numbers and leaves space to record details of the subjects.

An easy way of exposing a proof print is to use an enlarger as the light source. Set the enlarger to project the aperture of an empty 24 × 36 mm negative carrier to about 30 × 38 cm (12 × 15 in) on the baseboard, and the lens at $f/4.5$. A series of test exposures at, say, 2.5, 5 and 10 seconds on Ilfospeed paper, grade 2, should then yield a result from which the optimum exposure time for subsequent prints can be judged.

A single exposure time often has to be a compromise, resulting in some negative frames being underexposed and others overexposed. If the differences in print density are too great, so that some of the images are useless, another proof sheet has to be made to take care of the over- or underexposed frames. Although it takes a bit longer, the best way of making the second print is to expose it initially for about half the previous time. Then, after covering with small pieces of card those frames that have had sufficient exposure, expose the other frames for additional times, probably twice or perhaps three times the initial exposure.

Another, more elaborate, way of producing contact sheets showing uniformly dense images from widely varying negative densities is to use an electronic masking printer such as the Milligan. In those markets where they offer a processing and proof-printing service to users of XP1 film, Ilford in fact produces 'normalised' contact sheets in this way.

Because a contact print from a 24 × 36 mm negative is so small, it may sometimes be necessary to use a magnifier to examine it properly, particularly if only a part of the negative is to be enlarged. Another way in which the value of a 35 mm contact print can be enhanced is to inspect individual images through a frame-sized aperture in a viewing card. In this way adjoining images are covered, and the chosen picture can be assessed more confidently; this is particularly important when deciding how the negative should be 'cropped' when it is enlarged. Contact sheets should be marked-up with wax or chinagraph pencils so that the markings can be removed at any time. If a felt-tipped pen is used, changes may not be possible.

These contact proofs, from the author's 120 rollfilm negatives, have been roughly marked up to provide a guide when making the subsequent enlargements. The enlargement below is from the third frame of the top row

Although no longer contact sheets, proof sheets are sometimes made by projection from a whole set of negatives on to a large sheet of paper. This can only be done by using an enlarger that will cover a 20 × 25 cm (8 × 10 in) negative, so it is generally offered as a service to photographers by commercial printing houses. The larger individual images are of course easier to assess and to crop.

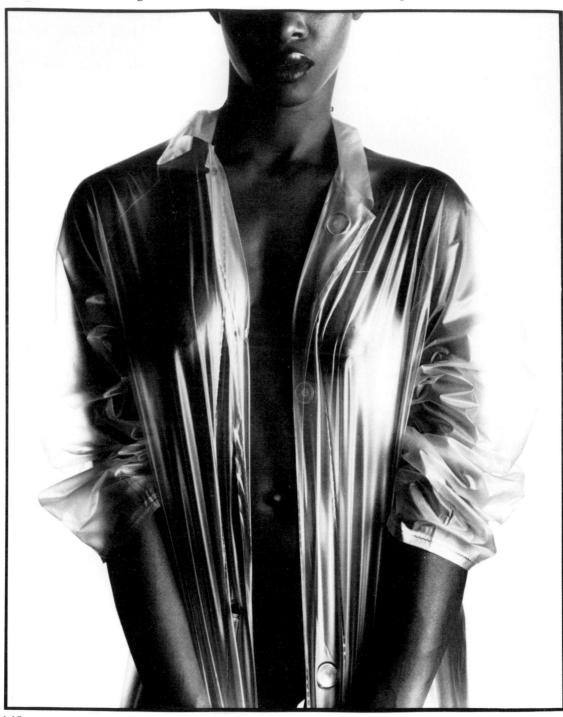

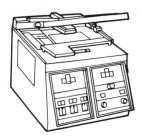

Contact printing box in which brightness of any of six lamps can be adjusted to control local density

Left: much of the quality of this print is due to the fact that the original negative was made on 8 × 10 in cut-sheet FP4 film, so that the print could be exposed in contact with it. Photographer Gary Bryan, printer Mike Campbell

Contact-printing from large negatives

Large negatives can be printed, one at a time, either in a large-format printing frame or on a printing box. When using a frame, it is better that it should be larger than the negative being printed; a mask can then be used to form a white border if required. Exposures can be made with an ordinary low-wattage tungsten lamp placed about a metre away. The distance should not be much less than this, to ensure uniformity of illumination and a controllable exposure time.

Local dodging or burning-in can be done while a print is being exposed in a frame, simply by interposing a suitably shaped piece of black paper or card between the lamp and the frame. As with any other form of dodging, the card must be kept moving slightly throughout the period of its use.

If contact printing is done regularly, a printing box makes the work more efficient and allows better control. A contact printing box allows exposures to be made without flooding the darkroom with white light during every exposure, and it usually incorporates a safelight as well as the exposing light so that the negative can be visually located and any masking easily arranged. It is also usual for an automatic exposure timer to be incorporated, so that

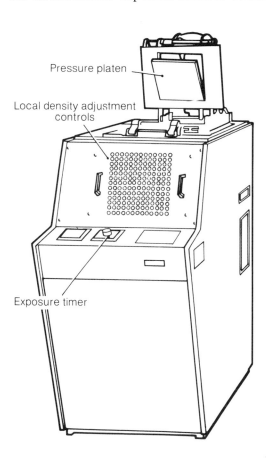

Pressure platen

Local density adjustment controls

Exposure timer

Friboprint contact printer allows density of large contact print to be 'modulated' in 195 local areas

149

exposures can be preset for any duration between, say, 0.25 and 60 seconds.

There are two ways in which local adjustment of exposure over the printing area can be achieved when using a contact printing box. If the box is fitted with a group of regularly spaced lamps beneath a diffusing sheet of glass or plastic material, the brightness of one or more of the lamps can be reduced with resistors, to lighten selected areas of the resulting print. Local shading can also be carried out by laying suitably shaped pieces of translucent material (such as tissue paper) on a sheet of glass located 2–3 cm beneath the negative plane. A second sheet of glass can be used to prevent the paper masks from moving. Because the translucent masks are displaced from the negative they do not cause sharp-edged shadows. Although this form of control requires some trial-and-error preparation, once it has been done any number of identical prints can be made quickly.

Extremely fine control of local densities can be achieved with the Friboprint contact printer, which uses 195 separate shading elements controlled by buttons; once a particular combination of shading adjustments has been made and checked, both visually and by means of a test print, the matrix of button positions can be transferred to a template which can be retained and used to reset the buttons whenever the negative has to be reprinted.

Electronic contact printing   A great deal of both aerial survey and reconnaissance photography is carried out with relatively large-format negative images that are printed by contact. Electronic masking printers, such as the Log Etronic and Milligan, can be used to compensate automatically for the local differences in negative density and contrast that frequently result from varying atmospheric conditions or cloud shadows. See page 188.

Edward Weston's negatives   The high quality obtainable by contact printing from a large negative is shown by the excellence of the work produced in this way by photographers such as Edward Weston, who always used large-format negative material.

However perfect the optical system of an enlarger, some deterioration of print quality is inevitable when the printing image is formed by projection. The difference may be small, but comparison between a contact print from a 20 × 25 cm (8 × 10 in) negative and the same size print enlarged from a small camera negative always favours the contact print. Some young photographers may not appreciate this subtle difference because they seldom see large contact prints; if they take the trouble to ask to see some of the earliest prints in the possession of museums such as the Victoria and Albert in London or the Smithsonian Institute in Washington, they will come to appreciate the perfection of detail and gradation that was achieved in the days when 8 × 10 in or even 10 × 12 in were common negative sizes.

Cole Weston has described how he makes prints from his father's world-famous collection of negatives, most of which are 8 × 10 in films.

'The negatives are coded in detail on each sleeve. The code may be, for example, "H−1, 100 watts, X15". That means Haloid paper, grade No. 1, 100 watt bulb, 15 seconds exposure. Dad loved Haloid, which was manufactured by a company that later became Xerox. The paper had a wonderful warm tonality. Ilfobrom is the paper that comes closest to Haloid.

'When I work in the darkroom, I place the paper and negative into a standard 8 × 10 inch wooden contact printing frame. I clean the glass in the frame with toilet tissue. The printing bulb is about three feet above the frame. I use ordinary frosted bulbs, and depending upon the density of the negative I use a 7½, 15, 25 or 60 watt bulb.

'To print "Nude 1936" (Neg No. 227N) I use a 15 watt bulb because the negative is not dense. Dad left instructions on the negative sleeve to use Haloid No. 1. The closest paper today would be Ilfobrom No. 0. I make a test strip at exposures of 5, 10, 15 and 20 seconds. On the negative sleeve, there are instructions to hold back on the shadow on the arm; the code also tells me to burn-in the right side of the print a little, because it is too bright. So I burn-in 6 seconds on the right side, 3 on the lower left corner and 4 on the foot. Usually I burn-in with my hands, although for small, difficult areas I sometimes cut a hole in a sheet of old photo paper.'

From Cole Weston's description of his method of printing it can be seen that the wonderful photographs obtained by Edward Weston resulted partly from what he did with his camera but also from what he did in the printing room.

Making prints by enlargement

It is likely that more than 95 per cent of all the negatives exposed in still cameras today are printed by enlargement. Apart from the fact that most negatives are now too small to yield useful finished prints by contact printing, projection printing is preferred because more controls are possible. For example:

1 The main area of interest in the negative can be selected and enlarged to almost any desired size.

2 Dodging and burning-in, to control local density, are easier to perform.

3 The quality of the projected image can be changed by overall or local diffusion.

4 Deformed or distorted negative-image perspective can be modified or corrected.

5 Two or more negatives can be used to produce one print.

While these possibilities are not all exclusive to enlarging, they are more easily achieved by projection printing.

Darkroom arrangement   Usually the most difficult part of fitting out a darkroom for printing is not where to put the enlarger, but where and how to carry out the 'wet' part of the process. Such problems are considered in Chapter 5, which deals with print processing.

For obvious reasons, prints must be exposed in a strictly dry area. Although the level of safelighting can be uniform throughout the room, there is an advantage in arranging things so that a maximum of safelighting is provided above the print developing area and much less light over the enlarging easel. The importance of this distinction is often overlooked, particularly if it is not recognised when the darkroom is first fitted out or taken into use.

The safelighting in the enlarging area must be sufficient to allow comfortable location and use of all the enlarger controls and fittings, and to enable paper to be placed on the baseboard or in the easel without fumbling. But the less ambient light there is, the brighter the projected image on the baseboard will be, and the better you will be able to focus, compose and manipulate it. One way of ensuring that the safelighting does not dull the image projected on the baseboard is to link the safelight (or at least the one over the dry bench) to the enlarger lamp switch, so that when one is on the other is off. Some darkroom timers can be wired so that they control both the safelight and the enlarger light at the beginning and end of any timed exposure.

Vertical enlargers

The earliest enlargers all worked with a horizontal optical axis (no doubt because of their very large size and the requirements of the early light sources), but the majority of enlargers now work vertically. There are still some large models, made for use in commercial or industrial darkrooms, that are mounted on rails and project on to a vertical surface (see page 185).

A vertical enlarger can be constructed in a variety of ways. Because it is important to avoid vibration during an exposure, a heavily constructed enlarger is generally preferable. But weight alone will not ensure high-quality prints: good design and accurate construction are also necessary. The basic requirement of any enlarger is that the negative and paper planes remain truly parallel to each other throughout the whole range of enlargement. The lens adjustment must also be smooth and positive, so that an image on the baseboard can be focused precisely with the confidence that the setting will not alter before the print is exposed. Evenness of illumination is another essential requirement, but is difficult to assess visually unless it is very bad. It is therefore worthwhile to arrange for a practical trial of an enlarger before deciding to purchase.

It has been said that a vertical enlarger, with its lamphouse raised to the top of the column, is an inverted pendulum just waiting to oscillate. For this reason it is extremely important that the bench or table supporting any enlarger should be rigid and substantial. The top of an enlarger column can sometimes be fastened to the wall behind with a bracket or a pair of wires, the tension on which can be adjusted with small rigging screws of the kind used on sailing dinghies. If a built-in bench is not possible an old but solid desk can serve well, and its drawers are useful for storing negative carriers, lenses, print dodgers and the packets and boxes of paper that always accumulate.

If the ceiling of the only room available is so low that the lamphouse of the enlarger cannot be raised to its maximum height, a recess can be constructed in the bench so that the paper easel can be located at a lower level when extreme enlargement is necessary from a small part of a negative. For this arrangement to work, the baseboard of the enlarger must be separated from its column.

Enlarger columns, and the ways in which they support the lamphouse, negative stage and lens assembly, vary greatly; each design is a compromise between cost, weight and complexity. The simplest arrangement is a tubular column supporting a lamphouse

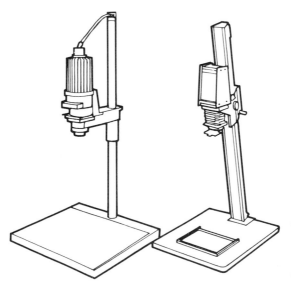

Left: Paterson enlarger, extremely simple yet adequate for the beginner. Right: Berkey C700 and 760 series enlargers can be used with condenser or diffusion head

that is light enough to allow its easy vertical adjustment without the aid of a counterweight or spring. The small Durst 'C' enlargers have tubular columns, but also incorporate a metal spline with which a friction drive engages so that the lamphouse can be wound up or down the column by means of a knob. Other designs, such as the Berkey C700 series, have a square-section sheet-metal column mounted at an angle to the baseboard and fitted with a spring-loaded steel band to take the weight of the lamphouse when it is moved up or down the column.

The more substantial, and of course more expensive, enlargers are typified by the Durst, Omega and De Vere models, which use solid machined metal columns. In one Beseler model, the problem of providing rigidity and parallelism between the negative stage and the paper plane is tackled with an inward-sloping frame support that transmits the load to the two rear corners of the baseboard.

Yet another type of design uses a vertical column attached to a parallelogram arrangement of arms that support the lamphouse, negative carrier and lens assembly at the outer end. A strong tension spring keeps the arrangement balanced, so that little effort is required to swing the lamphouse up or down through a vertical arc of quite a large radius. As the lamphouse assembly is moved, the centre of the projected image moves slightly in or out from the

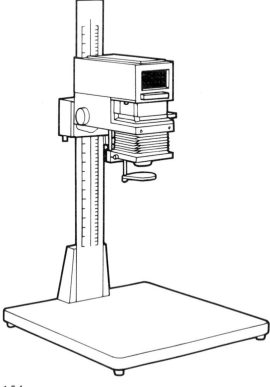

Durst 605 black-and-white condenser enlarger uses a 150-watt opal lamp with a pair of condensers that can cover 6 × 6 cm negatives. It can be used for copying, with its reflex finder

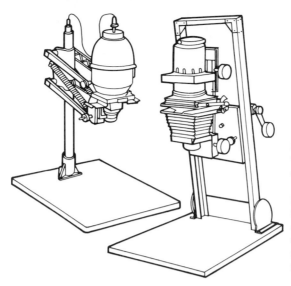

Left: Agfa Varioscop, one of the first automatic-focusing enlargers for 35 mm and 120 negatives. Right: Beseler 23C enlarger, with a rectangular frame instead of a single column to support lamphouse, negative carrier and lens assembly

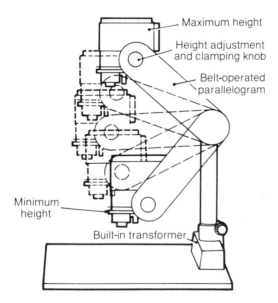

Maximum height

Height adjustment and clamping knob

Belt-operated parallelogram

Minimum height

Built-in transformer

Leitz Focomat V35 enlarger uses an endless belt to provide parallelogram movement and auto-focus

centre of the baseboard. Enlargers built like this include the older Leitz Focomats, Agfa's Varioscops and the Gamer.

The newer Leitz Focomat V35 works in much the same way as its predecessor, except that an endless band engaging two geared wheels replaces the earlier arrangement of four swivelling arms. The Focomat V35 can be fitted with a wide-angle lens, so that the range of enlargement, from 3× to 16×, is greater than it was with the earlier models.

The parallelogram system lends itself well to the provision of automatic focusing, since a cam can be made to move in unison with the position of the parallelogram, thereby controlling the location of the lens. Both old and new Focomat designs and the Agfa Varioscop work in this way.

There is often a division of opinion on the merits of automatic focusing on an enlarger. Certainly, if a printer doubts the performance of an auto-focus enlarger, so that he finds himself regularly checking the sharpness of the projected image, he might as well be focusing manually. There are a number of factors to be checked when an auto-focus enlarger is used for the first time. The lens must be the one specified for the job, and the designed distance between the enlarger head support and the paper plane must be achieved by careful adjustment to take account of the height of the paper easel that will be used.

Directed and diffuse light

The earliest enlargers depended upon daylight to illuminate the negative. In due course, artificial light sources were brought into use: oil lamps, gas lamps, arc lamps and eventually tungsten filament lamps. But all of these artificial sources were small in size and would not illuminate a negative uniformly unless located much too far from it. Furthermore, most of them were relatively ineffective compared with daylight, so the introduction of a diffuser to improve uniformity of coverage would have resulted in unacceptably long exposures. A solution to both problems was found by introducing a condenser between the light source and the negative.

The diagram shows a pair of plano-convex condensers placed in the optical path of an enlarger to direct light through the negative and into the object lens. When light from a small source is collected by a condenser system, passed through a negative and

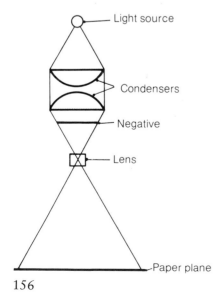

Basic elements of a condenser-type enlarger

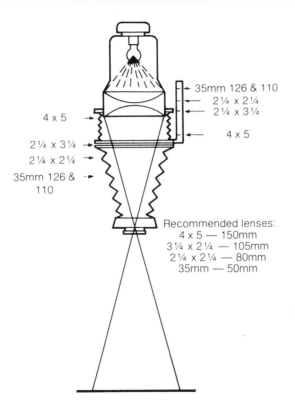

35mm 126 & 110
2¼ x 2¼
2¼ x 3¼

4 x 5

4 x 5

2¼ x 3¼
2¼ x 2¼
35mm 126 & 110

Recommended lenses:
4 x 5 — 150mm
3¼ x 2¼ — 105mm
2¼ x 2¼ — 80mm
35mm — 50mm

Negative plane of Beseler
4 × 5 enlarger can be
moved up and down to fill
enlarging lens aperture with
light

focused in the aperture of an enlarging lens, the illumination is
said to be directed or specular; the light efficiency of such an
arrangement is very high. The condenser system usually comprises
a pair of plano-convex lenses slightly larger in diameter than the
diagonal dimension of the largest negative to be covered. The
condensers are mounted just above the plane of the negative,
which is usually in a fixed position in relation to them.

It can be seen from the diagram that directed illumination only
works at its optimum light efficiency when the enlarger lens is in
one particular position relative to the condensers and the negative.
As soon as magnification requirements alter enough to require the
lens to be moved significantly, or changed for one of a different
focal length, the enlarging lens is no longer filled with light. The
directed light system also has the disadvantage that the aperture
settings of the enlarger lens are unlikely to influence exposure
times in a predictable manner, because the image of the source
focused in the lens by the condenser may sometimes be smaller
than the full aperture of the lens.

These difficulties can be overcome by adjusting the positions of
the lamp of the negative in relation to the condensers, to take
account of any changes in the position or the focal length of the
enlarging lens. One example of an enlarger in which the negative
carrier can be adjusted up and down is the Beseler 4 × 5 MX.

Another way in which the efficiency of a directed light arrangement can be maintained, despite changes in negative size and enlarging lens, is to have more than one set of condensers, or to add a supplementary lens to the basic condenser system to reduce its effective focal length. The Berkey Omega B66 enlarger is an example of the latter type. However, adjusting the lamp position is a nuisance, and provision of an adjustable negative stage or auxiliary condensers is a somewhat expensive solution to the problem.

Partially diffuse light   If the lamp in an enlarger has a tungsten filament in an opal-glass envelope, the light source is both large and diffuse; thus the full aperture of the enlarging lens remains filled whatever its position in relation to the condenser, and the negative is uniformly covered. This combination of a condenser and a diffuse light source has been adopted by almost every enlarger manufacturer at one time or another. The arrangement is a good compromise because it eliminates the necessity for additional movements or components and yet provides both adequate intensity and uniform illumination. A good example is the Kaiser 60 enlarger.

Quite often, particularly with small-format enlargers, a further simplification is made by using a single plano-convex condenser lens with its flat side facing the negative. The original Leitz Valoy and subsequent Focomat enlargers used the plane surface of a single condenser lens to clamp the negative to its carrier. Another, more recent, design that uses a single plano-convex condenser is the simple Paterson enlarger for 35 mm negatives.

All enlargers using directed light produce more contrasty prints from a black-and-white silver-image negative than those using

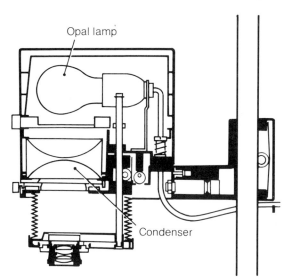

Opal lamp

Condenser

Kaiser 60 enlarger typifies modern diffuse light plus condenser system of negative illumination

diffuse light. This difference in the effective contrast of a negative varies according to the graininess of the image and the specularity/diffuseness of the printing light. The fact that a given negative can yield quite different prints on the same contrast grade of paper when printed on different enlargers can sometimes be a nuisance. The problem is peculiar to printing from silver-image negatives, since the non-scattering dye images of colour materials and of XP1–400 negatives print the same regardless of the type of enlarger illumination used.

The fact that a silver-image negative has a higher effective contrast when measured or printed by specular light is due to the Callier effect. The Callier coefficient or 'Q' factor is a means of expressing the ratio of specular to diffuse density of an image. For example, if an area of an XP1 negative has the same density to specular light as to diffuse light, it is said to have a Q factor of 1.0. If, on the other hand, an area of a negative on HP5 film has a diffuse density of 1.0 and a specular density of 1.25, the image has a Q factor of 1.25.

In practice, a negative made on a fast, grainy material and printed by diffuse light may require paper that is softer by one contrast grade to produce a similar print on a directed-light enlarger. A black-and-white enlargement made by diffuse light should have much the same contrast characteristics as a contact print from the same negative. The most likely cause of any difference is flare from within the bellows or the lens of the enlarger.

Contrary to the belief of some people, a print made in a diffuse-light enlarger can look just as sharp as one made from the same negative on a condenser enlarger, provided that they have the same contrast. This point has been made by George Wakefield, who made two prints from the same negative, one with diffuse illumination and the other with directed light. After adjusting the exposures and the paper grades to obtain prints that matched in both density and contrast, he found that: 'The most critical examination of the prints failed to reveal any difference in sharpness. In fact the precaution had to be taken of marking the backs of the prints to identify them as they were made, as otherwise it would have been impossible to tell them apart. It is worth pointing out that the enlarging lens used was of medium quality; it has been said that a diffused light enlarger demands a lens of the highest quality to give sharp results, but this is not borne out in practice.'

Printing black-and-white negatives with diffuse light has one great advantage, which assumes greater importance as the size of the negative gets smaller. Just as specular light is scattered by the silver grains comprising a negative image, any irregularity (such as retouching, scratches or dust on either surface of a negative) also scatters directed light and causes sharp images of the defect to be formed. A great deal of tiresome print finishing is then required.

Fully diffuse light   There can be many degrees of diffuseness in an illumination system, and so far only the arrangement in which an opal lamp is used in conjunction with a condenser has been considered. More complete diffusion generally becomes necessary when colour negatives are to be printed with filtration adjustment built into a lamphouse. The colour head, as we know it today, began with an idea of Aston of Pavelle Color in 1962. He saw that if the focused beam of light from a tungsten halogen lamp is partially and adjustably interrupted by one or more dichroic filters, and both the white light that passes by the filters and the coloured light that passes through them is subsequently thoroughly mixed together, the integrated light that results can be used to illuminate a colour negative for printing. The great advantage of this idea is that quite small dichroic filters can be used, because they resist high temperatures and can be located at the focused spot of light from the tungsten-halogen lamp. The system is entirely dependent on thorough integration of the light passing into a mixing chamber, which is usually lined with white polystyrene or some other highly reflective material.

A unique combination of optical elements is used in the Vivitar enlargers. Light from a tungsten-halogen lamp is directed not into the usual mixing chamber, but (via a mirror) into the upper end of a rod of Perspex or Lucite, which serves to integrate the light by total internal reflection throughout its length. The lower end of the rod therefore acts as an extremely bright secondary source, 2–3 centimetres in diameter, which can be picked up by a normal condenser system to illuminate the negative and be directed into the enlarging lens. The effective focal length of the condenser system is adjustable by means of an auxiliary element that can be located in several different positions relative to the fixed pair of lenses.

The combined effect of this diffuse/specular arrangement is to produce a printing contrast that is about the same as the older opal lamp and condenser enlargers, but with the much brighter illumination and uniformity of output that comes from a tungsten-halogen source. The illumination system of the Vivitar enlarger is also novel; to ensure even illumination, the lower of the two fixed condenser lenses is 'tinted' centrally to absorb just the right amount of light.

160

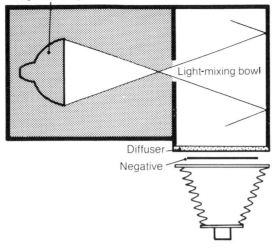

Tungsten-halogen lamp

Light-mixing bowl

Diffuser

Negative

Principle of diffuse light source using tungsten-halogen lamp and light-mixing box

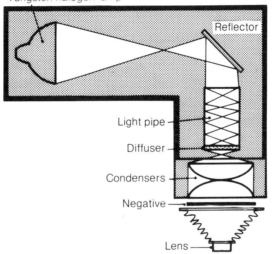

Tungsten halogen lamp

Reflector

Light pipe

Diffuser

Condensers

Negative

Lens

Light-pipe system of diffuse/directional illumination used in Vivitar enlargers

Many enlargers are now made to accept interchangeable lamphouses so that directed or semi-diffuse light can be used for black-and-white negatives and a fully diffuse mixing head for colour printing. Some manufacturers, including Leitz, have taken the bold step of using the same diffuse form of illumination for both black-and-white and colour negative printing, the only difference being the optional introduction of a colour-filter module between the tungsten-halogen lamp and the mixing chamber.

If, as now seems probable, increasing use is made of diffuse illumination for black-and-white printing, the slightly lower effective contrast that results can be offset in one of two ways:

161

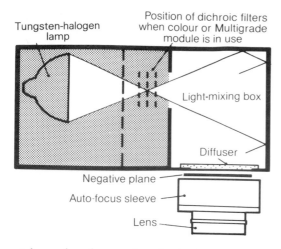

Tungsten-halogen lamp

Position of dichroic filters when colour or Multigrade module is in use

Light-mixing box

Diffuser

Negative plane

Auto-focus sleeve

Lens

Diffuse illumination system used in Leitz Focomat

either a harder grade of printing paper can be used, or the negative development time can be extended just sufficiently to produce negatives that will print satisfactorily on the same paper grade as was previously used when printing with a diffuse-light enlarger.

Lamps used in enlargers

Before the advent of colour mixing heads, the most common light source for a small to medium-size enlarger was an opal lamp. The kind of opal lamp required is different from the domestic 'pearl' bulb in two respects: its glass envelope is a far more efficient diffuser and it has no imprint on the end of the bulb, which would of course result in uneven illumination in an enlarger.

Sometimes a negative is so badly overexposed that it requires an inordinately long exposure time and more light in the enlarger would be welcome. A useful increase in output can sometimes be arranged if the lamp is supplied with a slightly higher voltage than its nominal rating, say 240 volts supplied to a 220 volt lamp, or 120 volts used with a 110 volt lamp. Over-running a lamp by about 10 per cent of its rated voltage increases its effective printing speed by some 40 per cent, although continual use at the higher voltage reduces its life to about half.

It is tempting sometimes to use a Photoflood lamp of the kind intended for lighting. These lamps produce up to five times as much light as an ordinary tungsten lamp, but they generate a lot of heat and should certainly not be used for long exposures.

Whenever tungsten filament lamps are used in enlargers, there is a problem in dissipating the heat generated. With a single lamp it is usually possible to keep the lamphouse at a reasonable operating temperature by encouraging heat transfer to the air by both radiation and convection, the former by making the lamphouse black and the latter by introducing light-trapped ventilation holes in the base and top of the lamp housing.

When a tungsten-halogen lamp is used (see below), the precise nature of its shape and dimensions offers the possibility (taken by Leitz in their Focomat V35 design) to use a heat sink to carry heat away from the lamp by directly contacting it with a cast metal surround equipped with cooling fins.

The power of the lamp or lamps required to print a large negative (e.g. 20 × 25 cm, 8 × 10 in) may amount to 2000 watts or more, equivalent to an electric fire! In such cases it is necessary to force air through the lamp housing in order to carry the heat away quickly enough. The blower supplying the air need not be mounted on the enlarger itself if there is a risk of vibration; instead, it should be mounted on the wall or floor nearby and connected to the lamphouse by flexible ducting.

Some further safeguards can be taken against unnecessary heat reaching the negative in an enlarger. If the negative plane is illuminated indirectly by reflection from a mirror, the mirror can be constructed so as to transmit infra-red radiation preferentially and reflect visible light, thereby getting rid of a large part of the heat from the lamp before it can reach the negative. This reflex system of illumination has been adopted by several manufacturers, including Durst, almost all of whose small enlargers are constructed in this way.

As a final precaution, an infra-red-absorbing filter can be inserted in the optical path between the lamp and the negative plane. Heat-absorbing glass filters can withstand very high temperatures and can therefore be located quite close to a small but intense light source, such as a tungsten-halogen lamp. Keeping the temperature of a negative as low as possible during a printing exposure is particularly important when the enlarger is used with a glassless negative carrier, with the attendant risk of negative 'popping'.

Cold-cathode lamps   These produce very little heat and are generally arranged in the form of a grid to print large-format negatives. A cold-cathode lamphouse is often available as an alternative to a condenser head, and produces lower-contrast images because of its extremely diffuse character. Unlike the older mercury-vapour tubes, cold-cathode lamps can be switched on and off at will, since they do not have a warm-up period during which light emission gradually increases. Because its emission is mainly at the blue end of the spectrum, a cold-cathode source of modest current rating enables large prints to be made with quite short exposures.

Tungsten-halogen lamps   The light source that has had the greatest influence on enlarger design and printing practice in recent years is the tungsten-halogen lamp (or, as it is sometimes called, the quartz-iodine lamp). Introduced in the 1960s as car headlamps, these low-voltage, high-intensity, compact sources were soon adopted for photographic applications, firstly in projectors and then as the basis of a completely new kind of colour mixing head for projection printing of colour negatives and transparencies.

The characteristics of the tungsten-halogen lamp that make it so useful for enlarging are:

1 It has a long life, with high and constant output of light.
2 The envelope does not blacken with use. A trace of iodine (chlorine, bromine or fluorine could also be used) is introduced into the envelope of the lamp; any tungsten that evaporates from the filament combines with the iodine to form tungsten iodide, which, instead of settling on the inside of the quartz envelope, is deposited back on to the filament, releasing the iodine to recommence the cycle.
3 The lamp can be small in relation to its output of light, and the compact source can be focused by a built-in reflector, making it possible to design very compact enlarger heads.

One slight disadvantage in using tungsten-halogen lamps is their need for a low-voltage supply, usually between 12 and 24 volts. This means that in most cases a transformer is necessary, either supplied as an accessory or built-in to the enlarger as with the Leitz Focomat V35. Berkey, however, have solved the problem by incorporating a solid-state power supply in the lamphouse of their C-700 dichroic head.

Evenness of illumination

If the negative aperture of an enlarger is evenly illuminated by fully diffused light, it might be thought that the image of a uniform density placed in the negative carrier would yield an equally uniform image on the baseboard. But because of the limitations of the enlarging lens this is not so. Fortunately the shortcomings of the camera lens complement to some extent those of the enlarger lens, and this tends to minimise the problem when printing with a negative-positive system.

Vignetting, as applied to a lens, is the tendency for the brightness of the image it forms to decrease towards the margins or corners; the effect is most pronounced at full aperture. The most obvious of several possible causes of vignetting is that the shape of the lens aperture, as viewed from the paper plane of an enlarger, changes from a circle (or at least a symmetrical geometric shape) to an ellipse of smaller total area, as the point of view moves outwards from the optical centre. This difference in illumination is greatest when the lens aperture is fully open; fortunately it usually becomes small enough to be disregarded when the lens is stopped down a couple of stops.

When a new or different lens is to be used for enlarging, it is worthwhile making a few uniformity test prints at a series of settings between full aperture and, say, $f/8$, to find out how much the lens needs to be stopped down to reduce vignetting to an acceptable level. The resulting information indicates which aperture to use whenever possible.

Although the eye is extremely sensitive when it is required to compare two different brightnesses or colours that are side by side, it is not so reliable when used to decide whether a large illuminated field varies significantly from one area to another. The uniformity of illumination of an enlarger has to be quite poor before it can be detected by direct observation. It is far better to see what happens when a sheet of paper is exposed just enough to produce a mid-grey density after processing. As the contrast of the paper used for the test is increased, the test itself becomes more critical; few enlargers yield uniform density across a print made on grade 4 paper. However, there should not be any serious difference between the density in the corners and the density in the middle of a print made on grade 2 paper.

If there is an obvious density difference between one side of the print and the other, some element of the illumination system is off-centre, probably the lamp itself. Sometimes, particularly with condenser enlargers, both the lateral and vertical positions of the lamp can be adjusted so that it can be centred first by visual observation and then by making test prints.

One easy way of improving the evenness of illumination of an enlarger is to introduce more effective diffusion between the light source and the negative, immediately beneath the condenser if there is one. The only snag is that this reduces the amount of light reaching the lens, and may make printing exposures unacceptably long. Using an opal-glass diffuser in place of ground glass can result in a tenfold increase in exposure.

Colour heads for black-and-white printing

Because many photographers are now using a mixture of black-and-white and colour films, the possibility of employing one enlarger for both colour and black-and-white printing has assumed great importance, but also poses several questions that will only be answered gradually as the two forms of photography progress alongside each other.

With one or two exceptions, colour enlargers (other than those that merely incorporate a filter drawer) are now based on fully diffused light emerging from a colour mixing box or chamber. This arrangement is successful because colour negative development and colour paper characteristics can be chosen to yield prints of a satisfactory contrast when printed with light from a colour mixing head. It would make very little difference if the negative illumination were specular; colour negatives, being composed of dyes, have a Q factor of 1.0, i.e. they print at much the same contrast with either diffuse or specular light. In the case of a silver-image black-and-white negative, the nature of the enlarger illumination significantly influences the effective contrast. Negatives of subjects that would print well on grade 2 paper on a condenser enlarger may well need grade 3 paper to produce an equivalent result when printed on an enlarger with a colour head.

It can be argued that any differences in paper contrast requirements can be economically met by using a variable-contrast paper such as Ilfospeed Multigrade. In fact the combination of a colour head with Multigrade paper does provide a flexible and convenient way of printing a wide range of silver-image black-and-white negatives. Nevertheless, if diffuse enlarger illumination is adopted permanently, it is advisable to extend negative development times just enough to make the difference between needing grade 3 paper and needing grade 2 (generally considered to be about the middle of the paper contrast range.)

Variable-contrast printing with colour heads   Because all enlarger colour heads contain both a yellow and a magenta filter, and usually a cyan filter that can be removed from the light beam by setting it at zero, they can obviously be used to expose variable-contrast papers by varying the proportions of blue and green light to produce different print contrasts. However, it is not possible to predict exactly what settings are required for the yellow and magenta filters to produce specific print contrasts with individual colour heads, since there are differences between the characteristics of the filters used, and none of them are intended primarily for use with variable-contrast papers. So the maximum potential contrast of Multigrade paper is unlikely to be obtained with the magenta filters used for colour printing. A broad indication of the settings that can be used as a starting point for practical tests with Multigrade is given on page 221.

The acceptance and rapid development of colour mixing heads has greatly influenced the introduction of convenient methods of exposing variable-contrast paper. It has always been something of a nuisance to have to deal with a variety of filters to achieve changes in contrast, and to have to recalculate exposure every time a change of contrast is required.

Ilford Multigrade 400 system   To be able to alter effective
contrast simply by pressing a button or adjusting a scale, without
having to reconsider exposure, greatly enhances the convenience
of using variable-contrast paper. This facility is achieved with the
Ilford Multigrade 400 enlarger head by using two
tungsten-halogen lamps to direct light through yellow and
magenta dichroic filters into a mixing chamber. The brightness of

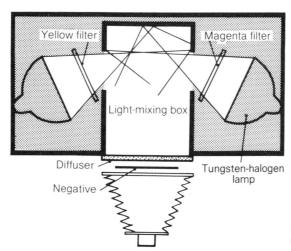

Illumination system used in
Multigrade 400 lamphouse

the lamps is controlled electronically through a series of
pushbutton switches; the light emitted by each lamp can be varied
between zero and a maximum, to produce any combination of
yellow (minus-blue) or magenta (minus-green) light. Further, the
electronic circuitry in the associated 400C control box and timer
ensures that whatever ratio of blue to green light is used, its actinic
effect remains the same, so that no alteration in exposure is
necessary when changes are made in print contrast.

There are two sizes of Multigrade enlarger head, the 400HL and
the 400HS. The former is designed for use on enlargers taking
negatives up to 10×13 cm (4×5 in), the latter for negatives up to
and including 6×7 cm. The larger of the two heads is supplied
with two mixing boxes so that 6×7 cm and smaller negatives can
be illuminated more efficiently. The combined control box and
exposure timer provides pushbutton selection of contrast in
half-grade steps; the whole-number buttons correspond to the
grades of Ilfospeed and Ilfobrom. The 400C control unit offers a
number of other features. A 'focus' button produces 'white' light
for composing and focusing, while the 'expose' button is
connected to the digital timer, which can be set to make exposures
between 0.5 and 99.9 seconds. There is a 'burn-in' button that
overrides the timer to allow additional exposure to be given to
local areas of a print, or even to produce areas of different contrast

167

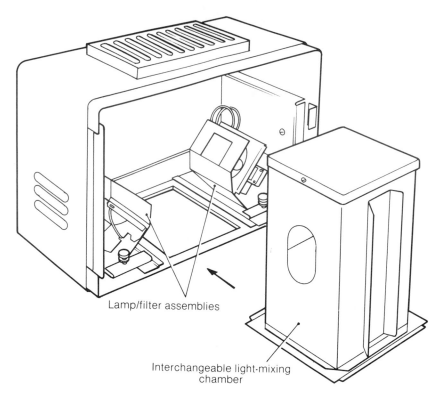

Lamp/filter assemblies

Interchangeable light-mixing chamber

Multigrade 400 lamphouses accept interchangeable light-mixing chambers to suit different negative formats

within the same print. An optional 'bleeper' is fitted so that audible timing can be used instead of the digital clock.

Other Multigrade enlarging systems   Enlarger manufacturers have also been working to improve the convenience of exposing variable-contrast paper. In collaboration with Ilford Limited, DeVere, Leitz and Berkey have all produced modifications or conversions to some of their designs. These make it possible to select any desired print contrast without having to readjust exposure and without the necessity for a range of different filters.

If a yellow and a magenta filter are butted together and mounted on a slide so that they can be moved to and fro across the beam of focused light from a tungsten-halogen lamp, it is possible to make a low-contrast print when the yellow filter interrupts the beam and a high-contrast print when the magenta filter is in that position. It is also possible to make prints having intermediate contrasts according to the position of the two-part filter in the beam. Whatever light passes the filters must of course be thoroughly mixed in an integrating box before it reaches the negative.

Unless something is done about it, more actinic light is transmitted by the yellow section of the composite filter than by the magenta part, so print density varies with contrast unless the

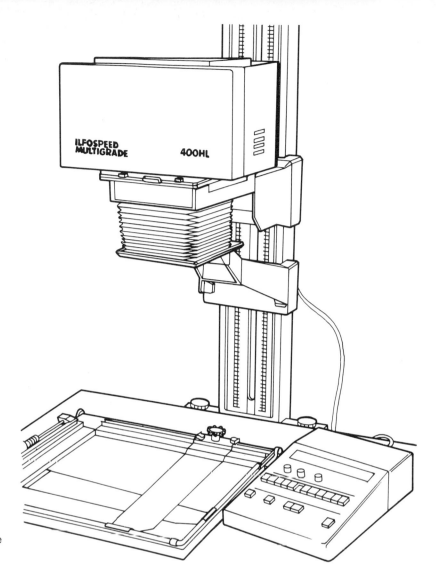

Multigrade 400 HL
lamphouse fitted to DeVere
504 enlarger

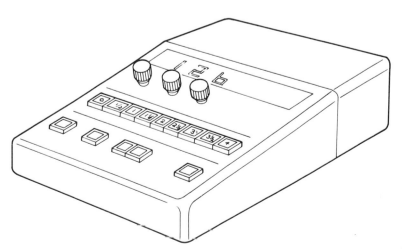

Multigrade 400C exposure
control box allows
pushbutton selection of
paper contrast. Three
knobs set exposure time in
seconds and tenths of a
second; five unmarked
buttons are for initiating
exposure, cancelling,
focusing at high brightness
level, burning-in, and
switching unit on/off

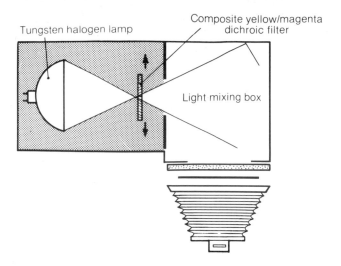

Tungsten halogen lamp

Composite yellow/magenta dichroic filter

Light-mixing box

Adjustable composite filter used with a tungsten-halogen lamp and light-mixing box

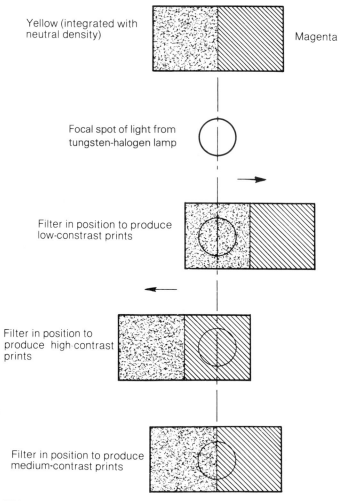

Yellow (integrated with neutral density)

Magenta

Focal spot of light from tungsten-halogen lamp

Filter in position to produce low-contrast prints

Filter in position to produce high-contrast prints

Filter in position to produce medium-contrast prints

Use of composite yellow/magenta dichroic filter to provide print-contrast adjustment with Multigrade paper

Multigrade lamphouses for DeVere 203 (left) and 5108 (right) enlargers

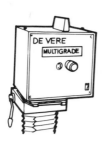

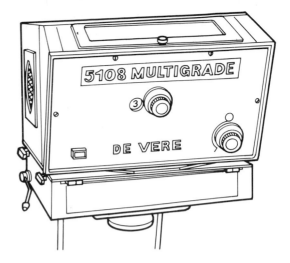

Multigrade filter module fitted to Leitz Focomat V35 auto-focus enlarger. One knob controls print contrast, and there is no need to adjust exposure when changing contrast

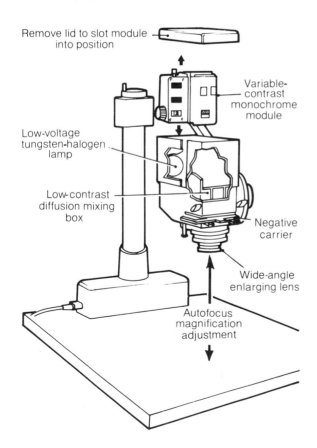

Remove lid to slot module into position

Variable-contrast monochrome module

Low-voltage tungsten-halogen lamp

Low-contrast diffusion mixing box

Negative carrier

Wide-angle enlarging lens

Autofocus magnification adjustment

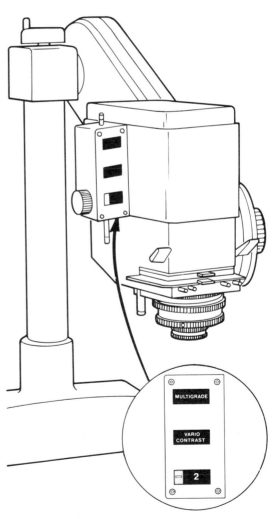

MULTIGRADE

VARIO CONTRAST

2

171

exposure is adjusted. If, however, some form of neutral density is incorporated with the yellow filter, it equalises the actinic light transmitted by each half of the composite filter; it is then possible to alter print contrast without having to worry about changes of exposure.

This compensated two-part dichroic filter arrangement is now incorporated in the DeVere 203, DeVere 5108, Leitz Focomat V35 and some other enlargers for the convenient exposure of Multigrade paper.

Enlarging lenses

When starting photographic darkroom activities, hobbyists often wonder whether a camera lens can be successfully used in an enlarger, to save the cost of buying a special lens for the purpose. In all the early Leica manuals it was assumed that anyone buying a Leitz enlarger would use his Leica camera lens in it; Leica practice has been influential in establishing the high standard of 35 mm photography, so it can hardly be doubted that camera lenses can be used successfully for enlarging.

More recently, W. D. G. Cox looked at the performance of some camera lenses (including a Pentax 50 mm f/1.8 and an Elmar 50 mm f/2.8) when used in an enlarger: 'At f/4 the camera lenses showed good central sharpness, suitable for focusing, with severe blurring away from the central third of the image. The enlarging lens (a four-element type) at its full aperture of f/4.5 showed poor performance all over, just adequate for focusing centrally, and with severe vignetting, which was completely absent from all the camera lenses by f/4. By f/8, all the lenses were giving good image quality across the frame, the Elmar being the best, with the enlarging lens slightly softer in the corners. *The best enlarging lenses, of course, performed better than any of these.*'

This last comment confirms that, while a good camera lens can be used for enlarging at a relatively small aperture, better results are obtained with a high-class enlarging lens, even when it is used at or near its full aperture. It is surprising that many photographers who spend as much money as they can afford on camera lenses still 'make do' with a cheap enlarging lens, thereby jeopardising the quality of the images they record so efficiently in the first place.

There are several ways in which the requirements of an enlarging lens differ from those of a camera lens. For example, the camera lens is designed to work at subject distances of a few feet to infinity, whereas an enlarging lens is usually designed to work best at enlargement ratios between 1:3 and 1:10. Furthermore, it is important for an enlarging lens to have a flat field, i.e. to

172

reproduce the image of a flat negative uniformly sharply on a flat sheet of paper.

At one time it was considered that colour correction was unimportant in a lens that would only be used for black-and-white enlarging. However, now that more variable-contrast paper such as Multigrade is being used, an enlarging lens should at least be sufficiently free from chromatic aberrations to focus both green and blue light in the same plane.

As with camera lenses, the performance of an enlarging lens depends largely on the complexity of its design and construction, and therefore on its cost. Just as many quite useful inexpensive camera lenses, such as the Triotar, are triplets, so a low-priced enlarging lens can be made with only three elements. The Rodenstock Trinar and the Schneider Componar-C lenses are typical examples. The limitations of a simple triplet enlarging lens are usually poor resolution at the corners of the image and bad vignetting; both of these defects can be improved by stopping down, although this may be inconvenient.

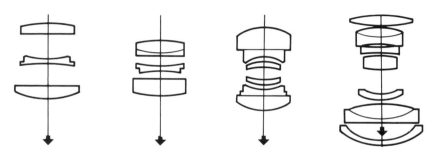

Enlarging lenses of different complexity and performance. Left to right: three-element Triotar type; four-element Tessar type; six-element Componon type; nine-element wide-angle lens

Four-element enlarging lenses, such as the Rodenstock Ysaron (now improved and called Rogonar) and the equivalent Omegaron in the US, are basically Tessar-type designs which, while capable of better performance than three-element lenses, still fall short of optimum requirements in two respects. First, their definition is slightly lower than it should be, even at the scale of reproduction for which the lens is corrected. Second, they are slightly more sensitive to scale variations. In other words, at magnifications other than the ideal scale of reproduction there is a risk of quality loss unless it is corrected by stopping down.

There are very few five-element enlarging lenses on the market, perhaps because they cost almost as much as the six-element (four-component) designs that are generally accepted as the best. Examples of six-element lenses include the Schneider Componons, Rodenstock Rodagons, EL-Nikkors, Leitz Focotars and Komuranons. These are all expensive lenses containing special glasses that are said to be 'worth their weight in gold'.

What focal length? The optimum focal length of a lens to be used in an enlarger depends primarily upon the size of the negative from which it is required to produce prints with satisfactory definition over their whole surface.

If it were not for the mechanical limitations of focusing arrangements and of the magnification obtainable with a particular enlarger, it would always be preferable to use a lens of longer focal length than absolutely necessary. This is because both uniformity of illumination and resolution are likely to be better when only the central area of the full image circle is utilised. In practice, however, it is more convenient to use as short a focal length as possible, consistent with satisfactory image quality, so that a wider range of enlargement ratios can be achieved without requiring inconvenient distances between the lens and the paper plane.

The rule that has been accepted over the years is that the focal length of an enlarging lens should not be less than the diagonal of the negative being printed. For example, a 50 mm enlarging lens is suitable for all negative sizes up to 24 × 36 mm, including 126 (26 × 26 mm) and 110 Pocket Instamatic (13 × 17 mm). A larger negative such as 6 × 6 cm is adequately covered by a lens with a focal length of 80 mm. A 6 × 7 cm, and certainly a 6 × 9 cm, negative requires a lens of at least 90 mm and preferably 100 mm focal length.

Some exceptions to this old rule are now emerging in the form of wide-angle enlarging lenses. These are designed to increase the range of enlargement that can be achieved with standard equipment and within restricted workroom dimensions. Several benefits come from using an enlarging lens with a shorter focal length than normal. Bigger enlargements can be made from a given negative size; but equally important, using the enlarger becomes more convenient because the reduced distance between the lens and the paper plane often makes it easier to reach the focusing adjustment of the lens while closely observing the sharpness of the projected image, either directly or through a magnifier. For example, a 40 × 50 cm (16 × 20 in) print from a 35 mm negative would require a lens-to-paper separation of 76 cm (30 in) with a 50 mm lens, but only 60 cm (24 in) with a 40 mm lens such as the Schneider WA-Componon.

A more extreme example of a really wide-angle enlarging lens is the 25 mm f/2.8 Computar-DL, with which a 40 × 50 cm (16 × 20 in) print can be made from a 35 mm negative with only a 48 cm (19 in) separation between the lens and the paper. An equally remarkable feature of this lens, which is described as a retrofocus type, is its relatively long back-focus distance; this

174

enables a very short effective focal length to be obtained without the need for a recessed lens panel or the risk of the lens fouling anything within the enlarger.

Vignetting has always been a serious problem with short-focus enlarging lenses when they are used at or near their maximum aperture. The problem has been dealt with in the 25 mm Computar-DL lens by coating the central area of one of the components to absorb central rays preferentially and thereby offset the unevenness of illumination that would otherwise result.

The construction of a modern wide-angle enlarging lens is necessarily complex; the Computar-DL, for example, comprises nine elements in seven components.

Zoom lenses for enlarging   Just as zoom lenses have been widely adopted for picture taking, they are gradually finding applications in projection printing. A number of high-quality photofinishing printers, such as those made by Gretag and Durst, already incorporate zoom lenses so that the effective focal length can be changed for different negative formats without the necessity to change the lens itself. This particular type of application was restricted to relatively small enlargements, but Schneider has designed an enlarging zoom lens to provide useful commercial enlargement ratios. The basic Betavaron lens provides enlargement ratios between 3× and 10×, while the addition of a supplementary lens provides a range between 5.3× and 17×.

With an enlarging zoom lens, the distance between the negative plane and the paper plane is set only once and then remains unchanged; thereafter the lens adjustment ring is used only to alter the ratio of enlargement, no focusing being necessary. Of course,

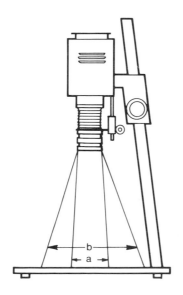
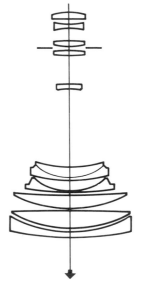

Left: projected image size range (from a to b) obtainable with fixed lens position using an enlarging zoom lens
Right: Schneider Betavaron 3.1–10× enlarging zoom lens for 35 mm negatives

as the effective focal length of the lens changes, so does the effectiveness of any given aperture. One way of overcoming this problem is to find, by trial, the relationship between exposure and aperture throughout the enlargement range of the lens, so that a scale of aperture settings can be found to give uniform exposure at any given magnification.

Aperture adjustment   Now that so many cameras incorporate automatic exposure control, there is much less need to know precisely what aperture is being used for any given exposure, particularly with shutter-priority systems. In any case, it is usually easy to see what aperture is being used if that information is required. With a lens used in an enlarger in a darkroom, it is a different matter. In fact, one good reason why a camera lens is not well suited for enlarging is that it is usually quite difficult to adjust and read its aperture setting when it is attached to an enlarger.

Fortunately, a good deal of attention has been paid to the improvement of aperture adjustment of enlarging lenses in recent years. Most lenses now incorporate an illuminated scale of apertures as well as 'click' stops that can be reliably felt and counted if that is the preferred method of working. Some designs also provide the further option of continuous adjustment of aperture to facilitate the use of null-reading enlarging exposure meters. One day, no doubt, a manufacturer will design an enlarging lens that will remain fully open for focusing and until an exposure is started, after which it will automatically close to any preselected setting.

Resolution of lenses   The performance of a lens in a photographic system such as an enlarger used to be stated in terms of its ability to resolve a certain number of lines per millimetre, but this told nothing of the quality of the lines, whether they were clear-cut and well separated, or fuzzy and hardly discernible. It is more usual nowadays to rate a lens, or any other part of an imaging system, in terms of its modulation transfer function (MTF) at a given number of 'cycles' per millimetre, thereby taking into consideration the contrast between adjacent lines in an image of a test chart.

Diffraction and the aberrations of any lens cause the image it forms of a pattern of closely spaced lines to be reproduced as strips of light with their brightness decreasing from the centre outwards. When the lines get very close together they begin to overlap, so that the light bands scatter light into the dark bands, thus reducing the difference between them. Finally, where the spacing between the lines of the test target is small enough, there is no measurable separation of lines in the corresponding area of the image, at which point the contrast transfer (the MTF) is zero.

176

In practice, the difference between the light and dark portions of an optically formed image of a test chart is noticeably reduced when compared with the original. This contrast loss can be quantified in terms of the transfer function; for example, if the original contrast is taken as 100 per cent and the measured contrast of the image is only 80 per cent of that, the MTF is 0.8. The higher the frequency of the lines in the target, the greater the tendency for the corresponding image lines to overlap, and the greater the loss of contrast, until finally the MTF reaches zero at that particular frequency.

The significance of thinking about lens performance in terms of image contrast as well as frequency is made clear by W. D. G. Cox: 'If a lens is well enough designed and constructed to be limited by diffraction, the absolute limit of its performance is given by the following figures, which do not vary with focal length:

$f/2$	1200 cycles/mm
$f/2.8$	900 cycles/mm
$f/4$	700 cycles/mm
$f/5.6$	450 cycles/mm
$f/8$	320 cycles/mm
$f/11$	220 cycles/mm
$f/16$	153 cycles/mm

'All of these look very respectable, but they represent the point at which contrast drops to one or two per cent. To avoid noticeably affecting the image, the contrast needs to be about 80 per cent and this will be obtained only at about 20 per cent of the limiting frequency. Thus a frequency of 700 cycles/mm on the film, corresponding ($10\times$ enlargement) to 70 cycles/mm on the paper, will be scarcely measurable at $f/4$. If it is required that contrast be degraded by only 20 per cent, then we are talking about 14 cycles/mm on a $10\times$ enlargement. This is the region of frequencies that make grain structure appear crisp or soft.'

Flare in enlarging

Any light that can affect the printing paper other than image-forming light is unwanted and lowers the quality of the finished print. Scattered light or flare cannot be entirely eliminated from an enlarger, but if the external surfaces of the enlarging lens are clean, the problem can be kept to an acceptable level.

Dust gradually settles on the upper external surface of the lens in any vertical enlarger, and causes light to be scattered within the lens itself. The result is that the highlight areas of any print become veiled, sometimes to the point where all subtlety of gradation is lost. Strictly speaking, the underlying resolution of the image may remain unchanged, but the tonal quality of the print is destroyed because it loses all sparkle.

The lower external surface of a lens in an enlarger is unlikely to attract much dust, but may well collect finger marks, particularly if the aperture adjustment ring is on the edge of the lens mount and the lens is not recessed. Whereas dust can be removed by gentle treatment with a soft camel-hair brush or with a blast of compressed air, a greasy finger mark must be wiped away with a lens-cleaning tissue and perhaps a trace of lens-cleaning fluid.

While the outer surfaces of an enlarging lens should be inspected regularly, a lens should only be wiped when it is really necessary to remove some obvious mark. Any wiping can cause scratches, which, if they accumulate, may spoil the lens permanently.

Negative masking to prevent flare The pre-exposed black surround of all 126 and 110 Instamatic image frames eliminates the effects of flare caused by non-image-forming light reaching an enlarging lens from around the negative image area. Because of the wide variety of image formats and the unpredictability of image positioning, neither rollfilms nor 35 mm films can benefit from this feature. Consequently light sometimes reaches an enlarging lens from the clear margins around a negative image, and whenever this happens some deterioration of the resulting image can result. Non-image-forming light can be prevented from reaching an enlarger lens if the area of the negative being printed is masked off by some means, such as a suitably shaped aperture cut in a piece of opaque material and superimposed on the negative. A more convenient technique is to use a negative carrier or negative stage, incorporating a set of four adjustable masking blades.

Because of cost, not all enlargers incorporate facilities for adjustable masking of a negative, yet if all other features were equivalent between two enlargers and one had negative masking, that enlarger would be preferable. Sometimes adjustable masking blades are incorporated in the negative carrier itself, sometimes in the enlarger just below the negative plane. The simplest way of adjusting the blades is to slide them in from either side and from

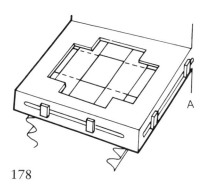

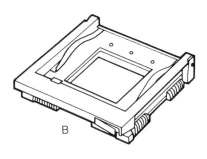

Adjustable masking blades can be incorporated in negative stage of enlarger (A) or removable negative carrier (B)

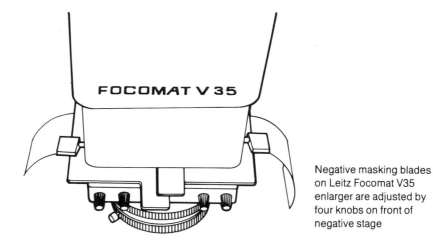

Negative masking blades on Leitz Focomat V35 enlarger are adjusted by four knobs on front of negative stage

back or front as required. If this is done with precisely fitted parts, it works well; but if the blades are badly fitted or become sloppy, then it is difficult to position them precisely. A better, but more expensive, method is to control the blades through a screw mechanism so that four small adjustment knobs can be used to position the blades independently. On the Leitz V35 enlarger, all four adjustment knobs are forward facing.

Negative carriers

Positioning a negative in a carrier would seem to be a fairly easy thing to do. In practice it can often be frustrating, particularly if the negative concerned is at the end of a strip so that the cut end of the film repeatedly springs into the opening in the carrier. Whenever possible, a negative should be positioned while the carrier is removed from the enlarger; its location can then be adjusted, and it can also be inspected for dust or hairs before being put into the enlarger for printing.

Above all, a negative carrier must help to keep the negative flat throughout the period of print exposure. One way of ensuring film flatness is to use a two-part carrier with glass in both apertures so that the negative is sandwiched between the glasses. But there are serious disadvantages in doing this. The four glass surfaces, added to the two surfaces of the negative itself, greatly increase the chances of dust or hairs settling on one or more of them. Furthermore, there is a good chance that sooner or later Newton's rings will be formed at the interface between the back of the film and one of the glasses, to provide one more unwanted image on the print.

Fortunately, glass can now be treated so that its surface is made sufficiently matt to prevent the formation of interference patterns (Newton's rings), but not rough enough for it to be recorded in the print as a granular structure, at least not when used in a diffuse-light system.

If it were not for the problem of negative movement (sometimes referred to as 'popping') during a printing exposure, it would always be better to use a glassless negative carrier. However, this is particularly risky with the larger rollfilm formats, unless a very cool light source such as a cold-cathode tube is being used, or each

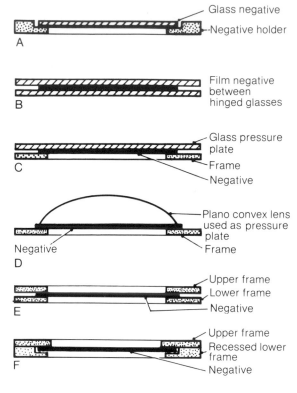

A: glass-plate negative rests, emulsion down, on locating aperture plate. B: film negative between two glasses. C: glass laid over film negative holds it flat against aperture plate. D: flat face of plano-convex lens holds film negative against aperture plate. E: film negative held around edges by two aperture plates. F: one of pair of aperture plates is recessed so that film can expand without buckling

printing exposure is deferred for a few moments until the negative has warmed up sufficiently for it to change position if it is going to do so.

It is safer to use a glassless negative carrier when printing from 35 mm or smaller negatives, as long as exposures are not prolonged. A number of enlarger manufacturers, including Leitz and Paterson, prefer to press a glass surface into contact with the back of the negative, either by lowering a condenser so that its flat surface clamps the negative into contact with the carrier or by sandwiching the negative between a hinged pair of aperture plates with a glass insert in the upper one.

Whatever the method of holding a negative in a carrier, a recessed track or a pair of stops should permit the strip or piece of film to be aligned and moved laterally without any risk of it being scratched once the clamping pressure has been released.

180

Enlarger alignment

For optimum resolution from any projection printer, the three principal elements of the optical system must be properly aligned so that the negative plane is truly parallel to the paper plane and the optical axis of the lens is exactly at right angles to those two planes. These requirements are usually taken for granted, certainly by the amateur, but they can and should be checked with a spirit level. Omega offer an enlarger alignment kit, which includes a special type of level that can be adjusted to match any unavoidable tilt the enlarger may have because of the bench on which it is used.

When an ordinary level is used, the baseboard should be adjusted, if necessary, to ensure that the bubble of the level is central when offered up in either the left-to-right or back-to-front direction. The parallelism of the negative stage can be checked by placing a stiff metal plate in the position of the negative carrier and noting whether this too is level. If it is not, it may be possible to slacken a few supporting screws to allow alignment of the stage to be adjusted. When there is no simple way to alter the angle of the negative stage, a strip or two of carefully located adhesive tape can be used on the underside of the negative carrier.

The third element in the system, the lens, should be mounted so that its optical axis is exactly at right angles to both negative and paper planes; this means that a straight bar or plate pressed up against the outer rim of the lens must register as level. If it does not, the lens panel (if there is one) can be packed slightly to correct a slight error.

All three sets of levelling tests must be made in at least two directions to detect any tilt from back to front as well as from side to side. Any decent enlarger should pass these basic alignment tests reasonably well, and only if the enlarger has been dropped or knocked should any significant misalignment be revealed.

Paper easels

It is no good ensuring that all the mechanical and optical elements of an enlarger are correctly aligned if the surface on which the image is to be recorded is not in the same plane as that on which it was focused. In other words, the surface on which the image is projected during focusing must be in exactly the same plane as the sensitive surface of the paper during exposure. Furthermore, this must apply to the whole area of the image, which is only the case when the paper is perfectly flat.

Printing paper that is not flat can not only lead to wholly or partly unsharp prints, but also cause incorrect positioning in a paper easel, which in turn leads to irregular white borders. Dependably flat paper is often used for enlarging without an easel, particularly in press darkrooms where every second counts and where white borders are of no consequence. All that is required to work this way is a baseboard marked out in paper sizes, usually 20×25 cm (8×10 in).

When borderless prints are required as well as precise positioning of the projected image, a borderless paper easel (such as the RRB from the UK or the Saunders from the US) can be used. These easels hold sheets of paper firmly between slightly undercut register bars and thereby allow the whole surface of the paper to be exposed. The magnetic corner pieces produced by Paterson also have serrated grips on their inside surfaces, but must of course be used on a metal baseboard.

Although more expensive, a vacuum frame is perhaps the best way to produce borderless prints, because the printing paper is bound to be held flat during exposure. But even with a rapid-action vacuum-release valve a little time is required for the pump to suck down and then release each sheet of paper, so printers in newspaper darkrooms tend to dispense with such a refinement. For precision work, however, the method has much to commend it, and it is well suited for use with a horizontal enlarger.

Masking frames   For most photographers, prints with white borders still seem to be more attractice than those in which the image is bled off the edges of the print. When there is no requirement for a range of non-standard image sizes, but bordered prints are preferred, a single-format paper easel can be used, the paper being slipped into the frame after simply lifting a front bar. This type of easel ensures that margins are always uniform and square.

An adjustable masking frame must be made with precision if it is to do its job properly and not be a source of frustration. White borders around a print only look effective if they are uniform and truly square. When they are neither, the print either looks poorly made or has to be carefully trimmed by hand to rectify the faults as far as possible. Even when this has been done the finished prints are unlikely to be exactly the same size and will certainly not stack well.

Most adjustable masking frames have two sliding arms so that image sizes can be changed and set by reference to scales on the left-hand and rear borders of the frame. This arrangement has the merit of requiring only two movable arms, but it means that the board itself must be moved whenever the size of enlargement is altered; this is not a serious matter, and is unavoidable with any enlarger that depends on a system of parallel arms to raise and lower the enlarger head, because the movement of the parallelogram causes the optical axis of the system to move inwards and outwards as the height of the lens is changed. Nevertheless, some masking frames have four adjustable arms so that the easel itself need not be moved whenever a particular area of a negative is to be enlarged to a greater or lesser extent.

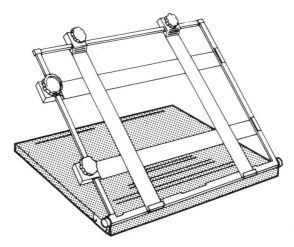

Four-bladed masking frame

It is the seemingly minor features of a masking board that determine whether it will be a pleasure or an irritation to use. So make sure that:

1 You can repeatedly insert sheets of paper into the easel and be confident they they will all be accurately positioned.
2 The movable blades are perfectly square to each other and to their supporting arms.
3 The movable blades can be smoothly and precisely adjusted.
4 The movable blades make proper contact with the paper along their whole length.
5 The easel does not slide around too easily on the baseboard.

Roll-paper easels The widespread use of rolls of paper for printing and processing in photofinishing has influenced industrial and commercial photographers; they too are tending to use paper in roll form whenever they can, because a great deal of time and labour can be saved if printing, processing and cutting can be done automatically. The first requirement of roll-paper operation is a means of exposing the paper while it is in roll form. If the prints are to be enlargements of varied size, there must also be some way of changing both the width of the roll and the pitch or travel between successive prints. These requirements can be satisfied by a motor-driven roll-paper easel that can stand beneath an enlarger lens instead of the normal paper easel.

Smaller types of roll-paper easels can simply be placed on the baseboard of an enlarger, but if the roll size and the range of

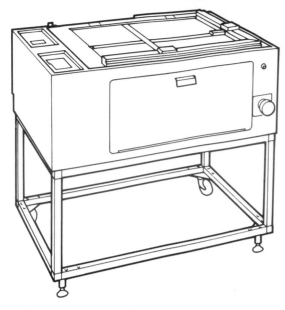

Durst ACS R16 roll-paper easel, for use with wall-mounted enlarger, provides any print format between 5 × 9 cm (2 × 3½ in) and 40 × 50 cm (16 × 20 in)

enlargement are to be large, the unit is usually freestanding and may be either permanently positioned under the enlarger or moved there on castors. Typically, the Durst ACS roll-paper easel takes up to 150 metres (500 feet) of 40 cm (16 in) wide paper, and can be set for any paper travel between 5 cm and 50 cm (2 in and 20 in) in steps of 6 mm (¼ in). The range of print sizes is therefore between 5 × 9 cm (2 × 3½ in) and 40 × 50 cm (16 × 20 in).

Easels for exposure control   With this kind of enlarging easel, integrated measurement of the light falling on the paper during exposure is used to terminate that exposure automatically. As with any other kind of integrated measurement of a large area of a photographic image, the success of the method can never be complete because it cannot take account of any abnormal distribution of subject brightness. This problem has led manufacturers of photofinishing printers to design image-scanning systems that measure negative transmittance at more than a hundred different points across a 35 mm frame, in order to provide the additional information required to determine the correct exposure of atypical negatives. Such printers can cost more than £100 000!

Nevertheless, despite its limitations, the large-area integration method of assessing print exposure can be usefully applied where the type of subject matter is unexceptional and the printing must be done by relatively unskilled operators. The Agfa Variomat easel depends on light transmitted through the printing paper being sensed by a photo-cell, while the Revomatic easel uses light reflected from the surface of the paper to drive a photo-cell and through it to terminate the exposure at a predetermined value.

184

Horizontal enlargers

Large horizontal projection printers of the kind used for exposing mural prints are often the most sophisticated enlargers of all. To be used to full advantage they should be housed in a separate room, one wall of which supports the printing paper, which is often cut from wide rolls and held against a white-painted steel sheet by magnetic bars.

The DeVere 810H is typical, and can be equipped with several different light sources to cover any negative size up to 20×25 cm (8×10 in), including aerial negatives in roll form. It can also be used as a copy camera (see below). Because the distance between the image plane and the enlarger itself is often greater than a man's reach, remote drive and focusing controls are essential. Even a cableless, sonic-control version is available so that there need be no physical connection whatever between the enlarger and the operator. The precise positioning and re-positioning of the enlarger and of the negative is indicated by digital readout, and a large digital countdown timer is available. The lamphouse normally used on the 810H for black-and-white printing is the Difcon, which is a diffuse source rather like that of a colour head.

`When directed light is preferable, a four-element condenser set made by Rodenstock can be attached to the horizontal slide of the

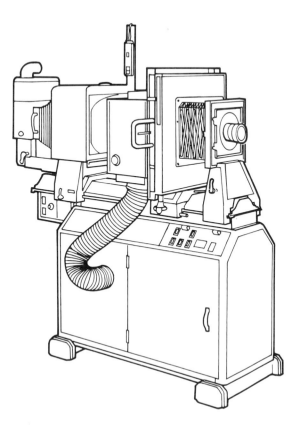

DeVere 810H horizontal enlarger can be used with condenser or diffuse system of negative illumination

185

810H enlarger as a separate runner unit, so that optical adjustments can be made to ensure that the projection lens is exactly filled with light. This is suitable for negative sizes between 20 × 25 cm (8 × 10 in) and 10 × 12.5 cm (4 × 5 in); with smaller negatives an auxiliary condenser lens must be added. The light source is a 1000 watt tunsten-halogen type, cooled by air from a blower in the base of the trolley.

Copying facilities

One facility that comes easily with any horizontal enlarger is the use of it as a copy camera. All that is needed is a 'copy back' to accept film holders or a focusing screen, and some lamps to illuminate the copy board. The film back replaces the lamphouse, and the lamps, on vertical stands, can be rolled into and out of position as required.

It is usually preferable, or even essential, to use a horizontal enlarger when very large prints are required, particularly from large negatives, but there are applications such as aerial photography where relatively small prints are made from large film negatives, commonly 23 × 23 cm (9 × 9 in). In such cases vertical enlargers are preferred because they take up less floor

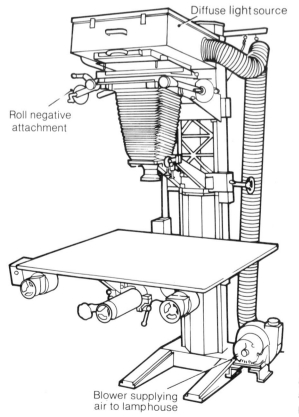

Diffuse light source

Roll negative attachment

Blower supplying air to lamphouse

DeVere 108AF vertical enlarger with roll-negative attachment, often used for printing aerial negatives

space and can be housed in separate areas but not necessarily separate rooms. However, such enlargers have to be geared to the large negative and are consequently very massive pieces of equipment, incorporating baseboard-located remote controls (sometimes motorised) for negative-stage and lens-stage adjustments, and a lamphouse that consumes enough current to make forced air-cooling imperative.

Copying is not so straightforward with ordinary vertical enlargers, and unless copying facilities have been designed into an enlarger it may be difficult or impossible. First, illumination of copy on the baseboard requires some kind of framework to support four lamps, or at least two fluorescent tubes. Second, focusing the image formed at the negative stage is difficult unless done via a mirror.

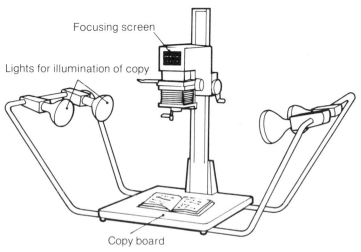

Focusing screen

Lights for illumination of copy

Copy board

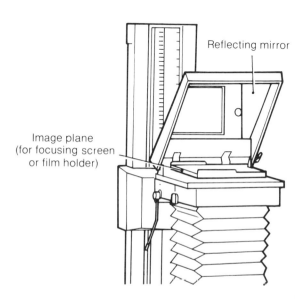

Reflecting mirror

Image plane
(for focusing screen
or film holder)

The Durst M series of enlargers lend themselves well to copying since a tubular lighting frame with four lamps is available, and the base of this slips easily under the enlarger itself. These enlargers also incorporate film holders that can be easily fitted on the negative stage, and focusing is done via a built-in, front-facing mirror.

The DeVere 504 and 507 enlargers can be used for copying simply by removing the lamphouse and inserting a film holder or ground glass on the negative stage. Focusing is done with a ground-glass camera back, viewed at right angles through a mirror.

Some enlarger designs, the Kaiser for example, are not intended for copying via the optics of the enlarger itself, but simply offer a lighting unit for attachment to the baseboard and an arm or bracket to support a 35 mm camera so that it can be raised and lowered on the enlarger column after removal of the enlarger head.

Special-purpose enlargers

One of the problems peculiar to aerial photography is that the contrast of negatives exposed from the air varies widely according to altitude and prevailing atmospheric conditions. These variations are further complicated by differences in density within a negative, due to cloud shadows on the terrain. The wide range of negative densities and contrasts makes it difficult by normal techniques to produce the uniformity of print quality that is required by an interpreter or a surveyor if he is to extract maximum information from the photographs.

The problem can be solved by using an electronically controlled enlarger (or contact printer), of which there are two basically

Log Etronic ED-54 projection printer, with schematic diagram

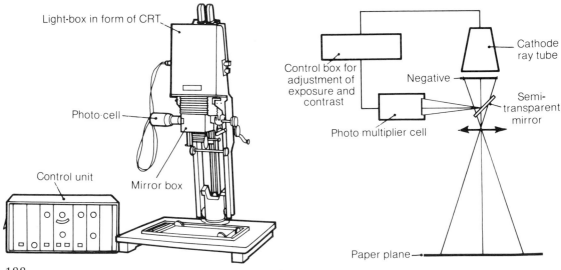

Light-box in form of CRT

Photo cell

Control unit

Mirror box

Control box for adjustment of exposure and contrast

Photo multiplier cell

Negative

Cathode ray tube

Semi-transparent mirror

Paper plane

similar types, the Log Etronic and the Milligan. In simple terms, both these enlargers expose a print by means of a flying spot of light, the brightness of which is modulated not only by the negative being printed, but also by any desired degree of 'feedback' that may be applied to the circuitry. The brightness of the exposing spot could be controlled in such a way as to eliminate completely all density differences so that a uniformly grey print

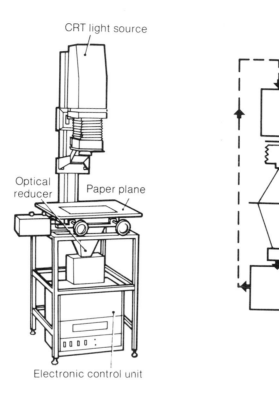

CRT light source

Optical reducer

Paper plane

Milligan 1427 projection printer, with schematic diagram

Electronic control unit

CRT (scanning light source)

Negative

Projection lens

Image plane

Paper

Optical reducer

Photo-cell

Electronic 'feed back' control unit

would result, even though the spot had scanned the whole surface of the negative image. In practice the 'feedback' is much less dramatic in its effect, and simply serves to reduce any extreme differences in density; thus detail is retained in areas of terrain that would otherwise be too dark because they happened to be in the shade of a cloud at the moment of exposure.

An electronic masking printer, whether projection or contact, uses a spot of light to traverse the negative in much the same way as an electron beam scans a television screen. A photo-cell monitors the light that passes through the negative (and the paper in the case of a Milligan printer) and simultaneously adjusts or modulates the brightness of the flying spot itself. The extent and direction of this control of brightness can be determined electronically, which means that print contrast can be increased or decreased at will.

Size of enlargements

What size should an enlargement be? This is not quite such a foolish question as it might seem, since strictly speaking there is only one size of print that correctly represents the perspective of an original scene when the print is viewed at the generally accepted shortest convenient viewing distance of 25 cm (10 in).

Put simply, the perspective of an image (on a focusing screen, for instance) appears to be correct only when that image is viewed from a distance equal to the focal length of the camera lens. So, now that so many of us use 35 mm cameras, we should be viewing any contact prints we make from our negatives from distances as short as 5 cm (2 in) or sometimes even less!

Clearly this is neither practical nor necessary, because we can enlarge the negative images to produce prints of a more useful size and look at them from a more convenient distance. Even then, there is a theoretically correct relationship between the size of print, the viewing distance and the focal length of the camera lens. The degree of enlargement necessary to produce a print that seems to be in correct perspective when seen from a distance of 25 cm varies according to the negative size and the focal length of the camera lens. Some examples are given in Table 1.

Table 1   Optimum enlargement for natural perspective at a viewing distance of 25 cm

Negative size	Focal length of lens	Diameters of enlargement	Size of print (approx.)
13 × 17 mm (110)	28 mm	7.5	10 × 13 cm
28 × 28 mm (126)	40 mm	6.0	17 × 17 cm
24 × 36 mm (135)	50 mm	5.0	12 × 18 cm
4.5 × 6 cm	75 mm	3.5	16 × 21 cm
6 × 6 cm	80 mm	3.0	18 × 18 cm
6 × 9 cm	100 mm	2.5	14 × 20 cm
10 × 13 cm	150 mm	1.7	17 × 22 cm

These considerations lead to some quite surprising results when we calculate the theoretically correct viewing distance for prints made from 35 mm negatives taken with lenses of different focal lengths. A range of examples is given in Table 2. Clearly, most of these theoretical relationships have to be ignored in practice. In fact the extent to which artificialities of perspective have come to be accepted and even cultivated in photographs may be seen as one of the freedoms that distinguishes photography from other forms of graphic representation.

Table 2   Theoretically correct viewing distances for prints from 36 × 24 mm negatives

Focal length of lens	Theoretical viewing distance for a 13 × 18 cm (5 × 7 in) print
21 mm	10 cm (4 in)
28 mm	13 cm (5¼ in)
35 mm	17 cm (6¾ in)
50 mm	25 cm (10 in)
90 mm	56 cm (17½ in)
135 mm	63 cm (25 in)
180 mm	89 cm (35 in)
300 mm	142 cm (56 in)
500 mm	254 cm (100 in)

This point has been well made by Edward Weston: 'Photography is not all seeing in the sense that the eyes see. Our vision, a binocular one, is in a continuous state of flux, while the camera captures and fixes forever (unless the damn prints fade!) a single, isolated condition of the moment. Besides, we use lenses of various focal length to purposely exaggerate actual seeing, and we often "overcorrect" colour for the same reason. In printing we carry on our wilful distortion of fact by using contrasty papers which give results quite different from the scene or object as it was in nature.'

The visual impact of a photograph often increases with its size. This is particularly true of landscapes, which are probably more satisfying when the print is large enough to require our eyes to scan it in somewhat the same way as we would look across a landscape scene. In practice the size of an enlargement is generally dictated by its purpose. The amateur wanting pictures of his family for framing and display around the house may choose 10 × 13 or 13 × 18 cm (4 × 5 or 5 × 7 in) prints, while the freelance journalist, needing to illustrate an article, submits 20 × 25 cm (8 × 10 in) prints with his manuscript. An advertising or display company needs 40 × 50 cm (16 × 20 in) or larger prints for an exhibition stand, and may also require photographic murals.

Composing the picture

Almost 50 per cent of the cut sheet paper sold by Ilford is in the 20 × 25 cm format. This is rather surprising because the proportions of a 20 × 25 cm print are not a good match for the shape of the most widely used negative format, 24 × 36 mm. It can therefore be assumed that not many 35 mm negatives are

191

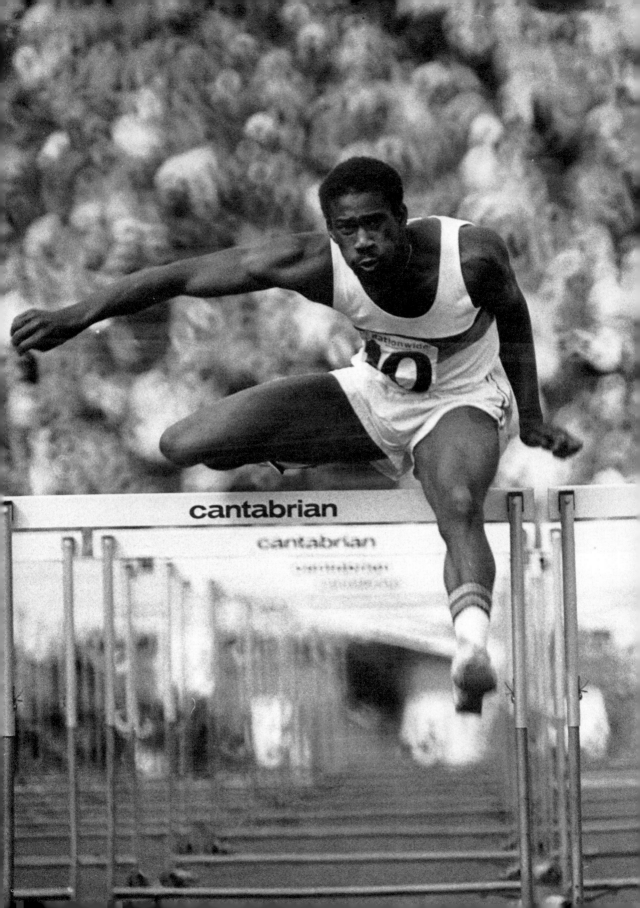

printed in their entirety, and that composition of the finished photograph often takes place at the time it is enlarged.

There are a few purists who still preach the doctrine of Edward Weston that photographs should be composed in the camera and that the whole of the negative should always be printed. (Denis Thorpe, for example, makes a point of composing his pictures in the viewfinder of a Nikon, and frequently prints the whole of the 24 × 36 mm negative frame.) But Weston would sometimes spend days exposing two or three 8 × 10 inch negatives, using a view camera on a tripod. Stieglitz on the other hand, who preceded and greatly influenced Weston, is reported to have rarely composed his pictures in the camera, and his final images were always cropped.

Certainly the widespread use of small hand-held cameras has brought about great changes. It has recently been said that some professional photographers are satisfied if, on average, they obtain two good pictures from each roll of 35 mm film they expose.

Unless the viewpoint and the focal length of the camera lens were chosen perfectly at the time the negative was exposed, it is necessary to decide the content of the picture when the print is being made. Adjustments to composition are carried out by raising or lowering the enlarger head to obtain the required size of image on the easel, then locating the easel suitably on the baseboard and

'Lowryland waits for demolition' is the title Denis Thorpe chose for this award-winning picture. As usual, he printed the whole of the 24 × 36 mm FP4 negative frame

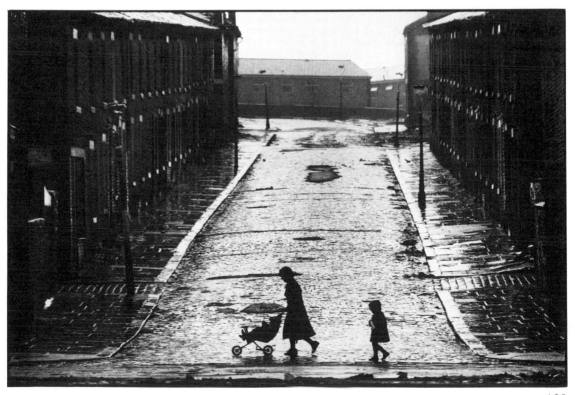

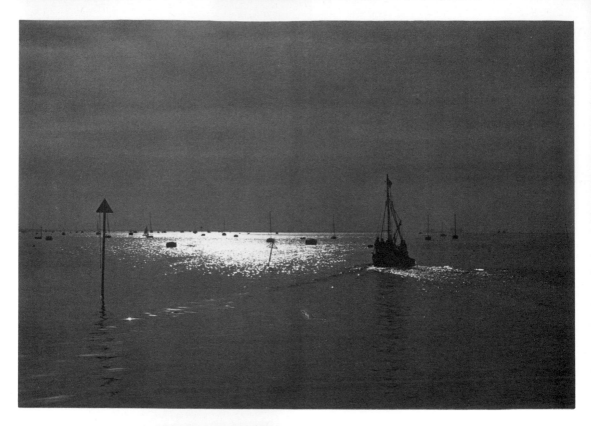

Mike Walden's negative of
Leigh Creek provides two
equally good pictures,
composed in the enlarger

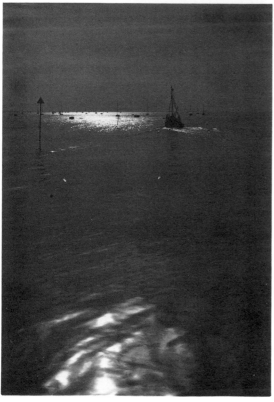

adjusting its masking blades to include only the part of the negative image that is to be printed. The negative itself should also be masked off with the sliding blades that are usually incorporated in the enlarger or negative carrier. This masking is not quite as tight as on the paper easel, but it is sufficient to prevent extraneous light passing through the negative to cause unnecessary scatter within the enlarger and the lens. If the enlarger has no facilities for masking the negative, a black paper cut-out mask can be placed over the negative.

If a contact print has already been made and marked-up, it acts as a guide during the positioning and adjustment of the image on the easel. The back of an old sheet of printing paper can be used for arranging and focusing the image.

While arranging the image on a focusing sheet, some obvious corrections can be made immediately. Tilted horizons can be levelled, and unnecessary intrusions into the picture area, either unavoidable or unnoticed at the time the negative was exposed, can often be eliminated by cropping the image a little tighter.

Converging verticals   In all that has been said about positioning the paper easel it has been assumed that the projected image lies normal to the optical axis of the enlarger, an important prerequisite for almost all kinds of work. However, the paper easel can be deliberately tilted whenever it is considered necessary to alter the 'perspective' of a subject from the way it was recorded on the negative. The most obvious example is to reduce or eliminate the convergence of the vertical lines occurring in street scenes or architectural subjects, when they have been photographed with the camera pointing upwards.

When an image displaying parallel instead of converging vertical lines is obtained by tilting the paper plane, this does not itself ensure that the proportions of that image are the same as in the original subject. If, for industrial or commercial purposes, rectification of scale is important, several other conditions must be

To avoid using extremely small lens apertures when enlarging negatives needing correction of verticals, negative, lens and paper planes should intersect at a common point

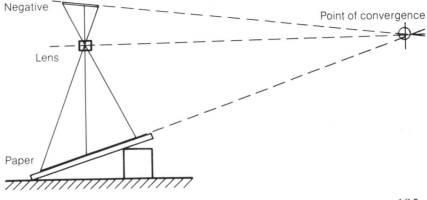

Negative

Lens

Point of convergence

Paper

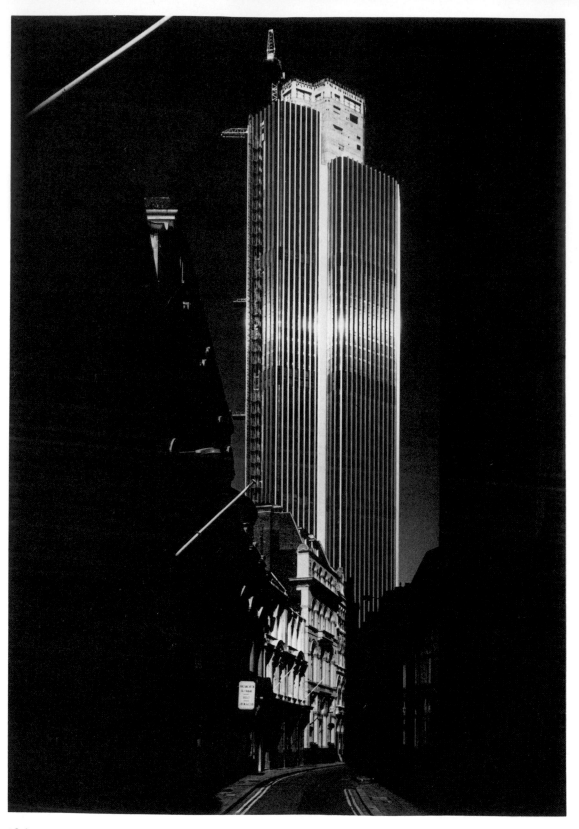

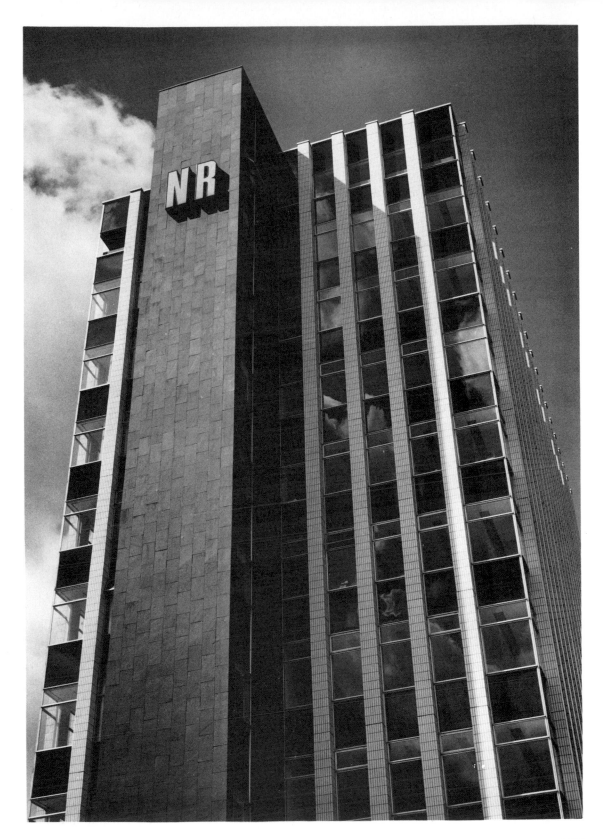

fulfilled. Although the precise conditions can be worked out mathematically, the necessary formulae involve precise relationships between the focal lengths of both camera and enlarging lens and specific degrees of enlargement.

As an alternative, David Charles, who was a practical photographer of great experience, worked out this empirical procedure: 'The enlarger is first adjusted to the required magnification with both negative and paper planes at right angles to the axis of the lens in the usual way. The negative and the paper easel are then tilted in opposite directions until the verticals are parallel in the projected image and definition is uniform over the whole of the image area. Next, the negative carrier and the paper easel are moved laterally and in opposite directions until the proportions of the image are judged to be correct. The lateral movements of the negative and paper plane will disturb parallelism and necessitate slight readjustment of tilts, but by trial and error positioning and tilting of the negative and paper planes, the image can be made to display parallel verticals and rectified proportions.'

This is only possible if the negative or part of the negative that is to be printed is appreciably smaller than the aperture in the negative stage, and if the enlarger lens adequately covers the negative when it has been moved sideways.

Working print   The important subjective decisions about the composition of the picture are not easy to make. It is often worth making a reference or working print, which can be viewed with a pair of L-shaped masks to examine several different ways of cropping the final enlargement. When the composition of the print has been decided, its edges can be marked on the work print with a chinagraph pencil. If the card from which the 'L' masks are cut is black or grey on one side and white on the other, the effect of a light or dark surround for the print can be judged.

Some printers take the trouble to make a good-quality work print; for others, almost any kind of print helps when deciding how to crop the negative and how it may be improved by shading or burning-in. The optimum exposure for the final print can be established when making the work print, though it may mean making a few test exposures in the first place. It will have to be decided whether to make the work print the same size as the finished print or whether, in the case of large prints, this would be too expensive. If the cost of materials is not a consideration, it is certainly preferable to make the work print the same size as the finished print; for one thing, the information on exposure is then directly applicable.

Page 196: Len Dance used the movements of his Sinar camera to ensure that he had parallel verticals on the FP4 negative he used for this print, which he calls 'Third encounter.' Page 197: Barry Traill pointed his camera upwards and disregarded the converging verticals in his picture 'The citadel.' Who is to say which of the prints is 'right'?

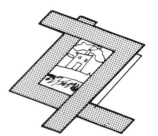

Pair of L-shaped masks help decisions on image cropping

Aperture-setting and focusing

Many factors must be taken into consideration besides a desire to use the enlarging lens at the aperture that will produce its optimum performance. If exposures become too short because the lens aperture is large, shading or burning-in is impossible. Furthermore, if a large aperture is used there is greater risk of an unsharp image if either the negative or the paper, or both, is not perfectly flat and the depths of field and focus are too small to take care of such conditions. Conversely, whenever a large print is required from a dense negative, exposure times may be kept within reasonable limits only by using the lens at or near its full aperture.

A reasonable procedure is to use an enlarging lens at one to three stops less than its maximum aperture, whenever conditions allow a choice. Consideration must also be given to any results that are obtained from checking the uniformity of illumination over a range of lens apertures, since many enlarging lenses have a tendency to vignette at large apertures.

A projected image should be focused with the lens aperture wide open. Quite apart from the greater brightness that results, this is also the condition under which the depth of focus is least; the in-focus and out-of-focus effects are most abrupt and optimum focus can be more confidently determined.

Whether a focusing magnifier is used or not must remain a personal decision for the printer. Some with perfect eyesight may scorn any artificial aid. Others, even with excellent eyesight, may choose to play safe by habitually checking their enlarged images with a focusing magnifier.

One new factor that is playing a part in black-and-white enlarging practice is the use of dye images in monochrome negatives such as Ilford XP1–400. Printers who habitually depend on the grainy appearance of the enlarged image to assist them in determining optimum focus will find that they can no longer work in this way. Instead, they will have to learn how to focus using the enlarged image of some detail of the subject itself, rather than the structure of the image.

Focusing magnifiers depend upon a magnified aerial image of the negative being reflected into an eyepiece via a front-surfaced mirror. Their accuracy relies entirely on the supposition that the base of the magnifier is in exactly the same plane as the sensitive surface of the printing paper when it is exposed. This means that a sheet of the paper that will be used to make the print must be in position on the baseboard or in the easel while the image is being focused.

The image seen through the eyepiece of a focusing magnifier is usually bright enough to allow the lens aperture to be set at whatever value it will be when the print is exposed. This may have some advantage, since the precise focus of a lens can shift slightly when it is stopped down.

When very large prints are being made with a vertical enlarger and the enlarger head is high above the baseboard, it is sometimes difficult to lean over a focusing magnifier and at the same time reach up to the low adjustment knob. To deal more comfortably with this situation, Paterson make a magnifier with an eyepiece that stands 36 cm (14 in) above the paper plane.

Negative 'popping' When using a glassless negative carrier there is always a risk that the negative may move slightly or even 'pop' during the time a print is being exposed. If exposures are quite short, say 10 seconds or less, the increase in the temperature of the negative may not be enough to cause any significant expansion, but as exposure continues movement may well occur and cause an unsharp print. The behaviour of a negative in a particular enlarger should be examined with the aid of a focusing magnifier before large prints are made with long exposures. Stopping down the enlarging lens cannot be relied on to help, since this extends exposure time still further and may be self-defeating.

Flatness of paper The image of a negative having been arranged and focused on a sheet of white paper held in an easel or laid on the baseboard of an enlarger, it is usually assumed that the image will still be in focus when the focusing sheet is replaced by a sheet of printing paper. This assumption must be questioned whenever there is any doubt about the flatness or the stability of a particular batch of paper or the humidity of the darkroom in which it is being used. Stability is important; even slight movement of the paper during a long exposure can cause mystifying areas of relative unsharpness within a picture area.

Modern photographic printing papers show much less tendency to curl than was once the case. Many printers, particularly those working on newspapers or for press agencies, regularly work without a paper easel, simply laying a sheet of Ilfospeed paper straight on to the baseboard of the enlarger. However, no paper coated with an emulsion layer on one side only can be expected to remain quite flat under all conditions of humidity. If there is any doubt about flatness, and the risk of unsharpness cannot be dealt with by stopping down the enlarging lens, the use of a vacuum easel should be considered for critical work.

Even with the image carefully focused on a flat sheet of paper, the resulting print can still be unsharp if there is any vibration during the exposure. Amateurs, who sometimes have to improvise darkrooms and support their enlargers temporarily on benches or tables, should be particularly careful to see that nothing moves or vibrates while prints are being exposed. The construction of the enlarger itself plays an important part in providing a stable optical system; generally speaking, the heavier the enlarger the less susceptible it is to accidental movement.

Determining the exposure

There are several ways of finding out what exposure to give a print. Some of them save time, others save paper. The professional printer, whose time is usually worth more than the materials he uses, can call on his experience to estimate an exposure after briefly assessing the brightness of the projected image of the negative on the baseboard or easel. He may not guess right every time, but he discovers very quickly whether the exposure was a long way out or whether the print can be made acceptable by shortening or extending the development time. In this way he makes use of the valuable development latitude of most black-and-white paper/developer combinations. Even if the first estimate of exposure was a long way out, the professional quickly discards the first sheet and exposes a second, with much greater certainty that the adjusted exposure will yield a good result.

By working with full-size sheets, the professional also enjoys the advantage that every exposure he makes results in a complete picture, not just part of one. This makes it easier to decide what changes will improve the print. The amateur printer, however, has to be more careful. He does not have the confidence or the experience of the professional, and his materials are often more valuable to him than his time. He therefore needs to be as sure as possible, when exposing a large sheet of paper, that the exposure is correct.

Timing the exposure   There are at least four ways in which printing exposures can be timed. The time-honoured and simplest of them is to count in one's head 'one hundred, one hundred and one, one hundred and two', and so on. The printer who still counts out exposures in his head is not likely to be giving absolute exposure times, but provided his mental metronome is reasonably consistent this will not matter. Other ways are to look at a watch or a clock, or to count the visible flashes or audible signals emitted by a 'bleeper' at one-second intervals. More often nowadays a preset clockwork or electric timer is used, either to sound an alarm or to switch off the enlarger lamp at the end of the required exposure.

The large luminous dial of the Gralab timer makes it popular, and since it has a timing range from 1 second to 60 minutes it can be used for enlarging or processing. This timer also has an outlet that can be connected to the enlarger so that the lamp is automatically switched off at the end of the preset period, leaving both hands free for shading or burning-in during the latter part of an exposure.

A footswitch can be used to start and end an exposure, leaving both hands free from the time the lamp is switched on. This is also the case when a battery-driven 'bleeper' is used. The Paterson bleeper offers the choice of visible or audible signals at one-second intervals, and has the further advantage of requiring no connecting wires.

Test strips or prints   The idea of a single 'correct' exposure in printing is really a misconception, since print exposure depends largely on the particular effect the printer or the photographer wishes to produce. Both the prints from which the illustrations on page 203 were made could be considered to have been correctly exposed, yet they are very different and it is a matter of opinion which is better.

In order to decide what exposure should be given to a final print, some preliminary evidence is necessary, usually in the form of test strips or prints. The evidence can also be in the form of density or transmission measurements taken from the negative, either before or during the time it is being printed; these methods of print exposure control are considered later (page 205).

The temptation for most amateurs, anxious to save paper, is to make the smallest possible test strips. This is a mistake, because the part of the image that is recorded on the strip may not be truly representative of the picture as a whole. The positioning of any test strip in relation to the important elements of a picture is important. Consider a quite ordinary example: a landscape in which the upper part of the picture is represented by sky while the lower part is open country dappled with shadows from clouds. With such a subject it would be quite misleading to expose a full-sized print solely on the evidence of a test strip that had been placed horizontally in the area of the sky. It would be better to use a long strip of paper placed diagonally across the picture to include both sky and parts of the foreground that are in both sunlight and shadow.

Normally, when using familiar equipment and materials, a range of test exposures with an overall ratio of about 10:1 proves adequate for most negatives. When an enlarger or a brand of paper or both are to be used for the first time, however, or when for some reason the negative is abnormally thin or dense, it usually saves time to widen the range of exposure times for the initial tests.

While the upper print could be considered properly printed, and in fact conveys more information, the lower one (given twice as much exposure and a burned-in sky) is far more striking and much preferred by the photographer, Janet Harber

202

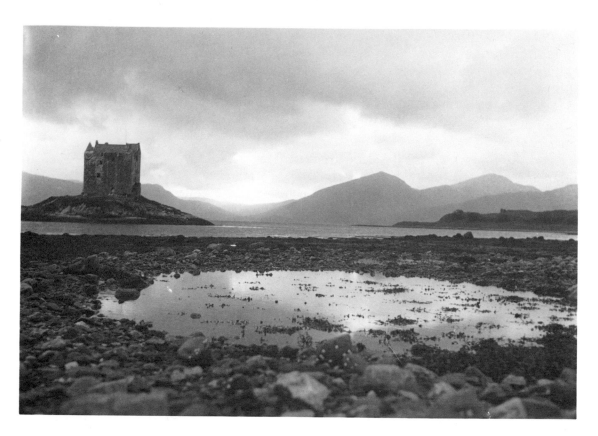

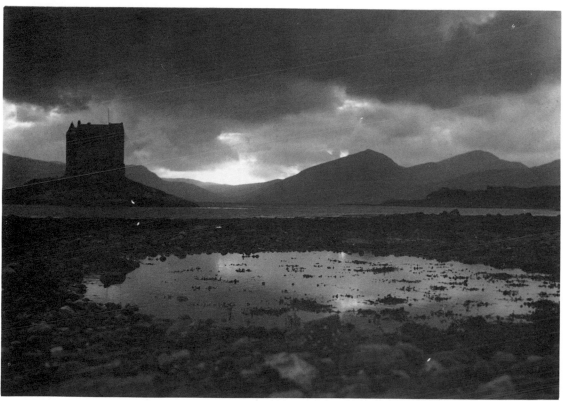

For example, after composing the negative image at full aperture and stopping the enlarging lens down to *f*/8, turn off the white light and place a sheet or part of a sheet of Ilfospeed or Ilfobrom grade 2 paper in the easel. Commence a series of exposures by giving the whole area of the test piece 5 seconds; then, using a sheet of black card or stiff paper, cover up about a quarter of the paper and give the rest of it another exposure of 5 seconds. After moving the card along to cover about half of the test piece, add another 10 seconds of exposure. Move the card once again, so that only about a quarter of the paper remains uncovered, and give it a final exposure of 20 seconds. This procedure produces a series of sectional exposures for times of 5, 10, 20 and 40 seconds. After processing, the test strip should include one section that has been exposed for something like the right time.

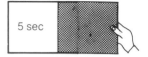

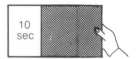

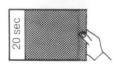

Should it turn out that even 5 seconds exposure was too long for the particular negative, the lens aperture can be reduced, perhaps to *f*/11. Exposures shorter than 5 seconds make it difficult to carry out any shading or burning-in that may be required. If none of the test exposures was long enough, repeat the sequence on another piece of paper, after opening the enlarger lens by one or even two stops. If the lens aperture cannot be increased without a risk of unreliable focusing at the paper plane, longer exposures will have to be tolerated, and the second test series should include sections at 20, 40, 80 and 160 seconds.

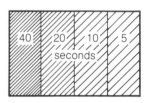

Series of four exposures when making a test print

When a negative includes some small but important area which, even after enlargement, is not large enough to be subdivided into differently exposed sections, squares or patches of paper can be sequentially exposed for different times and then processed

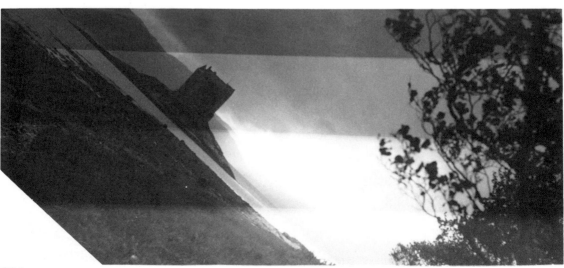

together. Test-strip printing devices are available, including one by Paterson for use with 13 cm (5 in) squares of paper and providing for five steps of exposure with thin dark lines between each exposed area.

Exposing very large prints   The problems of making very large prints such as mural photographs are mostly related to processing, but it is also important to have a sufficiently powerful enlarging light source to allow accurate focusing and to give reasonable exposure times. In any case, it is usually necessary to use much longer exposure times than normal enlargements require. This can introduce reciprocity effects (see page 51), so when making very large prints requiring minutes rather than seconds for exposure, it is not safe to assume that a straightforward relationship exists between the degree of enlargement and the exposure required. Careful tests should always be made before committing a large area of paper to a final exposure.

Integrated density measurement   Estimation or even automatic control of printing exposures is possible. If it were not so, there would be no photofinishing industry as we know it today. All the prints made from amateur negatives are printed on the basis of integrated measurements of the light transmitted by each negative at the time it is printed. This principle can be used when making enlarged prints, and often produces acceptable results. Unfortunately, some negatives do not lend themselves to printing on the basis of integrated density measurement; although such negatives are often referred to as 'subject failures', they represent a failure of the system.

Integration of the light transmitted by all, or substantially all, of the area of a negative is not the only way in which to assess the exposure most likely to produce a good print. Local 'spot' density measurements can be used to ensure that the print will contain a predictable density in any chosen area of the picture. In other words, the print density in a particular area of a sky or a face can be forecast from a measurement of the density of the corresponding area of the negative or of its projected image. By making two density measurements, one for the highlight area and the other for the shadows, the effective density range of the negative can be found. This enables a grade of paper to be chosen that theoretically fits the negative to best advantage, although it may not result in the best print when the result is judged subjectively.

George Wakefield has done a great deal of work in the determination of printing exposure by means of a whole-area negative density measurement. Provided that he had a choice of

An exposure test strip should be placed diagonally across a landscape picture in order to gain information about both foreground and sky

paper contrasts and could utilise the development latitude (or amplitude as he calls it) of a paper, by restricting or extending development, Wakefield found that he could obtain good prints from 178 out of 200 negatives. The negatives were of a wide range of subjects, including indoor and outdoor scenes and underexposed and overexposed examples. The prints were all developed by inspection.

From his work, Wakefield concluded that: '. . . the total density of a negative is a highly satisfactory criterion on which to base exposures in manual projection printing. Although it does not indicate the ideal exposure for every negative that may be encountered, a single correction factor equivalent to half a lens stop . . . applied when printing negatives having obviously large areas of high or low density . . . is adequate for ensuring prints of satisfactory density from most of the types of negatives likely to be encountered in general photographic practice.'

Enlarging exposure meters   The method used by Wakefield to measure the integrated density of his negatives was to place a Weston exposure meter in a fixed position above the negative, and then to measure the light reaching the meter from a Photoflood lamp after passing through both the negative and an opal glass diffuser.

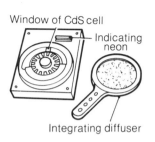

Window of CdS cell

Indicating neon

Integrating diffuser

Paterson CdS enlarging exposure meter

In everyday practice it would be inconvenient to have to measure the density of each negative before putting it into the enlarger to print it. Instead, equivalent measurements can be made in other ways. If a removable diffuser is mounted beneath the lens of an enlarger, a measurement of the integrated light passing through the negative can be made by placing an enlarging photometer on the baseboard. By prior testing, a speed rating can be obtained for the particular paper being used, and thereafter exposure times can be read directly from a scale on the meter. This is the method adopted for the Paterson CdS enlarging meter. It requires the temporary introduction of a diffuser into the light path and its removal before the print is exposed, but this is not much of an inconvenience except in a very busy darkroom.

Enlarging exposure easels   There are other ways in which integrated density measurements can be made while a print is being exposed, so that there is no extra operation involved. These methods of simultaneous exposure and measurement can also be used to terminate exposure automatically.

A proportion of the light used to project an image on to an enlarging easel can be collected, either by reflection from or transmission through the printing paper. This light triggers a switch controlling the enlarger lamp when some predetermined

206

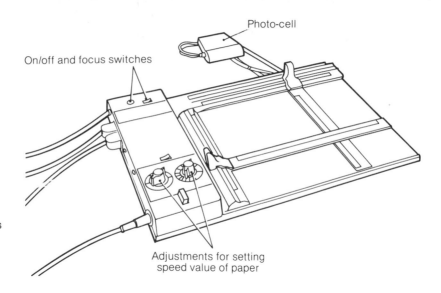

On/off and focus switches

Photo-cell

Adjustments for setting
speed value of paper

Revomatic enlarging
exposure easel integrates
sample of light that has
passed through negative
and been reflected from
paper into photo-cell

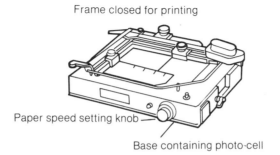

Frame closed for printing

Agfa Variomat enlarging
exposure easel integrates
light transmitted through
paper during exposure

Paper speed setting knob

Base containing photo-cell

amount of light has been received by the photomultiplier cell. When reflected light is used to energise the control circuit, the photo-cell is mounted somewhere above and to one side of the paper surface. With this type of exposure-control easel it is important to see that no light reaches the photomultiplier except that which is reflected from the printing paper.

When light that is transmitted through the printing paper activates the exposure-control circuit, the opacity of the paper must be consistent. If a change is made from single-weight to double-weight paper or to a different brand of paper, almost certainly the system will need to be recalibrated following a series of practical trials.

With an automatic enlarging easel, the exposure time is not known until the exposure has been terminated; thus shading or burning-in times are equally unpredictable, unless the trouble is taken to check the exposure time by trial before committing a sheet of sensitive paper.

Controlling print density

Larry Bartlett, an award-winning printer with the Daily Express, has commented: 'The most common mistake of inexperienced amateurs which I notice is that they produce prints which don't have good blacks. It may be because their developers are too weak, they don't develop long enough, or they use too soft a grade of paper. But in most beginners' work there is failure to get good, deep, rich blacks.' It is certainly true that inadequate development, whether caused by exhausted solution or shortened development time, results in poor print quality. All preliminary tests must be developed properly, with no short cuts taken in an attempt to save time.

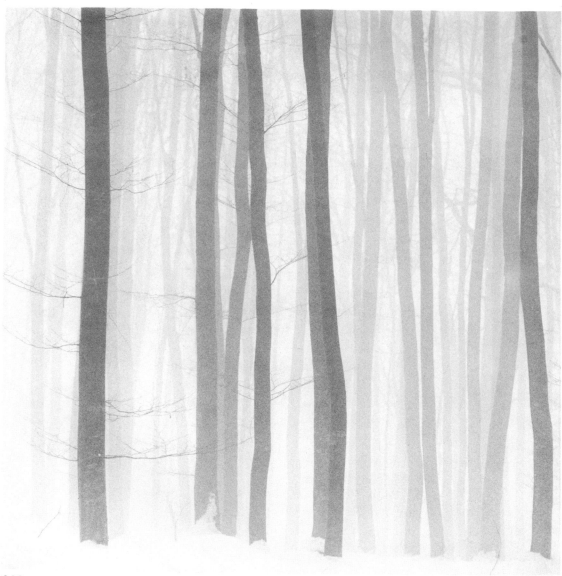

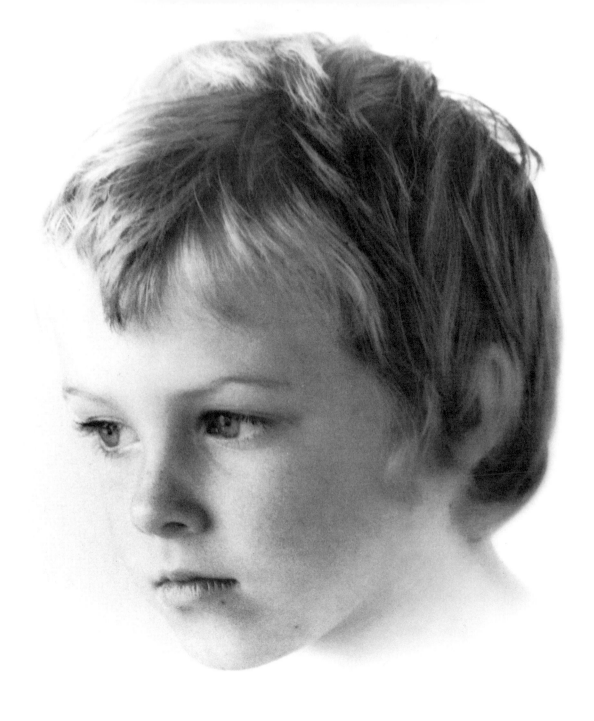

These two pictures, the
delicate woodland scene by
Hiroshi Shimura and the
vignetted portrait of 'Kirsty'
by Joan Salem, remind us
that not all subjects call for
maximum blacks

There are occasions when no true blacks are required in a print, for example in the beautiful study of trees by Hiroshi Shimura and the portrait of Kirsty by Joan Salem. High-key pictures of this kind, however, are achieved only by exercising full control of the photographic process throughout all its stages.

It may happen that when a test or work print has been exposed correctly and processed properly, it is unsatisfying in some way. Overall density may still not seem right even though great pains were taken to estimate the exposure correctly. But there can be several 'correct' exposures for a print, and sometimes the only way to be sure of finding the one that pleases most is to make several prints at different exposure levels so that they can be compared and a choice made.

A print may look flat and somehow uninteresting, or conversely it might have very little detail in highlight or shadow areas. In such cases, another print made on a harder or a softer grade of paper may bring about an improvement. Changing from one grade of paper to another is much less trouble than it used to be; with Ilford papers at least, there is no difference in speed between any of the grades from 0 to 4. Only if you have to resort to grade 5, the most contrasty paper of all, will you have to double the exposure.

If the print seems almost right, but could be improved by being just slightly softer or harder, it is sometimes possible to effect a small change by altering the development time. A slight increase in exposure followed by a shortened development (say two-thirds of the time used for the first print) usually gives a perceptibly softer result. To obtain a slightly harder result, shorten the exposure by about 25 per cent and extend development by 50 per cent, or more if necessary. These adjustments will not produce differences as great as changing from one grade of paper to another. They should be used only when enough experience has been gained to understand their limitations.

Local density control   The brightness range of some subjects leads to such extremes of negative densities that, even with a soft grade of paper, it is impossible adequately to reproduce both highlight and shadow detail in the same print by means of a single exposure. In any case, although printing a negative on to a soft paper may sometimes safeguard the reproduction of highlights and shadows, it may result in a rather dull-looking print because of poor tone separation in the rest of the picture.

There are two reasons for local manipulation of the densities of a print. The first, as has been explained, is to extend the amount of information depicted in a print by 'helping out' the photographic process. The other is to make a better picture in the aesthetic sense.

210

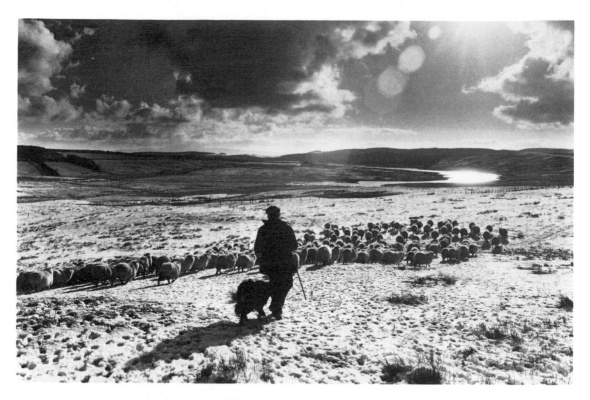

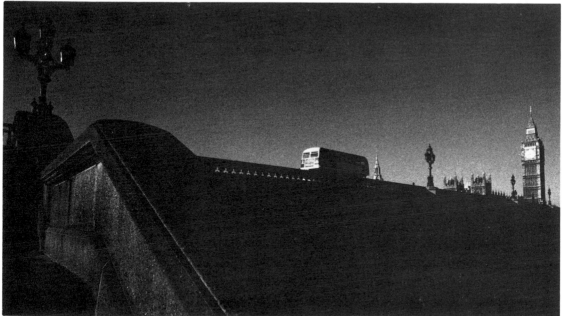

Top: the beautiful clouds enhancing Denis Thorpe's 'Shepherd of the year' would have been lost had the sky not been given much more exposure than the foreground

Above: the dramatic effect of Gene Nocon's 'London landscape' depends very largely upon the way he printed-in the dark sky

This is not necessarily related to the ability of a print to reproduce a wide enough range of brightness, but simply to do with subjective judgement of the preferred arrangement of the tone relationships between the principal elements of the picture.

For example, it is common practice to give a sky area more exposure than the foreground of a landscape subject. This is usually thought of as burning-in the sky, but it could be considered as shading the foreground. 'Shepherd of the year' by Denis Thorpe and 'London landscape' by Gene Nocon are two good examples of pictures in which skies have been emphasised by giving them extra exposure.

To shade or burn-in means to give less or more exposure to a particular area of a print than to the rest of it. Shading (dodging) and burning-in require a great deal of practice, however, and practice means using paper. As Larry Bartlett says: 'Getting the finest-quality prints from a black-and-white negative is an art which more amateurs should practise. Like a ballet dancer uses his feet, so a good darkroom printer should use his hands. Amateurs should have plenty of practice with their hands, forming different shapes in the light from the enlarger. This is much better than using artificial dodgers, as you get a more instinctive feel as you are exposing.'

Certainly the easier forms of shading should be done manually. Perhaps the simplest starting exercise is to use a negative of a landscape with a fairly well-defined horizon. With such a case the edge of the flattened hand, held in an appropriate position fairly close to the enlarger lens, can be made to cast a soft-edged shadow over the foreground after that part of the print has been given sufficient exposure. If the shadow of the hand is moved slowly to and from the upper edge of the picture during the additional exposure, the sky becomes darker at the top than nearer the horizon.

The basic or 'straight' exposure should be reasonably long, say 20 or 30 seconds, so that any shading or burning-in does not have to be done hurriedly and can be accurately repeated or reliably modified. If necessary, basic exposure time can be extended by stopping down the enlarger lens. Shading may sometimes have to continue for half or more of the time a print is being exposed, or it may only be necessary for a small proportion of that time. Similarly, burning-in may involve a short additional exposure or, in the case of dense local areas, might call for several times more exposure than the rest of the print.

Termination of exposure after burning-in is easily done if the enlarger lamp is controlled by a footswitch. Alternatively, one hand or the burning-in card can be used to blank off the light from

A straight print from John Downing's HP5 negative of Mother Teresa makes a good but not great picture. Larry Bartlett's interpretation of that negative, and his creative presentation, resulted in an award-winning print

212

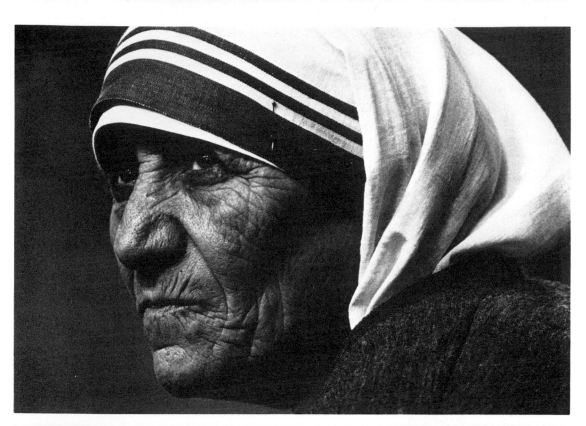

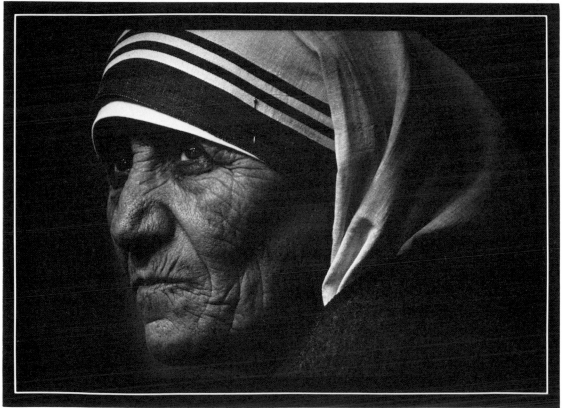

the enlarger lens while the enlarger lamp is switched off with the other hand.

Once the technique of shading a print has been learned and confidence gained, there is always a danger of overdoing it. If any suggestion of unreality becomes noticeable as a result of shading a particular area, it is usually time to reduce the treatment. The risk of excessive burning-in is not as great, but this too must be watched.

Shading devices   Although professional printers prefer to use their hands or fingers for both shading and burning-in, it is sometimes necessary, when shading small areas that are located well inside the picture, to use a dodging or shading aid. Usually this takes the form of a piece of black paper or thin card cut or torn to something like the shape of the area to be shaded, but smaller. The piece of paper or card is either taped or impaled on to the end of a thin but reasonably stiff wire holder so that the area requiring less exposure can be shaded without the wire leaving any evidence. In practice, the wire must be moved slightly but continuously throughout the period of shading.

For burning-in small areas, all that is required is a black card with a hole in it. The size of the hole is not very important since its effect can be altered simply by varying the distance it is held above the paper. Two or three different holes, 1.5, 2.5 and 5 cm (½, 1 and 2 in) in diameter, will serve most purposes.

The level at which to introduce any shading or burning-in device (or one's fingers) must be found by trial and error. A pretty good idea can be obtained by observation before a print is made; it will quickly be seen that the closer to the paper the obstruction is placed, the more accurate its location and shape must be. In general it is better to work as close to the lens as possible. Beginners often keep their hand or card in a fixed position while shading or burning-in, with the result that the edges of the shadows formed are too well-defined and can be detected in the finished print. Throughout any period of shading or burning-in, the hand or card should be kept moving with a slight circular movement.

Sometimes a print needs such a complicated combination of dodging and burning-in that it becomes necessary to enlist the aid of a second pair of hands. Denis Thorpe explains how he and Ken Hugill made the print of 'The miller':

'In printing this really difficult negative of the miller we were presented with the problem of preserving the rather delicately lit interior, which has a certain charm and subtlety, and trying to balance the tones with the harsh sunlight entering the doorway

214

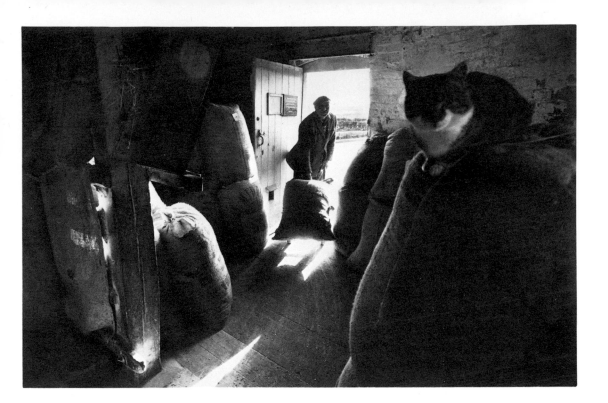

As explained on pages 214–216, Denis Thorpe and his printer Ken Hugill had to work hard, with four hands, to dodge and burn-in this print of 'The miller'

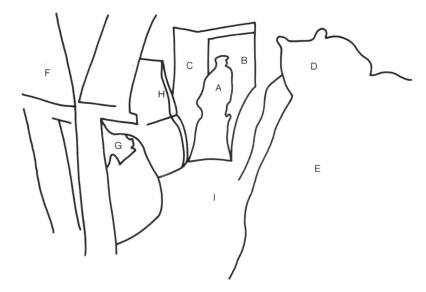

behind the miller and sack. I know exactly how I would have photographed the scene had I been able to set it up and with time to spare, but such is the nature of my job, working quickly for a daily newspaper, that we see and shoot for spontaneity.

'Ken Hugill and I prefer the accuracy of the Leitz Focomat IIc for our 35 mm printing. I think it superb even if it does look rather old-fashioned nowadays. With the really precision glass carrier essential in 35 mm black-and-white printing, and automatic focusing that really does work, we can work quickly.

'The miller print was done on Ilfospeed grade 3 glossy in Ilfospeed developer, warmer than usual because we like to know where we are with a print quickly; we also feel that the extra temperature gives us better blacks. This is a personal feeling that can probably be contradicted scientifically.

'The main interior was fairly easy to control, parts E and F (see sketch) receiving about 8 seconds at $f/8$ on the 50 mm Leitz lens, with light-shading by hand during exposure on the woodwork and toward the edges of the print. Ken Hugill crooked his right forefinger into a shape that kept the cat (D) just a little lighter, while all this time I had been shading back details in the miller and sack (A). This I did with a dodger made on the spot with a straightened-out paperclip and a rough shape torn from a piece of scrap paper. Otherwise we would have been left with a black silhouette at the outset.

'We needed 6 seconds extra exposure in area I, to accentuate the grains of corn against the light. We made a mask by cutting a slightly smaller doorway in a piece of card and then we both shaded the area BC, Ken with the mask and myself still with the paperclip dodger in area A. The right-hand top and side of the doorway where most overexposure occurred was done with a slightly smaller mask for at least a minute extra exposure, and the areas H and G, with sunlight hard on the top and edges of the flour sacks, were shaded for threequarters of a minute to one minute longer by hand, making the shapes though holes in our fingers. We looked like two mad magicians weaving spells! Developing was straightforward, with perhaps a cold tap running to wash developer away from the areas we thought were coming too quickly, but this sort of control was minimal, most of the effort going into manipulation at the enlarger stage. Very exhausting work, printing!'

Permanent shading   When a large number of prints are required from a negative that requires shading, it would obviously be laborious to have to follow the same shading procedure while making every exposure. In such a case it is worthwhile binding up the negative with suitably shaped and suitably spaced masks made from tissue paper or matt film; the required shading is thus built-in and has exactly the same effect throughout the run of prints.

The picture of a curtained window on page 219 was made from a 10 × 13 cm (4 × 5 in) negative; the masking was done by placing a number of suitably shaped pieces of fixed-out film and one piece of matt film (to deal with the foreground) in position on
216

the top surface of the upper condenser of the enlarger. The number, shape and density of these film overlays were determined partly by observation of the projected image, partly by making trial prints. The negative was used to produce thousands of specimen prints on Ilford Galerie paper.

A range of thin colourless matt film materials, known as Rosco 'Soft Frost' and 'Cine Frost' and intended for diffusing studio lighting, are very suitable for making shaped masks. On the assumption that only important negatives justify the time and attention required in making and positioning a shaped mask, it is worth cutting the single frame concerned from the series of exposures if the picture was shot on a 35 mm or roll film. The negative can then be handled more easily by being placed in a slide mount and protected by a pair of cover glasses. Appropriately shaped masking foils can then be sandwiched between the outside of one of the cover glasses and a third glass taped to the side of the mount to hold the mask flat and in position.

An ingenious method of achieving reproducible local density control when using negatives between 6 × 6 cm and 13 × 18 cm has been devised by Fribo. The Friboflex optomechanical shading head allows any combination of 354 shading 'elements' to be chosen to reduce the amount of light reaching the negative. The location and the effectiveness of the light reduction can be seen immediately on the projected image. Furthermore, once determined, the shading pattern remains constant throughout a production run and can be recorded on a 'storage master' for future use with the same negative.

Using variable-contrast papers

Throughout the foregoing section on local density control, it has been assumed that the results were confined to changes in density and not contrast. In fact, both density and contrast can be changed locally within the same print when a variable-contrast paper is used.

Black-and-white printing papers have been made in a variety of contrasts since the earliest days of photography, but it is also possible, as explained earlier (page 166), to achieve a wide range of different contrasts with a single type of paper, generally known as variable- or selective-contrast paper. All that has to be done by the printer to change the effective contrast of the paper is to alter the colour of the printing light. The simplest and cheapest way is to use a set of colour filters. This is how most variable-contrast papers have been exposed, despite the fact that it is often necessary to adjust exposure times when changing from one filter to another in order to alter the contrast of a print.

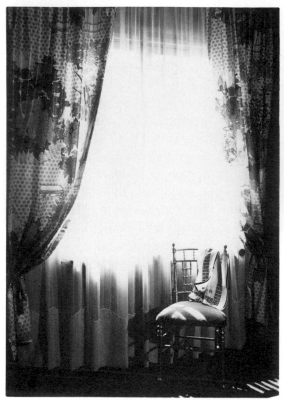

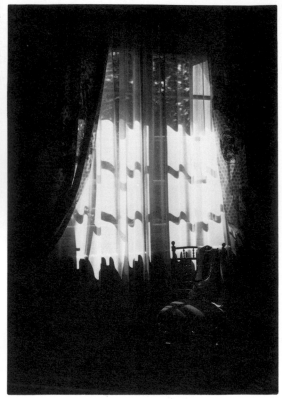

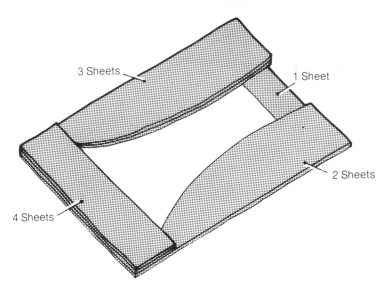

3 Sheets

1 Sheet

2 Sheets

4 Sheets

The print above left resulted from an exposure suited to the shadow areas of the picture. The print above right, requiring two to three times more exposure, successfully records the highlight areas of the window

By using tissue-paper masks (left) to restrict the light transmitted through shadow areas of the negative, sufficient exposure could be given to record the highlight detail of the picture while retaining open shadows (facing page)

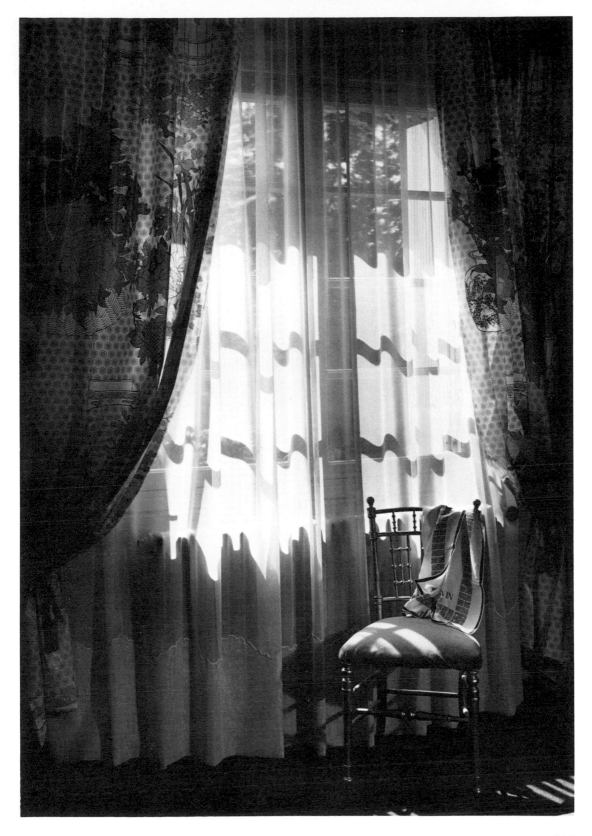

Multigrade filters range in colour from yellow to magenta, the yellow filters producing softer results while the magentas yield harder or more contrasty prints.

It is perhaps more useful to say that Multigrade paper used with one of the yellow filters produces normal-looking prints from a contrasty negative, while the same paper exposed through one of the magenta filters enables good prints to be made from low-contrast negatives. In other words, the primary purpose of a variable-contrast system is to enable the printer to obtain good results from a negative that is lower or higher in contrast than normal, either because of the subject matter or because of the way it was exposed or processed.

Although the filters originally supplied for use with Multigrade (Mk 1) paper were numbered 1 to 7, those numbers bore no relation to those usually associated with graded papers such as Ilfospeed. During 1982 Ilford plan to introduce an improved Multigrade paper, together with a new set of filters. There will be either 10 or 11 filters, numbered from 0 to 4½ or 5, thereby permitting direct comparison with the grade spacing of Ilfospeed and Ilfobrom papers. The new filters will be spaced at half-grade intervals to allow finer control of print contrast, and all except two of them will yield uniform print densities without any necessity to adjust exposure. When maximum contrast is required, one of the two deepest magenta filters has to be used, and exposure must be doubled.

Variable-contrast papers depend upon part of the emulsion assembly being sensitive to green (or at least greenish-blue) light, as well as to the blue light to which all emulsions are sensitive. This poses the question of safelighting. Fortunately, the same safelight recommended for use with Ilfospeed and Ilfobrom papers (Ilford 902, light-brown) can be safely used with Multigrade. The safety of any other safelight should be checked by experiment.

Contrast range with Multigrade   The range of contrast obtainable with Multigrade Mark 1 paper and the original set of seven filters was equivalent to the difference between rather less than grade 0 and grade 4. The range will be extended at the high-contrast end with the introduction of Multigrade Mark 2 paper and the new set of filters. Multigrade paper is often exposed without a filter in position, and then the effective contrast of the paper is slightly softer than grade 2 Ilfospeed or Ilfobrom.

When used without a filter Multigrade is a little faster than Ilfospeed or Ilfobrom, but when filters are used the paper requires more exposure. In order to make it easy to determine the new exposure when a print has been made on Multigrade and another

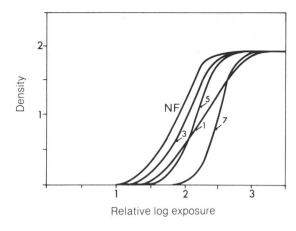

Effective speed of Multigrade paper changes when filters are used to alter contrast. Filter numbers on graph apply to set of filters sold with Multigrade Mk 1 paper

one is required with a different contrast, Ilford provides users with a simple rotary calculator. The extreme difference in exposure between the yellow and magenta filters involves a ratio of 1:4, but when working around the middle of the range of available contrast the exposures are about the same.

Use of colour head   Because most colour printing heads incorporate a yellow and a magenta dichroic filter (plus a cyan one), they can be used to obtain variations of contrast with Multigrade paper. The precise values of yellow and/or magenta that are required to produce paper contrasts equivalent to those obtained with standard Multigrade filters, or by using graded papers, must be determined by trial. In the same way, the adjustment in exposure necessitated by changes in contrast needs to be found empirically. In general, these changes are smaller than with polyester filters, because dichroic filters are more efficient. As a starting point the following table can be used:

Equivalent paper grade	Filtration
0	40 yellow
1	30 yellow
2	30 magenta
3	60 magenta
4	130 magenta

From the introduction of the original Multigrade in 1940, it has been usual practice for printers to readjust their exposures whenever they change filters to obtain a significant alteration in the effective contrast of a print. This has always been an inconvenience, and a particular nuisance when a negative requires

221

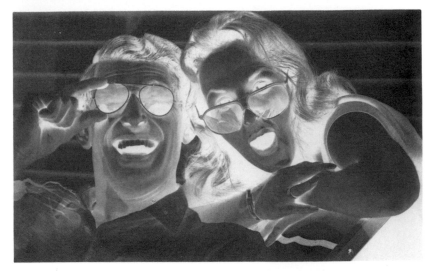

These three negatives were all exposed correctly, but they differ in contrast, the top one having been underdeveloped and the bottom one considerably overdeveloped

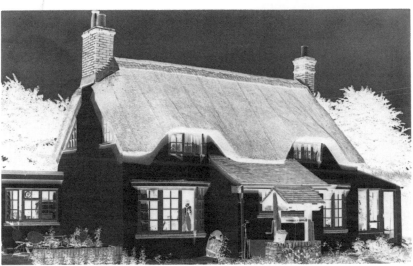

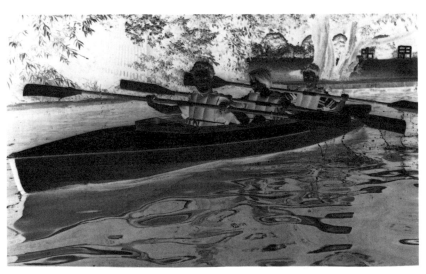

By using Multigrade paper with appropriate filters, excellent prints can be obtained from all three negatives. Top: printed with a yellow filter. Middle: printed on Multigrade paper without a filter. Bottom: printed with a magenta filter

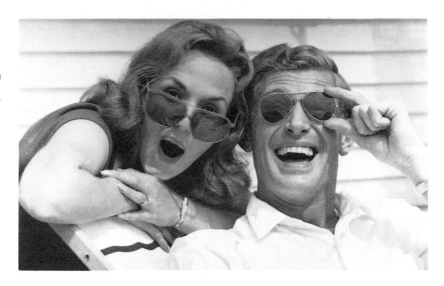

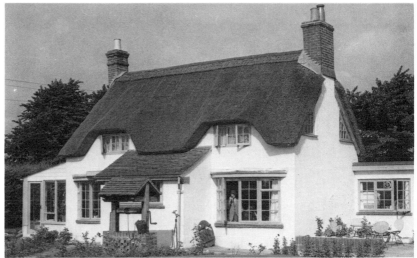

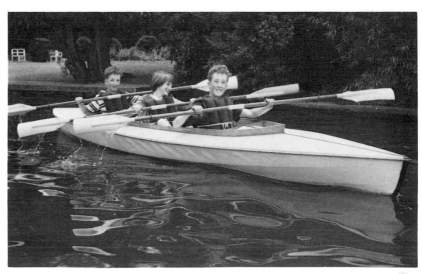

complicated shading or burning-in, because a change in overall exposure requires proportionate changes in the periods of local manipulation during exposure of the print and these times too have to be recalculated.

To solve this problem, Ilford invented and introduced the Ilfospeed Multigrade 400 system, which enables a printer to select any one of nine half-grade contrast steps on Multigrade paper at the push of a button (page 167). The nine selector buttons of the control unit are marked from 0 to 4 in half grades, and the resulting contrasts are similar to the equivalent grades of Ilfospeed and Ilfobrom papers.

If a print needs extra exposure locally, the 'burn-in' button can be used to re-start the exposure, which can be timed separately with the digital timer or audibly with the aid of a 'bleeper'. An optional footswitch is available so that both hands can be used for shading or burning-in. Unlike any previous method of exposing a variable contrast paper, however, the burning-in stage can be carried out at a different contrast from that used for the rest of the print, simply by pressing the desired contrast button. Furthermore, a change in contrast *involves no change in the effective speed of the Multigrade paper*. Because of this, either shading or burning-in can be done as easily with the Multigrade system as with graded papers, but with the added advantage of having two or more contrasts available for use within the same print.

Victor Blackman has commented on the value of the new facility for printers. Of a particularly difficult negative he said: 'Using a high-contrast paper to bring out their image would have ruined the rest of the picture. So darkroom technician Melvin Mann used Multigrade. Then, by skilful shading and switching of filters in the enlarger, he got the effect of printing the couple in the turret on contrasty paper, while the rest of the print was effectively on soft paper.' A straight print from the negative is reproduced together with the Multigrade print on page 225.

Alternative method of exposing Multigrade   Believing that it is important for the printer to be able to utilise the full range of contrasts available with Multigrade paper without having to think about adjusting exposure, Ilford devised another way in which this can be achieved.

As described on page 168, a yellow and a magenta filter are juxtaposed and can be moved across the focal point of a tungsten-halogen lamp; the user can choose any combination of yellow and magneta light and thereby obtain a full range of contrasts using Multigrade paper. Since the yellow or minus-blue sector of the composite filter is relatively more efficient in passing

Victor Blackman was concerned that the two World War II pilots were not clearly seen behind the perspex of the gun turret (upper picture), so he asked his printer to use Multigrade to obtain two levels of contrast within the same print

224

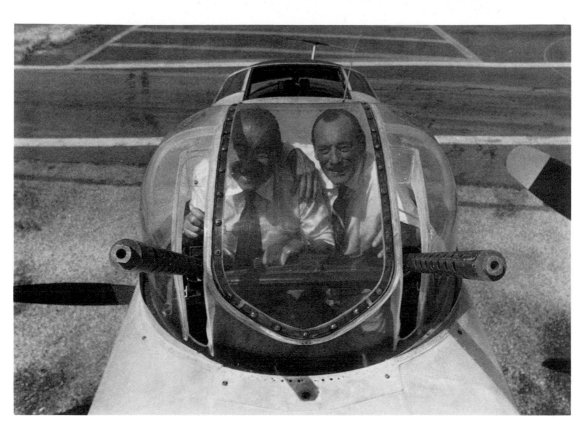

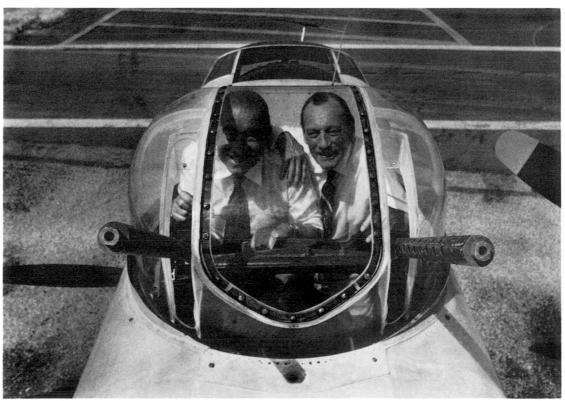

green light than the magenta sector is in passing blue light, the light transmitted by the yellow filter has to be reduced by the addition of neutral-density; this makes it possible to equalise the effective exposures through the two filters as they are moved across the light from the lamp.

Several enlarger manufacturers have adopted the two-part dichroic filter idea. One of the most interesting results is that the Leitz V35 enlarger can be obtained with an Ilfospeed Multigrade module as an alternative to the colour module. The Multigrade module is adjusted by a single knob, while the contrast setting is indicated on a scale seen through a window in the module. As with the V35 colour module, the filters can be temporarily removed from the optical path so that focusing may be carried out with the brightest possible image, but the preselected filter setting is regained when the white-light control rod is released.

By using Multigrade paper and one of the exposing methods that have been designed to enable contrast to be changed without having to alter exposure, it is perfectly possible for the professional printer to exercise all his skills and the amateur to experiment with a wide range of contrasts without having to use more than one box of paper. In fact, it is now arguable that there is no longer much of a case for using graded papers.

5 Processing the print

Processing by inspection

One of the greatest advantages of making black-and-white prints is that the job can be done by sight rather than by touch. Results can be assessed and controlled during development and not, as with colour printing, only after completion of the processing cycle. As discussed in Chapter 4, there should be just enough light over and around the enlarger to enable a sheet of paper to be accurately located in the paper easel, but not enough to reduce the effective brightness of the projected image on the baseboard. The greatest risk of fogging a sheet of black-and-white paper comes during the time it is being exposed. Once the exposed print has been immersed in developer, however, as much safelight as possible should be used in order to be able to assess the image as it grows. If the image is judged in too low a level of safelight, the finished prints, when seen in daylight, will probably look too light. One can learn to compensate for the difference between the apparent density of a print examined under dim safelight and its final appearance in white light, but it is far better to use optimum safelighting.

Only a series of practical tests, with the type of paper you expect to use, can enable you to determine how bright the safelighting can be, but the time spent in finding this out will be amply repaid in the confidence you will have when deciding just when to remove a print from the developer.

It is important to remember that undetected safelight fogging can occur in the image area of a print without it being visible in the unexposed margins. This is because excessive safelight exposure, *together with* the picture exposure, can add spurious density to highlight areas. For this reason it is necessary to allow some margin of safety when interpreting a safelight test, but do not overdo the safety factor and end up by working in an unnecessarily dim light.

There are differences between the colour of the safelight sources recommended by paper manufacturers, particularly for some variable-contrast papers. Fortunately, all Ilford papers (Ilfobrom, Ilfospeed, Multigrade and Galerie) can be safely used under the same light if it is transmitted via a 'light brown', Ilford No. 902, safelight screen.

Although they are sometimes used in very large printing rooms, sodium lamps are too powerful for use in a darkrom that is used by only one printer, since the 'safe' distance is about three metres.

Properly filtered fluorescent lamps are likely to become increasingly popular for safelighting because they can be obtained in lengths between 0.6 and 1.8 metres (2 to 6 feet), and some fluorescent fittings can be plugged straight into a bayonet lamp fitting. The Encapsulite 'amber' filter can be safe with Ilfospeed and Multigrade papers. This form of illumination is much less directional than any small source of safelight, and one well-placed unit lights the whole room.

Print viewing light   Even when the development of prints is judged under as much safelight as is permissible, their quality cannot be finally assessed until they are seen under the much higher level of white light in which they will be used. Whenever possible, therefore, a 'white' inspection light should be available in the printing room so that prints can be examined while wet, after a brief wash, to see what modifications may be required in exposure or shading, should another print be necessary. A short 'daylight' fluorescent tube, located perhaps under a shelf behind the processing sink, serves very well as a viewing light and in that position will not flood the rest of the room with enough light to penetrate any boxes or packets of paper that may not have been closed or sealed adequately. A light level of between 500 and 1000 lux (50–100 foot candles) at the print viewing position is about right.

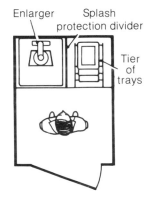

Enlarger   Splash protection divider

Tier of trays

Temporary darkrooms   It is not as easy to improvise a working space for print exposing and processing as it is for developing a roll of film. Because prints are exposed separately and often processed singly in dishes or trays, a good deal of space is required and relatively large volumes of solution are used. Nevertheless, it is possible to use a bathroom or some other room in the house temporarily, provided that daylight can be blocked out or the room is used only after dark.

The tiniest closet or cupboard that can be pressed into service as a printing darkroom needs to be about 1 × 1.2 metres (3 × 4 feet) in area, allowing just enough space to locate an enlarger on one half of a bench and a tier of three or four dishes for developer, fixer and water stacked alongside. Prints would have to be carried out in a dish to be washed elsewhere, possibly in the bathroom.

A bathroom is often the only place an amateur can manage to use as a temporary darkroom. It is usually preferable to the kitchen because it is less likely to be required by other members of the household during the evening; water is easily available, with at

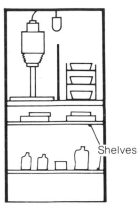

Shelves

Squeezing a darkroom into a 1 × 1.2 metre area

228

least one drain outlet. A stout plastic-surfaced board rigged up above the bath, at a higher level to avoid stooping, can be used to take the enlarger and three or four dishes. The enlarger should be shielded from the 'wet' side of the bench by a vertical partition or splash board, otherwise it will sooner or later be splashed with developer or fixer. Alternatively, and preferably, a stand fitted with castors can be used to take the enlarger, together with its accessories and printing paper, so that they are kept well away from the wet bench and from the brighter safelight that should be used over the processing area.

Anyone who has a large room that cannot be given over entirely to photographic work might consider using it in conjunction with a foldaway darkroom occupying a space 0.6 × 1.2 metres (2 × 4 feet) when closed and 1.2 × 1.5 metres (4 × 5 feet) when extended for use. Water generally has to be carried into this kind of darkroom and the waste water carried out, but a compensating advantage is that the enlarger, boxes of paper and bottles of solutions can all remain in place with the structure closed.

Permanently fitted darkrooms For those who are fortunate enough to have the space available, and those who earn a living by photography, the chance will come from time to time to lay out

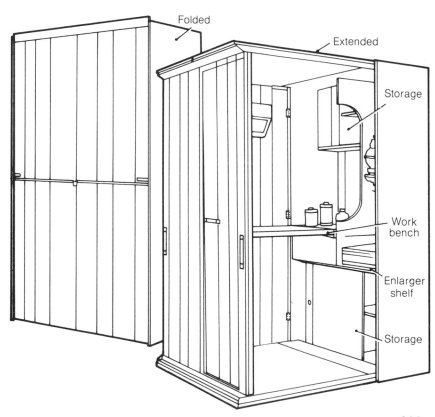

Foldaway darkroom, 0.6 × 1.2 m when folded and 1.2 × 1.5 m when extended for use

and equip a darkroom from scratch, but most of the idealised darkroom layouts shown in textbooks on photography are reminiscent of the beautiful kitchens illustrated in advertisements, and should not be taken too seriously.

No arrangement of working space or selection of printing and processing equipment will serve indefinitely without change. Looking back over the past decade, one can see that dramatic changes have taken place in darkroom methods. Glazers have been almost entirely replaced by RC paper dryers, while more and more enlargers are now fitted with diffuse light sources. Nevertheless, there are some fundamental considerations to be borne in mind, if working in the room is to be satisfying rather than inconvenient or frustrating.

All books on darkroom design stress the importance of having a wet and dry side to the active area. If space allows, this certainly is good advice, since processing prints in dishes or trays causes a certain amount of splashing, particularly when solutions are being mixed or transferred from one container to another. If a room is only large enough to allow a bench along one side, a vertical partition or splash board should be erected between the printing and processing areas.

There are a number of different kinds of purpose-made processing sinks available, made from materials such as polypropylene, rigid PVC or glass-fibre-reinforced resin. Gone are the days of lead-lined sinks. The new standard sinks vary in length from about 1 to 2.5 metres (3 to 8 feet), although any size can be fabricated to suit a particular space. Most designs incorporate a raised splashback to protect the wall behind the sink from attack by hypo. As a guide, a sink long enough to accommodate three 30 × 40 cm (12 × 16 in) trays with a built-in washing section is about 1.5 metres (5 feet) long. In some specially designed sinks, water is supplied to the print-washing section through submerged spray pipes and overflows through holes in a partition at a higher level, to ensure efficient use of the water. Because of the way they are assembled, welded PVC sinks can be made L-shaped to fit into small and awkward spaces.

Called dishes in the UK and trays in the US, they are simply shallow containers into which solutions can be placed so that exposed sheets of photographic paper can be processed by inspection by being transferred at suitable intervals from one dish/tray to the next. The simplicity and economy of this form of print processing is peculiar to black-and-white photography and is one of its greatest attractions. Processing dishes should be larger and deeper than might at first seem necessary. If a dish is only slightly larger than the prints that are developed in it, it is difficult

230

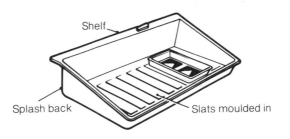

One-piece moulded-plastic processing sink

Shelf

Splash back

Slats moulded in

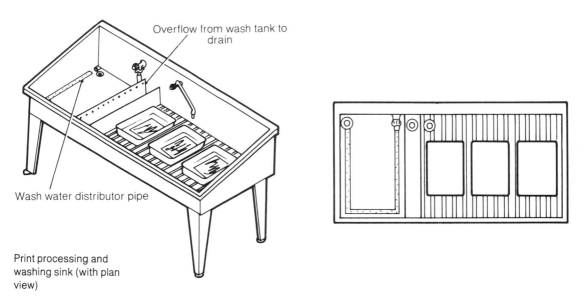

Overflow from wash tank to drain

Wash water distributor pipe

Print processing and washing sink (with plan view)

to get hold of a sheet of paper when the time comes to stop development by transferring it to the stop bath or the fixer. A shallow dish prevents the use of sufficient solution to cover the prints adequately, particularly when they collect together in the fixer; it also limits the amount of agitation that can be given by rocking, since the developer would simply spill if the dish were tilted too far. So large, deep dishes or trays are well worthwhile.

Right-handed people usually find it slightly easier to work with the developing dish to their left, so that an exposed print is held in the right hand for immersion in the developer and then, after each processing step, is transferred by the right hand to each successive dish or tray.

Most books on photographic printing stress the importance of using tongs when processing a print. This is good advice if you are not developing more than one print at a time, but it may happen that you want to make a number of prints from the same negative. In that case, after having found the correct exposure by testing you will probably expose the prints one after the other and develop them in batches to save time. Print tongs are then less convenient than your fingers for moving prints successively from top to bottom of the stack to ensure uniform development. If you are using a Phenidone/hydroquinone developer such as Ilfospeed, PQ Universal or ID62, there is not much danger in occasionally handling prints throughout processing without the protection of gloves, but the practice cannot be encouraged. Fortunately there are cheap, light, disposable gloves available now to replace the heavier and clumsier rubber types that were once commonly used.

Processing large prints   If a very large print has to be made and for some reason the work cannot be given to a specialist laboratory, there are ways of improvising processing troughs to make the job a little less cumbersome. If the size of the print is not too big, some of the plastic troughs used for wallpapering may be used; otherwise plastic drainpipe can be cut down the middle to provide a pair of troughs, once end caps have been added. Purpose-made troughs up to 25×168 cm (10×66 in) are made by Deville in France; some of them are intended for use with a mechanical roller assembly, enabling the paper to be wound back and forth through the processing solutions.

   More and more prints of all sizes are being processed in continuous roller machines, some of which are wide enough to take the full width of a manufacturer's parent roll. These machines allow no local manipulation of a print during development, but they produce consistent results and the prints are dry when they leave the machine. Print processing by machine is dealt with on pages 244–254.

Variables in print development   There are one or two things about print processing that distinguish it from negative processing. A print is usually developed fully, in the sense that its maximum contrast is reached, but when the growth of the image is being observed in a dish some control is possible over its final density. In other words, although an optimum print exposure requires a predictable development time, a useful result may be obtainable from a print that is slightly underexposed or considerably overexposed, if development time is extended or shortened accordingly.

   Optimum development time varies according to (a) the development characteristics of the paper, (b) the developer formulation, (c) the developer concentration, (d) the temperature of the developer, and (e) the exhaustion of the developer. From this list of variables it can be seen why an experienced printer, once he has settled on a combination of paper and developer, is seldom anxious to change. The other variables he knows he must control.

232

Ilfospeed and Multigrade prints

Not so long ago, any textbook on photography would state that a bromide print should be developed for two minutes at 20°C (68°F) in any normal print developer. This remains true for what might be called traditional paper and developers, but the introduction of the Ilfospeed system with a total 'dry to dry' processing time of four minutes changed things for those who wish to produce high-quality black-and-white prints in the shortest possible time. The recent growth in the use of polyethylene-coated paper such as Ilfospeed and Multigrade has been so great that they now represent much the larger part of the market for black-and-white paper.

The induction time of Ilfospeed paper used in Ilfospeed developer at 20°C is around six seconds for a correctly exposed print, compared with some 20 to 30 seconds with older papers and developers. It is amusing to estimate how much time is lost by printers who develop by inspection and accept induction times that are at least 15 seconds longer than they need be. Many thousands of man hours are wasted each year by printers gazing at blank sheets of paper!

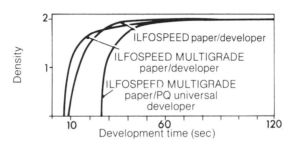

Times of induction and complete development for three combinations of paper and developer

The rapid initial appearance of an Ilfospeed print image is followed by its steady growth until, after about 30 seconds for the softer grades and 40 seconds for grade 5, no significant further change in contrast occurs, although there can be a slight increase in density if development is extended up to even two minutes.

Whenever possible, exposure should be adjusted so that a good print results after about 60 seconds development in Ilfospeed developer (diluted 1:9) at 20°C. This advice, to keep exposure to a minimum consistent with achieving adequate print density after full development, applies particularly when a number of prints are being developed together in the same dish. If they are overexposed, they need to be removed from the developer quickly and at just the right time if they are to match in density.

When development time is as short as one minute, it is essential to ensure prompt and even wetting of the print emulsion by the developer, followed by effective agitation. Although individual printers cultivate their own particular ways of working, the following sequence of steps will serve to get the beginner started – after which he will surely develop his own procedure.

1 Holding the exposed sheet by its right-hand edge and emulsion up, slide the the opposite edge into the developer in one smooth action.
2 Rock the dish several times in both directions to ensure a flush of developer over the emulsion.
3 Note mentally the time taken for the first sign of an image to appear, because from this you will soon come to tell whether the print has been seriously over- or underexposed. (With Ilfospeed, if the first sign of the image appears in six to eight seconds you know that your exposure was not far out.)
4 Turn the print face down for the next 20 or 30 seconds, but still rock the tray.
5 Turn the print face up again; while still rocking the tray in both directions alternately, allow development to continue until the image looks right.
6 After letting surface developer drain off the print for two or three seconds, rinse it briefly in a tray of cold water before transferring it to the fixer. Make sure that the emulsion side is completely covered with the fixing solution, then turn the print face down in the tray.

Because Ilfospeed Multigrade paper has special emulsion characteristics, it was necessary to formulate a special developer in order to maintain the short induction period that is characteristic of the Ilfospeed system and to ensure a maximum range of available contrast. Ilfospeed Multigrade developer requires a slightly longer time for the first appearance of an image (about 10 seconds) but the time for complete development remains the same as for the Ilfospeed paper and developer combination, namely 60 seconds at 20°C. Multigrade developer is a liquid concentrate to be used at a dilution of 1:9 in the same way as Ilfospeed developer.

Developer temperature   An Ilfospeed print only develops fully in 60 seconds if the temperature of the Ilfospeed developer is at or close to 20°C. If the developer is allowed to fall significantly below the recommended temperature, there is a temptation to increase exposure to compensate for the resulting drop in developer activity and to maintain the short development time; but if this is carried too far the quality of the resulting prints, in terms of their contrast and maximum density, begins to suffer.

As with many other kinds of processing, the most satisfactory (but not the cheapest) way of maintaining solution temperature is to have the whole workroom at that temperature; of course this is not always possible, particularly for the amateur. An alternative is to heat (or cool) the developer by placing the dish or tray containing it in contact with water at a slightly higher or lower temperature than that required for the working solution. The tempered water required for this method of working can be mixed and adjusted in a large outer container just before the start of development, and then re-adjusted from time to time during the working session. A more convenient but more expensive way is to provide a pumped supply of thermostatically controlled water flowing continually through the sink in which the developing tray is standing.

Thermostatically controlled electric dish warmers provide heat by direct contact with a developing tray, and can usually be adjusted to work between 15 and 30°C with an accuracy of ± 1°C; this is more than adequate for black-and-white print processing.

Fixing RC prints   If each print were fixed separately, the fixing process would give little trouble. In practice several, often many, prints are collected together in the same fixing tray, and there is some risk that one or more of them will not get adequate treatment. One way of guarding against this is to transfer fixed prints as soon as possible into the washing tray or tank, so that the number of sheets remaining in the hypo is always kept to a minimum. This precaution is fairly easy to take because the fixing time for an Ilfospeed print in fresh Hypam need not be more than 30 seconds. In any case, the tray used for fixer should be a deep one.

Although fixer temperature is not as important as developer temperature, remember that (roughly speaking) a change of 10°C in the temperature of any photographic solution either halves or doubles the time required for an equivalent reaction. An Ilfospeed print is properly fixed in Ilfospeed fixer (diluted 1:3) in 30 seconds at 20°C, *provided that the emulsion surface of the print is in free contact with the fixing solution throughout this time.* In other words, the print must not be thrown face up into the fixing tray so that parts of it are exposed to the air. Neither must the prints be left face down unless care is taken to ensure that no air is trapped beneath them. These are relatively simple precautions to take and in practice fixing should present few problems.

Thiosulphate solutions (particularly those such as Ilfospeed fixer and Hypam, which contain ammonium thiosulphate) not only dissolve the residual silver halides left in a print after development, but also slowly attack the silver image itself. The time taken for enough silver to be dissolved for a difference to be noticed is fortunately long enough to permit any normal processing cycle, but if prints are left overnight in a warm fixing bath they will certainly lose a measurable and probably noticeable amount of density.

Treatment with Farmer's reducer   The judicious use of ferricyanide bleach on a black-and-white print can convert it into an award-winning photograph, and the skill required to do so makes the printer a special kind of artist. As with any other manipulative treatment of a photographic image, whether it be dodging during projection printing or negative retouching, only practice brings confidence. Fortunately there are usually plenty of scrap prints around on which to experiment.

Eugene Smith, a famous exponent of the 'ferricyanide' art, said this about it: 'I don't feel that bleaching is dishonest to the reality of the image, because it helps me state clearly what I feel the true reality to be.' Of his technique, he said: 'Basically, I bleach to bring back what is not held strongly in the film or paper. For instance, just a touch along certain highlight areas on a face or arm will give an almost three-dimensional feeling. It can also produce a much greater sense of texture. I want a piece of cloth to feel like cloth when you look at it. Bleach can be used to remove that sheet of grey that comes over print papers sometimes.

'I fill the little cup in the palm of my hand with ferricyanide (crystals), and mix it with ¼ cup of water. (If I'm in a hurry I add more ferricyanide). I wipe the hypo off the print with my hand (you can blow it off also) then I paint the ferricyanide on with a sable brush or cotton ball, or Q-Tip. Oftentimes, I leave large areas of the print covered with hypo, float it off with ferricyanide, and set it back down into the hypo, fast, before the bleaching has truly set in. Afterwards, I like to put the print through a second, fresh hypo bath.'

Clearly this describes the methods of an expert. The amateur will be less bold, but may care to start like this. Remove the print from the fixing bath and lay it on an inclined flat surface under a good white light. Wipe or squeegee surface fixing solution from the area you intend to modify. Then apply a weak (light yellow) solution of ferricyanide to the area you wish to bleach, using a swab of cotton wool on the end of a cocktail stick or something similar. When the print has become slightly stained by the ferricyanide, rinse it in water and transfer it to a plain fresh hypo bath. The stain then disappears and the reduction in density can be assessed. If, as should be the case, further reduction seems necessary, the procedure can be repeated. If a drastic change is required and the rate of reduction is too slow, a stronger solution of ferricyanide can be used.

236

Washing RC prints   The processing step that is shortened most dramatically by the use of polyethylene-laminated papers is the final wash. At one time it was not at all unusual for photographic paper manufacturers to recommend that prints should be washed

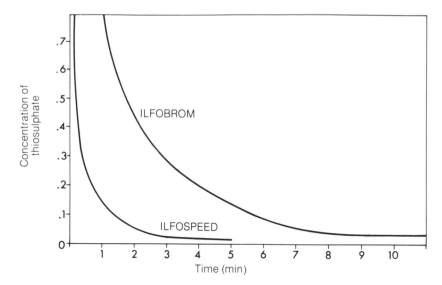

Concentration of thiosulphate

ILFOBROM

ILFOSPEED

Time (min)

Rate of removal of thiosulphate from resin-coated and fibre-based papers

for at least 30 minutes, if permanence was at all important. With a resin-coated paper such as Ilfospeed, the time required for adequate washing is only two minutes in running water. However, washing still has to be done properly; simply to leave a pile of prints in a tray with water running over them means that sheets in the middle of the stack will not be fully washed.

Drying RC prints   In the early days of 'waterproof' papers, mechanisation of the drying operation was neglected, probably because polyethylene-coated papers can be dried quite quickly by laying them out or hanging them up. But since RC papers *cannot* be dried on rotary or flat-bed glazers in the way that all glossy prints used to be dried, there was for a time no adequate mechanised method of drying these new prints, even though they had been processed more quickly and conveniently than had ever before been possible. Then came the Ilfospeed Dryer, capable of drying 20 × 25 cm (8 × 10 in) glossy or pearl-surface prints at the rate of 400 an hour and at the same time imparting a better surface to glossy RC papers than can be achieved by any other method.

The Ilfospeed 5250 dryer accepts Ilfospeed or Ilfospeed Multigrade paper (and most other polyethylene-coated papers) up to 60 cm (24 in) wide, or the equivalent width made up with narrower prints. Unlike the glazing drums it replaces, the Ilfospeed dryer can be ready for use in 1½ minutes from the time it is switched on. The speed of operation is adjustable and the optimum setting can be found for each make or surface of paper by ensuring that prints emerge neither damp nor curled because of overdrying.

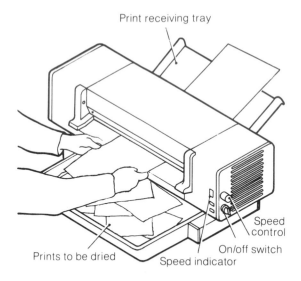

Print receiving tray

Speed control

On/off switch

Prints to be dried

Speed indicator

Ilfospeed 5250 dryer

The Ilfospeed dryer comprises three pairs of feed/squeegee rollers driven by a variable-speed motor. The first two pairs of rollers feed a print between three radiant heater bars, one above and two beneath the print, while two centrifugal fans supply air to lower the surface temperature of the print and remove water vapour. The third pair of rollers are soft and deliver the dry print to a receiving tray at the back of the machine.

An Ilfospeed dryer is a relatively expensive piece of equipment, usually only bought by professionals. Fortunately the amateur can mechanise the drying operation to a modest extent by using one of the dryers that blow warm air over the surfaces of small batches of prints laid flat on closely spaced grids. A typical drying time in small units of this kind is two minutes and the maximum print size is about 30×40 cm (12×16 in). Some of these dryers incorporate a manually operated roller squeegee for the removal of surface water before drying is commenced.

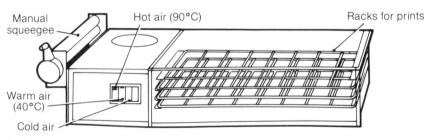

Manual squeegee

Hot air (90°C)

Racks for prints

Warm air (40°C)

Cold air

Simple dryer for RC papers. After being squeegeed, prints are placed in racks and warm or hot air is blown over them

238

Even with no machine at all, it is quite easy to dry Ilfospeed prints. Provided the surface water is removed by squeegeeing or wiping, prints dry quickly when laid out in a reasonably warm room. The Paterson RC print squeegee has a pair of soft rubber blades, one of which is spring-loaded; a single stroke completely removes surface water from both sides of a 20 × 25 cm (8 × 10 in) print. Larger prints need to be squeegeed section by section. After squeegeeing, prints can be laid out on newspaper or on specially constructed net-covered trays, or stood on edge between the separators of a plastic print-drying rack of the Paterson type.

Ilfobrom prints

Ilfobrom papers were the first to be made with equal speeds throughout the five contrast grades between 0 and 4. The success of this innovation, together with the excellent sensitometric properties of the emulsion, won worldwide support for this range of traditional fibre-based papers. By their nature, unprotected paper-base products require a different and longer processing cycle than polyethylene-laminated papers. Since fixing, washing and drying an Ilfobrom print takes much longer than the four minutes required to finish an Ilfospeed print, there is little point in cutting 60 seconds or so from the developing stage.

An Ilfobrom print developed in PQ Universal developer diluted 1:9 needs 1½ to 2 minutes treatment; if Ilford IF23 diluted 1:5 is used, it needs five minutes fixing. Hypam would hasten fixing, but then washing would take longer to reach a given level of residual thiosulphate. Some printers argue that the longer development time allows better control of the image during development; this may be so, particularly if the print needs to be manipulated in the developer to enhance local densities.

For the enthusiast who would like to mix up a print developer that will require between 1½ and 2 minutes when used with Ilfobrom, here is the formula for ID62.

sodium sulphite (anhydrous)	50 g
sodium carbonate (anhydrous)	60 g
hydroquinone	12 g
Phenidone	0.5 g
potassium bromide	2 g
benzotriazol	*0.2 g
water to	1000 ml

* or 20 ml of a 1% solution of benzotriazol

For use, mix one part of the solution with three parts of water.

Ilfobrom Galerie prints

In the mid-1970s, soon after polyethylene-coated black-and-white papers were introduced, there was a body of opinion (held mainly by journalist/photographers in the US) that high-quality fibre-based papers were becoming an 'endangered species', and that papers using waterproof base were not a satisfactory substitute in terms of quality or permanence. The introduction of Ilfobrom Galerie did much to allay these fears, although there is growing evidence that prints made on RC papers will prove to be as good as those made on fibre-based materials.

Galerie papers can be developed in just the same way and in the same solutions as would be used for Ilfobrom. Development latitude is such that longer-than-optimum exposures can be compensated by shortening development time (to as little as 60 seconds) without significant loss of either contrast or maximum density, while underexposure can be partially dealt with by extending development for as long as four or even five minutes in extreme cases.

Unlike Ilfobrom, Galerie papers, both glossy and matt, are made in only four contrast grades (1, 2, 3 and 4), but while grade 2 Galerie just about matches grade 2 Ilfobrom for contrast, grade 1 Galerie is slightly softer than grade 1 Ilfobrom, and grades 3 and 4 Galerie are slightly harder than the equivalent Ilfobrom grades. Because of this slightly wider gap between grades, it can be useful to have what is in effect a variable-contrast developer with which the effective contrast of Galerie paper can be pitched midway between two grades. Dr Beer's two-part developer comprises stock solutions that are mixed in varying proportions to give different levels of contrast. These are the two formulae:

A	water (at 50°C)	750 ml
	metol	8 g
	sodium sulphite anhydrous)	23 g
	potassium carbonate (anhydrous)	20 g
	potassium bromide	1.1 g
	water to	1000 ml

B	water (at 50°C)	750 ml
	hydroquinone	8 g
	sodium sulphite (anhydrous)	23 g
	potassium carbonate (anhydrous)	27 g
	potassium bromide	2.2 g
	water to	1000 ml

For use, the stock solutions are diluted with water according to the following table:

Contrast:	low			normal	high		
	1	2	3	4	5	6	7
Parts of:							
Solution A	8	7	6	5	4	3	2
Solution B	0	1	2	3	4	5	14
Water	8	8	8	8	8	8	0
Total	16	16	16	16	16	16	16

Note that the metol in stock solution A can cause dermatitis if print tongs or protective gloves are not used.

One great advantage that comes from taking two or three minutes to develop a print is that there is enough time not only to assess the image carefully as it grows, but also to effect some local changes where required. When using Dr Beer's developer, selected areas of an image can be darkened simply by treating them with a swab of cotton wool that has been dipped in stock solution B. This can best be done if the print is removed from the dish temporarily and placed on a sheet of Perspex or Plexiglass.

Stop bath   Although it is not absolutely necessary, fibre-based prints should be briefly immersed in an acid stop bath between developer and fixer. The volume of developer carried over with a fibre-based print is many times more than with a polyethylene-coated material; if the alkalinity of the developer is not neutralised by an acid stop bath, the fixer will steadily deteriorate until eventually instead of fixing prints it begins to stain them. Ilford IN1 is a concentrate that can be diluted with 40 parts of water to make a working stop bath, or one can simply use a two per cent solution of acetic acid.

Fixing and washing   Until Ilford devised a novel 20 minutes fixing and washing procedure for Galerie paper, there had been no significant change in the way that traditional fibre-based papers had been processed since the turn of the century. Protracted fixing and washing times had become an essential part of print processing, particularly when image permanence was important. Since the photographers who use Galerie papers are likely to be those who must be assured of maximum print stability, the new fixing and washing recommendations have been thoroughly tested and the results conform to the ANSI standard for optimum print stability. The key to the new procedure lies in the use of a rapid ammonium-thiosulphate fixer, Hypam, together with a 'washaid'

241

to facilitate removal of residual chemicals from a print. The sequence is:

1 Fix in Hypam (1+4) for 30 seconds.
2 Wash in running water for 5 minutes.
3 Immerse in Galerie Washaid (1+4) for 10 minutes.
4 Wash in running water for 5 minutes.

The temperature of both treatment solutions and the wash water must be around 20°C for the times given to be applicable, since even with a washing aid the time required for washing increases significantly as the temperature of the wash water decreases.

The amount of thiosulphate remaining in a Galerie print following this recommended fixing and washing treatment is about 0.2 micrograms per square centimetre, which can only be detected by careful analysis. The idea of using a wash aid to speed up the removal of thiosulphate when processing negatives or prints may have come from the observation that water containing salts (for example the sodium chloride in sea water) removes residual fixer chemicals from a print or film much more quickly than ordinary water. It has also been found that a two per cent solution of sodium sulphite facilitates washing.

In general, Ilfobrom Galerie is used by photographers who make relatively large prints in limited numbers, so the short but meticulous fixing and washing treatment can be given to each print. When large numbers of prints have to be processed, longer fixing and washing times might be more convenient; two-bath fixing is then recommended, carried out as follows. Make up two separate fixing baths, using either Hypam (1+9) or IF23 (1+5), fix the prints in the first bath for about two minutes and then transfer them to the second bath for another two minutes. Continue working this way until the first bath has fixed an area of emulsion equivalent to forty 20 × 25 cm (8 × 10 in) prints; then discard it and replace it with the second bath, after replacing the second bath with completely fresh fixer.

Washing and drying fibre-based prints

When conventional fixing is used without a washing aid, Ilfobrom and Galerie prints need to be washed for at least 30 minutes. Even then care must be taken to see that fresh, or at least changing, water reaches the prints continuously.

If only a few prints are being washed at the same time, it is not very arduous to lift them briefly one by one from the wash water, to ensure that they are all reached by a change of water and do not cling together in the dish or tray. A simple siphon hung over the edge of the washing tray also helps by periodically removing all the chemical-laden water from the prints. Alternatively, a specially

242

designed print-washing tank can be used so that, without any attention, each print remains separate from the others and water passes freely between them. The various Paterson Auto Print Washer units are good examples of this kind of rack and tank; one model takes a dozen prints up to 25 × 30 cm (10 × 12 in) held vertically, and the other takes the same number of 30 × 38 (12 × 15 in) prints.

When large batches of prints are to be washed some other method must be used. One way is to have a series of three or four trays arranged so that water entering the highest one overflows

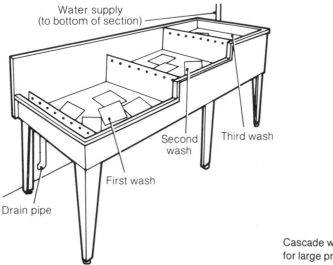

Cascade washing set-up for large print batches

into the next, and finally goes to waste after flowing through the bottom tray. This cascade system depends on someone regularly transferring prints from one tray to the next one up, and removing those from the top tray when they have been there the allotted time. If prints are not transferred regularly, the washing is no better than if it had taken place in a single tray.

Another way of ensuring that prints are washed properly is to put them into a deep tank through which water is swirled so as to carry the prints round in an ever-moving cycle. This type of tank is sometimes fitted with an automatic siphon so that all the water is drained away at intervals.

There is no way of drying an Ilfobrom or Galerie print as quickly as one made on Ilfospeed paper. About ten times as much water is absorbed by the base and the emulsion of an unprotected print material as is taken up by a print made on polyethylene-laminated base.

The usual way of speeding up a drying process is to use heat and moving air. Traditionally heat alone has been used to dry

243

photographic prints; it has been applied to wet prints by pressing them into contact with a heated metal drum or plate. The surface of the drum is highly polished and prints are applied with their emulsion surfaces in contact with the polished metal; after the water has been driven off through the paper base of the prints and they become dry, they leave the drum or plate having a highly glazed surface. Hot glazing, as the process is called, if carried out successfully yields prints with an extremely high gloss, although the care that must be taken to maintain a perfectly clean and polished metal glazing surface is considerable; also the process is very slow compared with the seconds required to dry a glossy Ilfospeed print using an Ilfospeed dryer.

When a highly glazed surface is not required, or when a matt-surface paper is used, prints can easily (albeit slowly) be dried by being suspended by clips from stretched lines or by being laid out on trays or racks. Muslin net or plastic mesh materials can be stretched over simple wooden frames to make trays of any size, and these may be hoisted up out of the way if space is restricted. Surface water should always be squeegeed from prints before they are put to dry. This not only speeds up drying but prevents the formation of drying marks.

Processing by machine

The Graber continuous paper-processing machine was introduced in the UK around the turn of the century and became widely used for the production of view postcards and the portraits of Victorian and Edwardian music-hall stars. These 'genuine' photographic cards were produced with permanence very much in mind. As an advertisement of the time explained: 'The New Perfected Graber machine develops, rinses, fixes, washes, bleaches, rinses, tones, rinses, hardens and finally washes.' These early processors were fed with continuous rolls of exposed paper and could be linked directly with the contact printer at one end and a hot drying drum at the other end, no mean achievement for those days.

While the motion-picture industry was at its height and black-and-white movies were still being made, there was an enormous demand for 'stills' to be printed from 8 × 10 inch negatives, and these were all produced on machines of the Graber type. With the advent of colour films and television this outlet disappeared, as did the market for view cards when they began to be produced in colour by the offset-litho printing process.

There was renewed interest in the continuous processing of black-and-white prints when the photofinishing industry expanded so rapidly after World War II, but soon the interest switched to the production of colour rather than black-and-white prints, so for a while the machine processing of black-and-white papers assumed less importance. Then, when 'waterproof' papers became available, someone began to wonder if it would be possible to process sheets of paper in the same way as sheets of X-ray film were being processed in X-Omat and similar roller processors. Before the introduction of polyethylene-laminated papers, the washing and drying times required for paper prints would have made a roller processor prohibitively large and expensive; but with fixing time down to 30 seconds or less, and the task of drying certainly no more difficult than for X-ray film with emulsions on both sides of its base, the prospect was promising. Consequently, roller processors geared to the requirements of black-and-white RC papers began to appear in the UK during the early 1970s.

Ilfospeed 2000 system

Because they had introduced the Ilfospeed dish processing system to reduce dramatically the time and effort required to make high-quality black-and-white prints by hand, Ilford soon turned their attention to providing an Ilfospeed machine processing system (Ilfospeed 2000 and 2001) that would deliver properly processed and dried prints in 90 seconds. (Strictly speaking, this was not the first time that Ilford had introduced a roller transport system for processing black-and-white prints. Ilfospeed papers, machines and chemistry had been on the market for some years, but this is an activation/stabilisation process: see later.)

Ninety seconds is about the least time in which an exposed sheet of Ilfospeed paper can be developed, fixed, washed and dried in a machine about the same size, cost and electrical loading as a

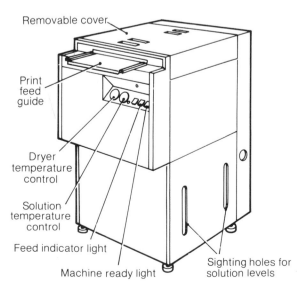

Removable cover

Print feed guide

Dryer temperature control

Solution temperature control

Feed indicator light

Machine ready light

Sighting holes for solution levels

Ilfospeed 2001 processor can process and dry 350 20 × 25 cm prints in an hour

245

medium-sized X-ray processor. The Ilfospeed 2001 has a transport speed of about 76 cm (30 in) per minute and accepts paper up to 40 cm (16 in) wide, or two 20 × 25 cm (8 × 10 in) prints fed into the machine side by side. Working in this way, 350 20 × 25 cm prints can be processed and dried in an hour. The shortest length of paper that can be safely handled by the machine is 15 cm (6 in).

Because of the success of the Ilfospeed 5240 and 5250 roller-transport dryers, the drying section incorporated in the Ilfospeed 2000 and 2001 machines is a counterpart of the 5250 and therefore produces the same excellent gloss when processing prints on Ilfospeed 1M paper.

Other brands of polyethylene-coated paper can be processed in the Ilfospeed 2001 machine, just as other processors may be used to process Ilfospeed papers. In fact companies specialising in giant enlargements often use Ilfospeed paper in wide roller processors such as the Hope, Hostert, Kreonite or San Marco.

When exposed sheets are posted directly into a roller-transport processor, there is no 'wet' side of the darkroom in the usual sense, since prints are dry when they enter the machine and dry again when they emerge. Furthermore, there is no need for more than the feed-in end of the machine to be located in safelight, so the feed-out or delivery end can be in a fully lit 'white' light or daylight area. However, the whole machine is often located in safelight so

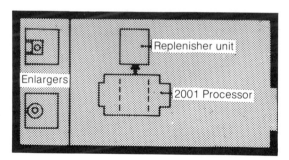
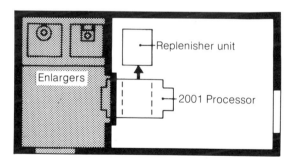

that test strips or prints can be inspected by the printer as quickly as possible after exposure. Much depends upon the nature of the work. In an industrial department where hundreds of prints may be required from the same negative, there is a good case for having the prints emerge into white light; but in a newspaper darkroom, where almost every print is made from a different negative, it would be inconvenient and take too much time to go out through a light trap into a fully lit area to see the first print or test from every negative.

The Ilfospeed 2001 processor (or any other similar machine) uses about three kilowatts of electricity, most of it for drying. A great deal of moist air is generated, and some thought must be

Print processor can be entirely within safelight darkroom or can be located so that emerging prints are inspected in white light

given to the effect this might have on working conditions if the machine is installed wholly within a darkroom. Some kind of extractor ducting or air conditioning may be essential.

Processing cycle   The processing cycle for Ilfospeed papers in the Ilfospeed 2001 roller-transport machine is:

Develop	30 seconds
Fix	23 seconds
Wash	17 seconds
Dry	10 seconds
Crossover time	10 seconds
Total 'dry to dry' time	90 seconds

A composite sectional stainless-steel tank is used for developer, fixer and wash water, and the roller-drive racks are the same in each section except for their path length; there are eight pairs of rollers in the developing rack and only six pairs in both fixer and washing racks. The roller racks are identified by colour: red for developer, blue for fixer, with an uncoloured rack in the washing section. The racks are easily lifted out of their tanks for inspection or cleaning.

Processing variables (temperature, circulation and replenishment) are all controlled automatically. Developer temperature is regulated to within ±0.5°C, and is generally set to

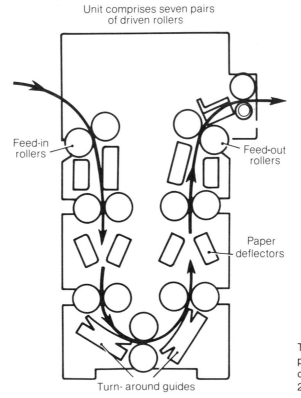

Unit comprises seven pairs
of driven rollers

Feed-in rollers

Feed-out rollers

Paper deflectors

Turn-around guides

Transport path followed by prints progressing through one section of Ilfospeed 2001 processor

operate at 30°C. Recirculation of developer is at the rate of 20 litres per minute; replenisher, controlled by a paper detector at the feed-in end of the machine, is introduced into the working bath by a positive-displacement pump that can be adjusted to deliver any volume between 0 and 400 ml per minute. Usually the replenishment rate is set at around 150 ml of developer replenisher per square metre of paper passing through the machine.

The temperature of the fixer follows that of the developer, with an accuracy around ±1°C. The fixing bath is replenished at the same intervals as the developer but at a separately adjusted volume, usually 250 ml per square metre of processed paper. Overflow from the fixing tank can and should be fed into an electrolytic silver-recovery unit before being released to the drain.

Both sections of the replenisher tank assembly hold 40 litres of solution. The whole thing is mounted on castors and housed within the processor, beneath the processing tanks.

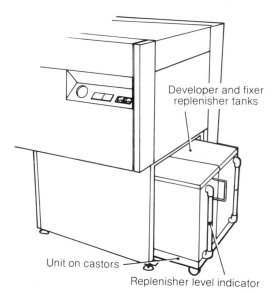

Developer and fixer replenisher tanks

Unit on castors

Replenisher level indicator

Replenisher tanks are beneath Ilfospeed 2001 machine's processing tanks; replenisher assembly can be moved out for refilling

While prints are in the machine, water flows through the washing tank at about six litres per minute. The temperature of the water is not important, provided that it is between 5 and 30°C, although some adjustment of its temperature is achieved by routing it through a pipe located in the bottom of the developer tank.

The roller configuration in the drying section of the Ilfospeed 2001 processor is similar to that used in the well-proven Ilfospeed 4250 dryer, and the prints are dried by four infra-red silicon-sheathed heater bars coupled to a pair of fans. There is a safety cut-out in case a print becomes stationary opposite the heaters.

248

Operation   When a print is fed into the processor, a detector system is activated by its leading edge. This starts the main drive, replenisher pumps, dryer heater and fans, and operates the water supply solenoid if one is fitted. The drive rollers then transport the print into the developing tank and the paper detector senses the trailing end of the print. All the services continue to operate while the print passes through the processor, with the exception of the replenisher pumps, which only run for approximately three seconds after the paper detector has been de-activated. An audible signal is made when the three-second delay has expired and a signal light simultaneously indicates that the processor is ready to receive another print. If no further prints are fed into the machine, it returns to a stand-by condition about 15 seconds after the last print has been processed.

Automatic stand-by ensures that the main drive motor, dryer heaters, fans and water supply are all turned off when no prints are in the machine. However, the solution heaters and circulation pumps continue to operate so that the processor is ready for immediate use. In order to prevent the crystallisation of developer or hypo on any exposed transport rollers, the machine drive is switched on for about 20 seconds at intervals of about 15 minutes during a stand-by period.

Continuous roll processing   Photofinishers have seen the advantages of processing their black-and-white prints in a roller-transport machine instead of continuing to use the larger and much slower 'festoon' type machines they installed years ago. All that is required to handle continuous rolls of paper 9 cm (3½ in) wide on the Ilfospeed 2001 machine is a reel stand for exposed rolls at the feed-in end, and a motor-driven re-reeler to

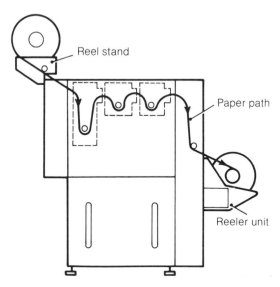

Ilford 2001 machine can process continuous rolls of exposed paper

249

take up the processed paper at the other end. Both units can be clipped on to the machine within minutes.

When a roll of paper is taken from a printing machine and transferred immediately to a continuous processor, the end of the roll that is developed first was exposed last. This has no significance if the paper being used has good latent-image stability, but if it suffers from latent-image regression, the first exposures to be made on the roll (the last to be processed) will be relatively light when compared with prints at the other end of the roll. The converse applies if the paper suffers from latent-image progression. A test should therefore be made to see whether it is necessary either to rewind the roll before processing it or to defer processing it for sufficient time for the latent image to have stabilised. Neither solution is likely to appeal to a busy processing department.

When prints are exposed and processed in rolls, it is often possible to automatically place a graphite mark on the back of the paper or print a small photographic mark on the front, each time an exposure is made in the printer or roll-easel. These marks can

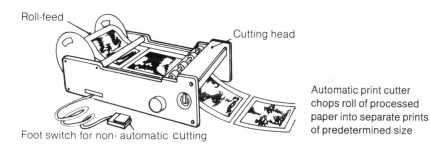

Roll-feed

Cutting head

Automatic print cutter chops roll of processed paper into separate prints of predetermined size

Foot switch for non- automatic cutting

be detected by a contact sensor or a photo-cell on an automatic cutter so that the roll can be cut up accurately and quickly. Some roll cutters can be operated without marks, to cut rolls of unexposed paper into sheets of any predetermined size. Paper in rolls is cheaper per unit area than paper bought in sheets, and also offers a way of obtaining special sheet sizes. For example, sheets can be cut to suit negative formats such as 24×36 mm.

Monitoring quality

Apart from the convenience and the short processing cycle, automatic print processing should ensure greater uniformity and reproducibility than can be achieved by manual methods, particularly when long runs of prints are required from the same negative. However, the very fact that results usually are so predictable can lead to too great a dependence on routine procedures; any variations, particularly slow drifts in quality, may therefore go unnoticed for quite a long time. To guard against overlooking the unexpected change that can result from a faulty pump or thermostat, some form of monitoring system, however simple, sooner or later repays the small amount of time and effort it takes.

If the supplier of the processor or the paper you are using provides pre-exposed control strips, it is a simple matter to run one of the strips through the process at regular intervals, certainly not less than once a day. It is not even necessary to make densitometric measurements of the processed strips; if they are filed in sequence alongside each other, with the reference or standard strip also on hand to make a side-by-side comparison, any drift will become noticeable after only a few days and a more dramatic, sudden change should be spotted immediately.

If there is difficulty in obtaining pre-exposed strips, an alternative is to run off a few hundred small prints from a good negative that can be retained for the purpose. A photofinisher will have no problem in doing this, but a professional or commercial processor may need to use a roll-easel and an accurate exposure timer. Provided that they are marked in some way, single exposures can be cut from the roll as required for processing checks. Each print may have to be taped to a piece of scrap paper to extend the combined length sufficiently to ensure that the print runs safely through the machine.

Developing and fixing machines

Paper processors such as the Ilford 2001 machine have a large capacity and cost thousands rather than hundreds of pounds. This prevents many photographers from using machine processing. For them a compromise is possible if they use a much smaller roller processor in which prints are automatically transported through developer, stop and fixer solutions before emerging for subsequent washing and drying away from the machine.

The Durst RCP 40 Variospeed processor can be set to run at any transport speed from 9 to 60 cm ($3\frac{1}{2}$ to 24 in) per minute, and the developer and fixer temperatures can be adjusted and maintained separately. This means that 20×25 cm (8×10 in) Ilfospeed prints can be developed and fixed at the rate of four a minute.

Activation/stabilisation processing

Although the idea of stabilising a silver-halide emulsion dates back to 1893, the first system of roller transport for sheet-fed processing of black-and-white papers was introduced in the 1950s and was based on the activation/stabilisation concept.

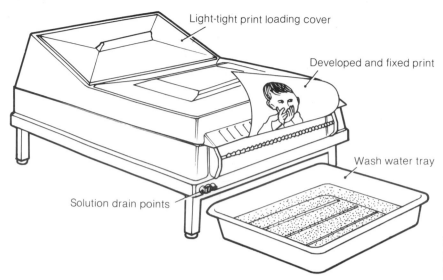

Light-tight print loading cover

Developed and fixed print

Wash water tray

Solution drain points

Durst RCP 40 Variospeed processor automatically develops and fixes prints

Activation is the term given to a method of image formation that depends upon a developing agent (usually hydroquinone) being incorporated in the emulsion when the paper is coated. After exposure of such a paper, which can have just the same sensitivity as any ordinary paper, contact with or immersion in an alkaline solution suffices to bring about reduction of the exposed silver to form an image. Then, instead of dissolving the residual silver halides in a thiosulphate fixer, a stabiliser (often ammonium thiocyanate) is used to convert the residual halides into relatively stable silver thiocyanate complexes that can be allowed to remain in the emulsion layer. The total time required is only a matter of seconds, and the two reactions can be carried out very satisfactorily in a small and inexpensive roller-transport machine.

The design of activation/stabilisation machines can vary in detail, but in principle they all work in the same way. A print is fed to a first pair of rollers, which immediately pass it into contact with a roller that is rotating in the activator solution. This is followed by a short squeegeeing action by rollers that transport the paper into the stabilising bath. The print is then squeegeed again between a pair of exit rollers and emerges 'touch dry' after about 20 seconds.

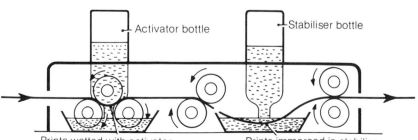

Activator bottle

Stabiliser bottle

Prints wetted with activator

Prints immersed in stabiliser

Two stages in activation/stabilisation processing

A material that has been stabilised instead of being fixed must not be washed, since this could remove the stabilising chemicals and accelerate deterioration of the image. Because the prints are not washed and dried, the machine can be small, needs no connections to either water supply or drain, and has a low current requirement.

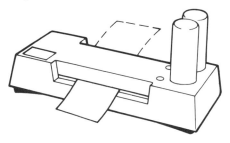

Activation/stabilisation machine produces 'touch-dry' prints in a few seconds

Another advantage of using activation rather than development to generate a silver image is that the alkaline solution dissolves the hydroquinone in the emulsion to form an 'immediate' developer adjacent to the exposed halide grains; thus development quickly reaches completion and is not very dependent upon temperature. This means that an activation/stabilisation machine can be used in almost any environment, although Ilford make two different activators for use according to ambient temperature. IA11 is intended for use with Ilfoprint YR and DR projection papers at temperatures up to 24°C, while IA12 should be used for processing when the ambient temperature is likely to be higher than 24°C.

Most machines deliver prints directly after stabilisation; at this time they are not really dry, but only 'damp dry'. Some machines therefore incorporate a heat-drying section, and Ilford provides a special stabiliser, IS22, for use with these. Solution levels in the two trays of a machine are usually maintained by using the simple 'chicken-feed' principle of upturned bottles of activator and stabiliser.

All Ilfoprint materials are coated on fibre-based paper because the paper base itself has to serve as a kind of 'sink' to retain the products of stabilisation; this could not happen if the base were 'waterproofed' with protective layers of polyethylene. There is no really satisfactory way of processing film-based materials by stabilisation, since the stabilising chemicals would simply crystallise out on the surface of the film.

Ilfoprint papers have the same image characteristics as conventional silver-sensitised papers and can be exposed in just the same way. Ilfoprint YR and DR have a speed similar to Ilfobrom and Ilfospeed and can be safely used under light from an Ilford 902 safelight screen. Ilfoprint YR glossy papers are available

253

in four equally-spaced contrast grades, grades 1 to 3 having the same speed and grade 4 exactly half the speed of the others.

Permanence   Depending on storage conditions, a stabilised print may remain unchanged for many months, but in practice, if the print is handled normally, it will probably not last for more than six months before showing signs of deterioration. Under really adverse conditions of high temperature and high humidity a stabilised print may become badly stained in a few weeks. However, a high degree of permanence can be achieved if, before any deterioration has occurred, a stabilised print is fixed and washed in the orthodox way. Some photographers regularly work like this, using an activation/stabilisation machine to process prints that they can almost instantly see, but then resorting to the much slower subsequent stages of fixing and washing. In this way, a small darkroom can be mechanised to a modest extent at relatively low cost.

It is even possible to design a machine in which an image is formed by activation rather than development and the print is subsequently fixed, washed and dried automatically. But since the fixer certainly and the wash water possibly would have to be heated to ensure short enough treatment times, one might just as well heat a developer so that development is complete in 10 seconds or so. In that way, the disadvantages of using a strongly alkaline activator are avoided and any type of resin-coated black-and-white paper can be processed, since it need not contain a developing agent.

6 Print quality and stability

The quality of any photographic print depends upon a long chain of choices and actions, starting with the type of film used in the camera, and upon an equally important series of precautions. Therefore it cannot easily be defined. Even Hurter and Driffield, despite their fervent desire to quantify the photographic process, declared: 'The production of a perfect picture by means of photography is an art; the production of a perfect negative is a science.' In theoretical terms they described a 'perfect' negative as one in which 'the opacities of its gradations are proportional to the light reflected by those parts of the original object which they represent'.

In similar terms, a 'perfect' print has been described as having 'such density and contrast that every tone in the original subject is exactly reproduced in the print when it is viewed under certain definitive conditions by an average viewer'. To comply with such conditions is generally impossible, for as Lloyd Jones has said: 'The theoretical relationships and practical methods necessary for computing in physical terms how closely the brightness differences in the original can be reproduced by a specified photographic process have been known for years. However, when an attempt is made to apply these methods in practice, it is usually found to be impossible, with available photographic materials, to obtain an exact physical reproduction of the brightness differences existing in many objects of which it is desired to make pictures.' In other words, it might work for a street scene on a foggy day but not for much else.

What then do people mean when they speak of a picture exhibiting 'excellent photographic quality' or say that 'the quality is very poor'? Probably, if the observation is made by a practising photographer, he is commenting on the properties of the print itself: on the depth of the shadows or blacks, and the clarity of the highlight or whites. Other factors, such as the sharpness of a print, can be assessed objectively, but without access to the negative it is difficult to decide whether any improvement could have been made by the printer.

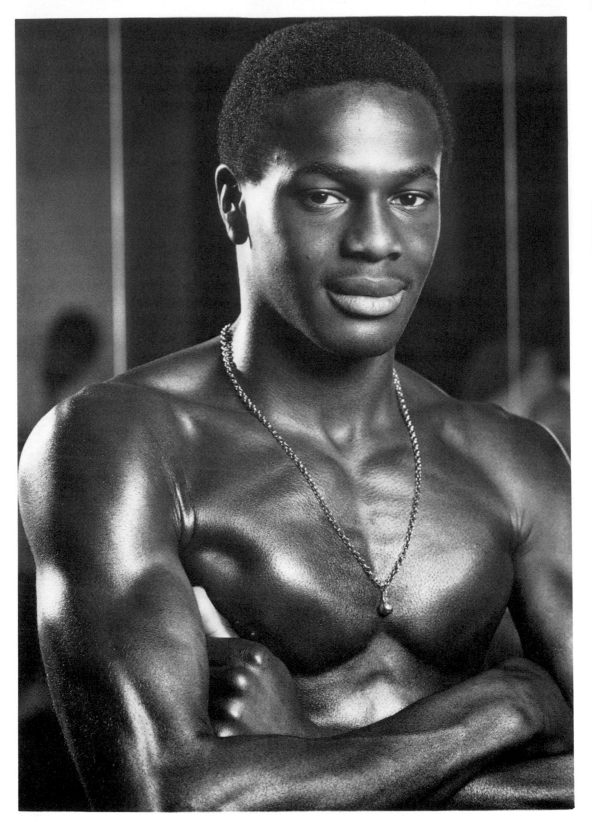

Objective and subjective factors

There are two different ways of judging the 'quality' of a photographic print. One is objective and has to do with measurable properties such as density, contrast and sharpness; the other is subjective and has to do with the way in which the photographer and or the printer chose to interpret the subject. After all, most prints are a combination of what the photographer actually saw and what he or his printer thought about it.

In the objective sense, a print is made to represent the subject as convincingly as possible within the constraints of the medium, while in the other case the subject may or may not remain

The striking portrait of the footballer Justin Fashanu, by Arthur Steel of the *Sun*, is representational photography at its best. The study below, by Hiroshi Shimura, is more concerned with the design formed by branches and leaves than with their precise representation

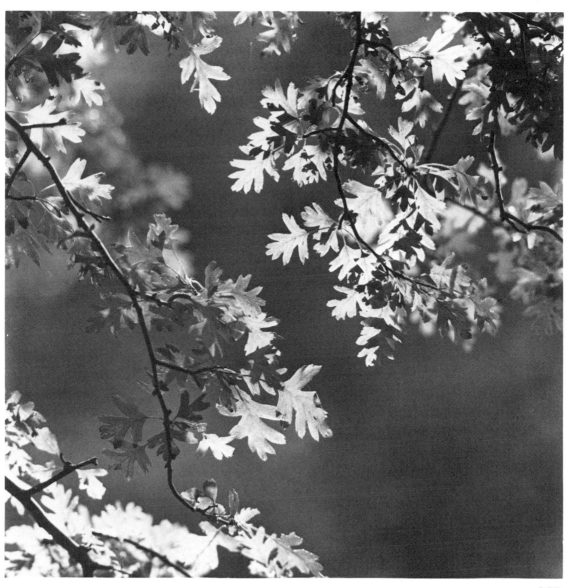

important, because the principal aim is to capture attention for the print through its aesthetic appeal.

To be convinced that there are plenty of subjective factors in the practice of black-and-white photography, it would only be necessary to hand the same negative to half a dozen printers in turn and to ask them to make the best print they could, using any paper and developer they chose. The six results would be unlikely to look the same. Some would certainly be darker than others and there would probably be differences in contrast. With a negative of a difficult subject, the prints might be expected to bear the individual stamp of each printer in terms of the dodging or burning-in he decided to employ.

In short, when a photographer or printer decides to express himself through a black-and-white print, there are no rules. However, if the intention is to produce a print that conveys as

This 'pattern' picture by Denis Thorpe looks almost as interesting when it is held upside down

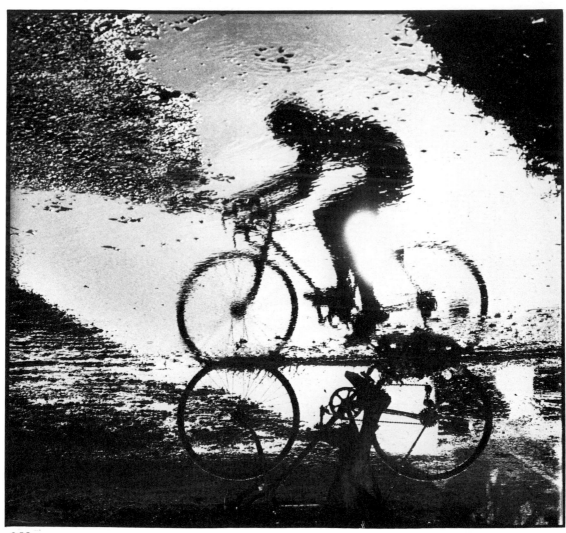

much realism as possible, a number of factors that can be controlled and quantified will determine the excellence of the result. Among them are:

1 Sharpness
2 Tonal separation
3 Highlight detail, including clear highlights
4 Shadow detail, including good blacks
5 Freedom from reproduced grain
6 Freedom from random defects

Notice that every one of these requirements depends to a greater or lesser extent on the negative image as well as on the properties of the print itself. This is simply a reminder of the truism that a first-class print can never be made from a poor negative.

Sharpness   Assuming that the resolution of the negative image is known to be adequate for the purpose, an unsharp print made from it could result from one or more of these faults:

1 Insufficiently careful focusing of the projected image.

Noel Palmer's job is to photograph Rolls-Royce cars, and in this shot of a Corniche saloon he has integrated a clear sharp image of the top of the car with a completely black, almost mysterious background. He used FP4 in a Sinar camera

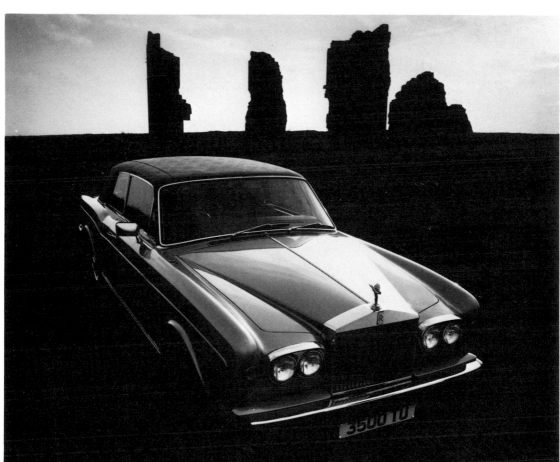

2 Movement of the enlarger lens between focusing and completion of exposure.
3 Part or whole of the sensitive surface of the paper not in the focal plane of the projected image throughout the exposure.
4 Inability of the enlarging lens (at the chosen aperture) to transfer the negative image adequately.

The possible remedies for these shortcomings are either obvious or have been discussed earlier in the book.

Tonal separation There has always been a tendency among amateurs, and perhaps even some professionals, to misunderstand the true meaning of the so-called 'contrast' of a printing paper. A negative, because it is an intermediate step in the photographic process, can be developed to any one of many different contrasts; but a print, if it is to display good blacks, must always be developed to practically the same contrast. However, the ratio between the exposure that produces a just discernible density and the exposure that is just sufficient to produce the best black the

There must be no kind of blemish on either negative or print material, and no mistakes in processing or printing if this kind of perfection is to be achieved. Only meticulous work could produce 'Ballet pupil' by Graham Davies

Now that wedding photographs are less formal, photographers look for more imaginative settings, and to deal with them they often need a film with great latitude. James Morrison shot 'The interlopers' with FP4 in a Mamiya camera

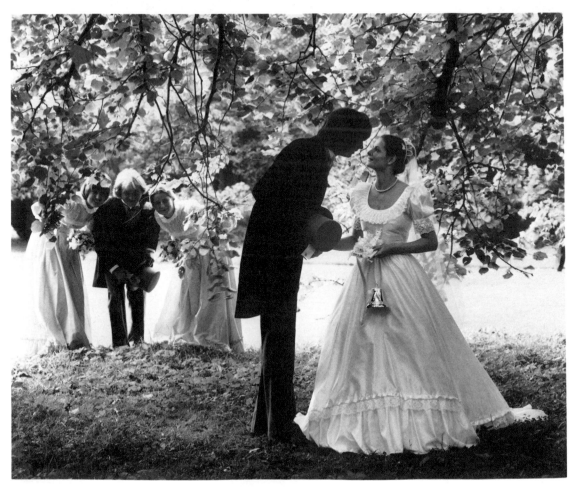

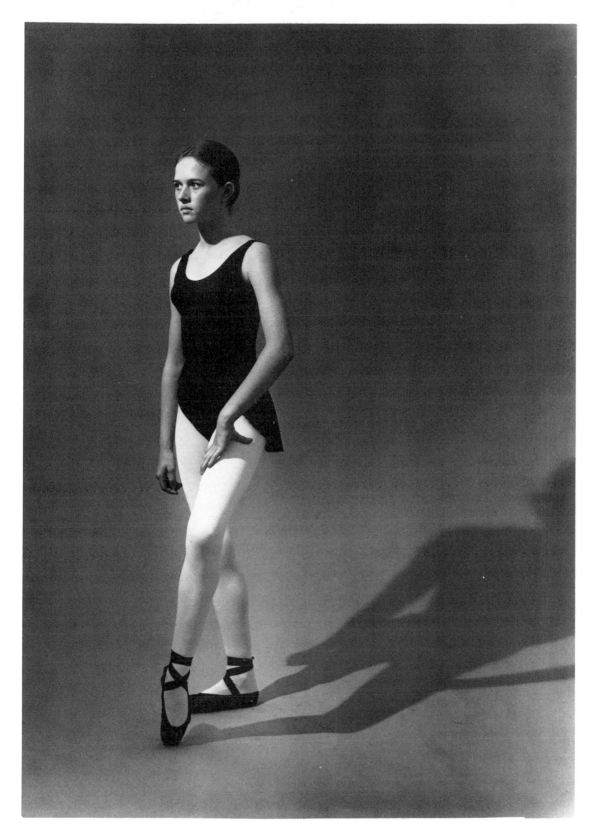

paper can give varies considerably from one grade of paper to another. In other words, all grades of paper of the same type can produce the same image contrast, but the exposure required to produce a good black on a grade 4 paper may be four times as great as that required to produce an equivalent black on grade 0 paper. Conversely, the maximum black density of a 'soft' paper might need 30 or 40 times as much exposure as is required to produce a just discernible density on the same paper. Therefore the so-called 'contrast' of a paper tells us nothing about the number of different tones of grey it can produce, but only the amount of exposure required to produce them.

When, in 1894, Driffield gave a lecture to the Widnes Photographic Society on 'The Principles Involved in Enlarging', he had this to say about matching paper to negative: 'The image gradation of the negative must coincide with the range of gradations of the paper if a satisfactory result is to be looked for. By the range of the paper I mean the ratio existing between the two exposures, one of which just falls short of producing any deposit, and the other of which just suffices to produce the deepest black which the paper is capable of recording.'

In practice, the suitability of a paper for use with a particular negative is usually determined by judgement, supported by trial and error, rather than by densitometry. This is of course made much easier when using a variable-contrast paper such as Ilfospeed Multigrade.

Highlight rendering The brightness range of the subject, together with the level of exposure of the negative, has more to do with the subsequent rendering of highlight detail on a print than any other factors. Apart from burning-in (the importance of which should not be underestimated) the only choices open to the printer are paper grade and print exposure; of these, the selection of paper grade is the more important.

Nevertheless, there are several ways in which the highlight rendering of a print can suffer because of what might be termed external factors. The first of these, lens flare, can be held at a minimum by using a top-class enlarging lens and keeping it scrupulously clean. If the information is available, it also helps to use the lens as often as possible at apertures that produce the least flare. The second danger is fog, caused either chemically during development or by unsafe safelighting.

David Brooks conducted some tests to find out how long Ilfobrom paper can be developed in Bromophen developer before the onset of chemical fog. Rather surprisingly he found that, although at 20°C (68°F) the standard or recommended time of development is between 1½ and 2 minutes, he could continue developing a print on Ilfobrom for more than seven minutes before running into any fog. From this it can safely be deduced that, with a developer in good condition (i.e. one that has not been worked to exhaustion), there is little risk of a print suffering from chemical fog during any normal period of development. However, any suspicion that a developer is causing trouble can be easily checked by making up a fresh working bath.

Safelight fogging can be more difficult to detect, since the usual 'penny on the paper' test may not be adequate. To be quite sure that absolutely no fogging is being caused by the safelight, turn it off and expose a sheet of paper with the enlarger lens stopped down and no negative in the carrier; allow just enough time to produce a light-grey density after development. Immediately after the exposure, and before moving the paper, cover half of it with a card and turn on the safelight or lights for as long as your longest print exposure is likely to take, including the time you need to remove a sheet of paper from its box and locate it in the easel. After that, process the exposed sheet and look *very* carefully to see whether there is any difference in density between the two halves.

The slightest degree of safelight fogging would have ruined the all-important highlight rendering of this silver replica of a Model T Ford. Photographer Ken Shipton, printer Mike Gill

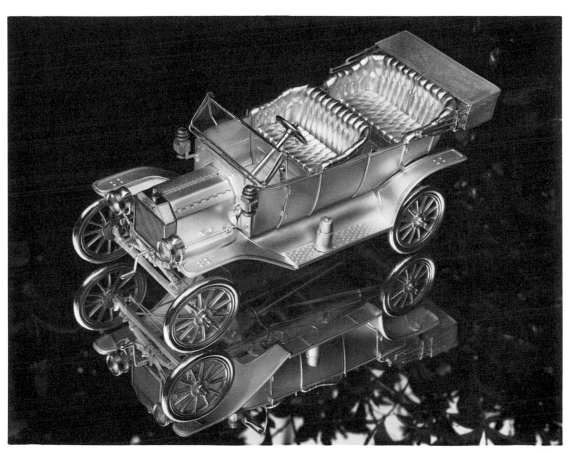

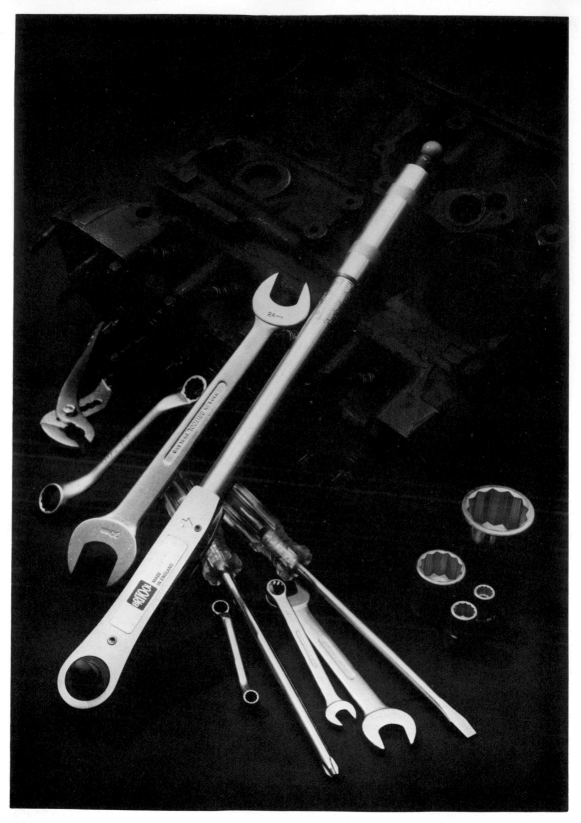

264

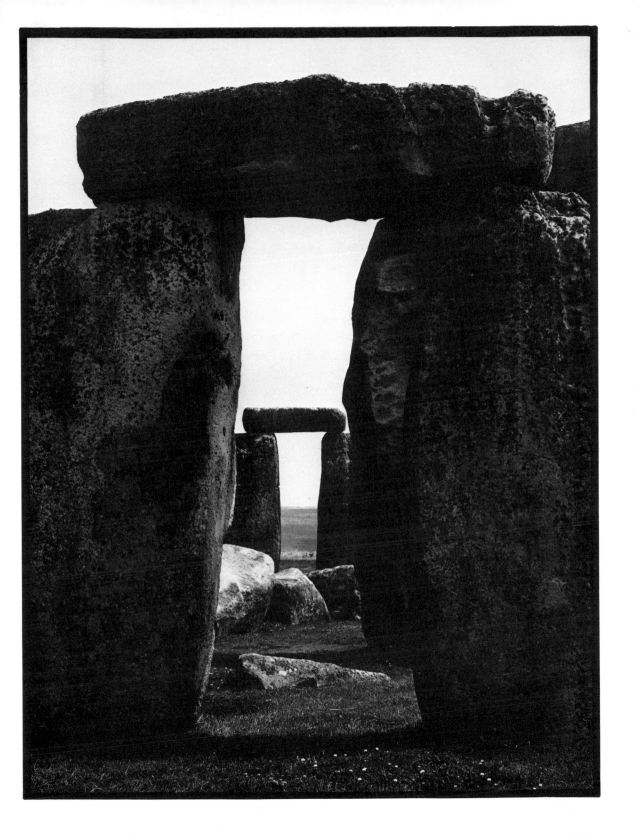

Shadow rendering   Probably the most frequent cause of mediocre print quality is the failure to make use of the full density range of the paper, in other words 'poor blacks'. The factors influencing the maximum black that can be obtained in a print are few. First, every paper has its own maximum black, depending on the emulsion properties and even more on its surface characteristics. A glossy paper always has an appreciably higher maximum density than one with a matt surface. Second, the developer that is used with a paper must be capable of yielding, *and be allowed to produce*, the best black the paper can give. Third, exposure must be sufficient for maximum density to be achieved.

Useful evidence of the best black that can be expected when using a particular paper/developer combination can easily be obtained by completely fogging a piece of the paper and developing it for twice the recommended time at the recommended temperature. After processing, the resulting patch can be used for comparison with the blacks obtained on subsequent prints.

From time to time, there are complaints that manufacturers are cutting down on the silver coating weight of their papers, and that consequently the quality of prints must be suffering. By way of contrary evidence it is interesting to note that the maximum densities usually indicated for the black-and-white papers of twenty years ago seldom reached 1.8, whereas none of the Ilfobrom, Ilfospeed or Multigrade papers made by Ilford has a maximum black potential less than 2.0. Galerie, with a glossy surface, easily achieves a maximum density of 2.2.

When David Vestal examined a selection of 'premium quality' fibre-based black-and-white papers, including Ilford Galerie, he made these observations: 'There's much talk among photographers about wanting rich papers, but I don't know of any established standards or measuring methods for that richness. On thinking about it, I decided that the useful range of densities is probably the logical measure for richness. There are certainly other aspects of richness, subjective ones that can't be measured or agreed on, so "useful range" isn't all there is to the matter. Yet the greater the useful range, as far as I can see, the richer the paper. So I devised a "richness index" (RI) on the useful range. I picked low-richness and high-richness end points, divided the space between them into 10 equal parts, and had an evenly spaced scale of "richness numbers".'

By applying his rules to Ilford Galerie paper, Vestal found that grade 1 Galerie has a maximum density of 2.2, a useful density range of 1.95 and a 'richness' factor of 5¾+. The 'richness' factor could be increased to 7+ by subsequent selenium toning.

Pages 264 and 265: recording shadow detail in the negatives and its subsequent retention in the prints was essential to the success of both of these pictures. That on the left is by Gordon Fidler, while 'Stonehenge' is the work of Ed Buziak: both used FP4

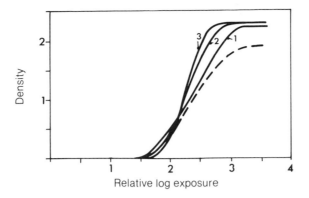

Characteristic curves for three grades of Ilfobrom Galerie glossy paper (1K); broken line is a typical curve for 1960s glossy paper

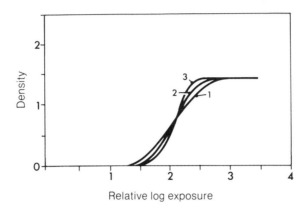

Characteristic curves for three grades of Ilfobrom Galerie matt paper (5K)

These independent results seem to show that modern black-and-white papers are the best there have ever been, and this is David Vestal's view: 'Five years ago things looked bleak. Most of the best non-RC papers had disappeared or deteriorated. We complained hard and long, and evidently we were heard. Today the devoted black-and-white photographer who cares enough to pay for extra-rich fibre-base paper can choose from new papers that seem even better than some of the ones we lost.'

Evidence of grain For all practical purposes, the intrinsic graininess of a printing paper can be completely disregarded. The 'grain' that is so often apparent in a print that has been enlarged from a small negative area is simply a faithful reproduction of the structure of the negative image, and must be considered undesirable when a photograph is intended to convey maximum information and realism.

Once a picture has been taken and the negative processed, there are only one or two things a printer can do to limit the grainy appearance of the prints he makes from it. He can restrict the scale of enlargement as much as possible consistent with requirements, and he can use an enlarger with a diffuse rather than a directional

267

light source. However, using a diffuse light source will probably lead to a requirement for a harder grade of paper, and this in turn nullifies the reduction in the grainy appearance of the finished print.

At this point, something must be said about a disadvantage of using a hard grade of paper to print a low-contrast negative. When this is done, the tone separation that results may be perfectly satisfactory and just the same as would be obtained from a more contrasty negative printed on to a 'normal' or 'soft' grade of paper, but the recording of the negative's graininess is usually much more apparent in the print made on hard paper. Furthermore, any defects present on a negative appear more prominent the harder the paper grade used for the print. So, within the limitations of the subject brightness range, negatives should be developed so that they print comfortably on a 'normal' rather than a 'hard' grade of paper.

Random defects   Many of the defects that occur in a print originate with the negative from which it was printed. This unfortunate fact has become more obvious as the average size of negatives has been reduced. Keeping a 35 mm negative absolutely free from dust, hairs and marks of any kind is extremely difficult, particularly when the negative is printed repeatedly. The effects of dust and scratches can be significantly reduced by using a diffuse light source in the enlarger, and it now seems probable that the trend towards this kind of enlarger illumination will be maintained.

A less obvious form of print defect can also originate in the enlarger, and takes the form of printed evidence of Newton's rings. These interference patterns are caused by partial contact between the back of a film-based negative and the glass surface used to hold it flat. The cure is to use a piece of glass of the kind that will not cause Newton's rings because one of its surfaces has been very lightly etched.

Other defects in prints are caused by careless handling or treatment of the paper during exposure or processing. Although all papers incorporate a very thin gelatin supercoat to protect the emulsion layer from physical damage, stress marking can occur if the paper is handled too roughly or is kinked or creased in any way. Mechanical damage can result in two quite different forms of stress marking, according to the emulsion characteristics of a particular paper. Desensitised stress shows itself in the form of irregular marks that are lighter than the surrounding densities, while sensitised stress results in dark marks wherever the emulsion has been damaged. A simple practical experiment indicates what

268

form stress marking will take with the paper you are using. Take a piece of paper and scribe marks on its emulsion surface with your thumbnail before developing it to see the result.

A bad case of contamination by finger marking can easily be recognised, and the culprit even identified! But less obvious marks due to the same cause are not so easily explained. If paper is being handled without gloves or print tongs there is a high risk of contamination unless a strict finger washing and drying routine is observed; this must include a plentiful supply of clean linen or disposable paper towels.

The inadequacy of reproduction   It is an unfortunate limitation, in any book on photography, that what is written about the finer points of print quality can never be backed up by convincing illustrations. Stieglitz, who started out by using the carbon process and later turned to platinum printing, felt the limitation so strongly that at one time he refused to allow his prints to be reproduced by photo-mechanical means; saying: 'My photographs do not lend themselves to reproduction. The very qualities that give them their life would be completely lost in reproduction. The quality of touch in its deepest living sense is inherent in my photographs. When that sense of touch is lost, the heartbeat of the photograph is extinct, dead. My interest is in the living. That is why I cannot give permission to reproduce my photographs.'

There is therefore only one way in which the student, of whatever age, can learn to appreciate the full potential of the black-and-white photographic process, and that is by taking the trouble to visit exhibitions, where he will be able to examine original prints as closely and for as long as he wishes.

Stability of prints

According to an article in 'Time' magazine, platinum prints by Paul Strand sold for about $125 in the 1960s, for $1500 in the early 1970s and for as much as $12 000 by the beginning of the 1980s. At such prices it is as well that they are Platinotypes, since their owners will certainly not expect to see any deterioration or change in the prints during the time they hold them.

Quite apart from the very high prices that are paid for the works of famous photographers, many less illustrious people are now increasingly aware that silver-image black-and-white prints do sometimes deteriorate. Strictly speaking there is no such thing as a permanent photographic print, only differences in the resistance of prints to deterioration. These differences can vary widely according to the processing history and the use to which a print is put. An attempt was made in the US to group prints in three

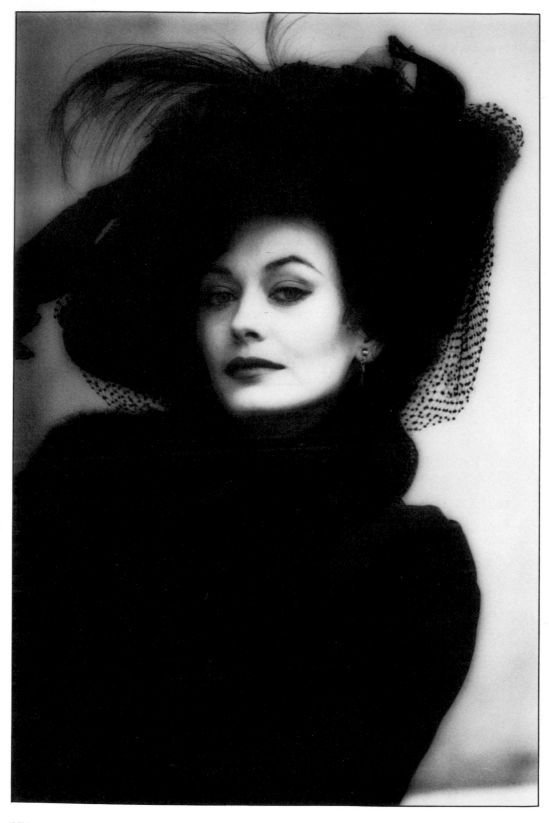

categories, 'stable', 'permanent' and 'archival'; but since the first two of these labels surely amount to the same thing and the third needs explanation, few photographers or print owners are likely to be helped by such descriptions.

Forms of deterioration   Before water-resistant polyethylene-coated papers came into use, the most frequent form of deterioration of black-and-white prints was staining or fading due to chemical changes that had affected the silver image. While these same changes can also affect a silver image on a polyethylene-coated base, an additional kind of deterioration in the form of cracking sometimes used to happen to the polyethylene layer itself. The past tense is used because, for reasons that are explained later, this particular trouble is not likely to occur in future.

Whenever thiosulphate ions are left in the gelatin and base of a black-and-white print, they eventually combine with the silver of the image to form yellowish-brown silver sulphide. Prints can also become discoloured or faded as the result of being treated in a fixing bath laden with the by-products of the fixing process. The silver complexes resulting from the reaction between silver halides and thiosulphate accumulate in a fixing solution during use; as more and more prints are treated in the same bath, the concentration of these silver compounds increases until, at a certain level, relatively insoluble silver compounds begin to be formed and cannot be removed by subsequent washing. Obviously these two causes of image deterioration can be avoided by ensuring that fixing baths are not overworked and that prints are washed adequately after being fixed.

Even when a black-and-white print, whether on a 'fibre' or on a 'water resistant' base, has been carefully fixed and washed, it may still suffer deterioration because of contamination by air containing high levels of industrial pollutants such as hydrogen sulphide and sulphur dioxide. The form of staining or 'bronzing' that can happen under such conditions can easily be mistaken for the results of inadequate fixing or washing, and this sometimes leads to confusion as to the real cause. The chances of fading or discoloration occurring due to external atmospheric agents can be reduced by protecting the prints with a waterproof lacquer and by ensuring that it is dry mounted rather than 'wet' mounted with a hygroscopic water-miscible adhesive. The emulsion maker too can make things better or worse according to the kind of 'stabiliser' he uses.

Storage conditions   Although the professional or commercial photographer cannot control the way in which the prints he sells are subsequently stored, the hobbyist or print collector certainly can. Even though poor storage may not be responsible for spoiling as many prints as poor processing, many negatives and prints do suffer from having been stored in contact with sulphur-containing envelopes, boxes or rubber bands. Fortunately today we have more convenient and less damaging synthetic materials in which to keep negatives and prints. Polythene sleeves or envelopes are not only inert but also allow the negatives or prints they contain to be examined without removal and consequent handling. However, polythene is impervious to moisture, so while it helps keep contents dry if they are dry, it also keeps them damp if they start damp. Under really moist conditions the polythene may even stick to the gelatin of a negative or print. To prevent this happening, a small amount of silica gel in a porous bag should be included in any box or drawer in which photographs are kept.

Standards for processing

In 1974 the American National Standards Institute recognised that there was a need for a means of predicting the permanence of photographs, and they published their 'Method of evaluating the processing of black-and-white photographic papers with respect to the stability of the resultant image'. The scope of the standard is described in the following terms: 'This standard specifies test methods for indicating the relative stability of the images of processed silver halide photographic papers as conditioned by the internal factors resulting from processing. It applies only to processed photographic papers containing silver particles in an organic colloid layer and not to dye images, or to tinted, toned, intensified photographs that have received a lacquer or other surface coating. *This standard does not define a finite time for useful life of the processed photographic papers.*'

It should be understood that the method of testing proposed by the standard is comparative and intended to provide an assessment of processing efficacy, which can only be indirectly related to the real-time stability of a print.

The necessary reference samples are prepared by successive treatment in a stopbath, a plain sodium-thiosulphate fixing bath, a hypo eliminator containing hydrogen peroxide and ammonium hydroxide, and a final 20-minute wash completing a total processing cycle of more than an hour.

The incubation treatment, to which both reference and sample are subjected, requires that they be suspended within a sealed glass desiccator in a relative humidity of 96 per cent at a temperature of 38°C (100°F) for either one day, 10 days or 30 days. The three different periods relate to three arbitrary criteria of processing

272

efficiency: 'short-term' (1 day), 'commercial' (10 days) and 'optimum' (30 days). In the phraseology of the standard itself: 'The process being evaluated shall be considered "optimum" with respect to stability if the resultant stability is in all respects as good as that of the reference sample for the maximum duration of the test.'

Similarly graded tests are used to assess the comparative stability of processed samples when exposed to simulated sunlight, i.e. 5400 foot-candles (58 000 lux). In this case, 'short-term' rating is given to samples showing a change in less than eight hours, the 'commercial' rating is given to those showing a change between eight and 24 hours, while 'optimum' rating is given to samples withstanding 24 hours of sunlight without change.

Ilfobrom/Galerie processing sequence

Knowing that Galerie papers would be used by such distinguished photographers as Ansel Adams, Arnold Newman, Donald McCullin and many others who would certainly want to depend upon the stability of their finished prints, Ilford decided to re-examine the whole business of processing fibre-base prints for maximum stability. The processing sequence that resulted from the study caused something of a stir, because the time required for fixing and washing was much less than all earlier recommendations.

Ilford started by deducing that, in the absence of a standard, a maximum of 0.7 microgram of thiosulphate per square centimetre is little enough to ensure archival permanence in a fibre-based black-and-white print, and then ended up by devising a processing sequence that leaves prints with a much lower thiosulphate concentration than their target.

Following development, which has no effect on the subsequent stability of a print, prints should preferably be rinsed in an acid stop bath before being transferred to an ammonium thiosulphate fixer (Hypam 1+4) for 30 seconds at 20°C. The shortness of this time in the fixer is important, because whether a print can be washed effectively depends on the extent to which the complexes formed during fixing have time to be absorbed by the fibres of the paper base. These complexes, given the time, form strong bonds that cannot be removed by washing or even by using a washing aid.

Next, the print is washed in running water for 5 minutes. Although 20°C is the generally recommended processing temperature, this wash and the wash at the end of the cycle can be done at temperatures as low as 10°C with negligible effect on results. Furthermore, washing time need not be extended because of the lower temperature.

The third step is to treat the print in Galerie Washaid (1+4) for 10 minutes (the longest step in the sequence). In a paper on 'The washing powers of water', Levenson pointed out that 'of all "waters", pure water emerges as much the poorest in respect of washing power'. By this he meant that the neutral salts normally found in tap water greatly accelerate the rate of removal of hypo from films and papers. Sodium sulphite and sodium sulphate are both effective in expediting the removal of hypo and silver thiosulphate complexes from photographic materials.

A final wash for 5 minutes completes a processing cycle of just over 20 minutes.

Dangerous possibilities arise at the print-drying stage if a photographer decides only occasionally to process a few prints on Galerie paper to ensure permanence, but at all other times takes rather less trouble with print processing because the results are for one-time use. If this happens, there is a risk that the carefully treated Galerie prints may be laid out on slightly contaminated blotters or racks, or even on newspapers that have been used before. Any print is particularly susceptible to contamination while it is wet, so probably the safest and simplest way to dry Galerie prints is to hang them up where they will not be disturbed before they are dry.

Toning

Toning can provide additional protection for a print by converting it into, or coating it with, some other material (often a metal) that will give it greater resistance to deterioration from external contaminants. Not all papers respond in the same way to toning. The grain size of the emulsion has a significant effect on the colour of the toned image, but at this point these differences are disregarded and only toners that bestow an improvement in stability are considered.

It is unfortunate that the toner that converts a silver image into one of silver selenide and seems to provide the greatest improvement in stability (judged by accelerated aging tests) is the 'nastiest' one to prepare, because of the toxic nature of selenium. In the earlier days of photography there was less concern with chemical hazards, and formulae for making up selenium (sometimes know as 'Flemish') toners from powdered selenium were to be found in most textbooks. But now the 'safe' recommendation is to use a made-up concentrate such as Eastman Kodak's Rapid Selenium Toner, a working bath of which can be prepared by diluting one part of toner with three parts of water. Prints to be toned can be transferred directly from their final wash into the toner and left there for five or six minutes at 20°C. The

274

colour of the toned image does not change dramatically, although the shadows and blacks may take on a slightly purplish appearance and the overall density of the print may slightly increase. After toning, prints should be washed thoroughly before being dried.

Sulphide toning provides slightly less protection against change than selenium toning. Conversion of a silver image to the more stable silver sulphide was extremely popular at one time, because of the rich sepia image colours it can produce. There are two or three ways of doing this. The old way involved the use of a hot solution containing hypo, alum and silver nitrate; although this may have been dependable and economic on a larger scale, it is not very convenient for the treatment of a few prints. A simpler, two-step toner working at room temperature can be made up as follows:

Bleach	water	500 ml
	potassium ferricyanide	50 g
	potassium bromide	50 g
	water to	1000 ml
Toner	sodium sulphide	5 g
	water to	100 ml

For use dilute one part toner with nine parts water.

On the assumption that any print to be toned will have had the fixing and washing treatment recommended for Galerie paper, it can be transferred directly into the bleach bath and should remain there until the black silver image has been completely converted to faintly visible yellowish-white silver bromide. Next the print must be washed until all traces of yellow ferricyanide have disappeared, and then transferred to the toner until the image has been completely re-formed and shows no further change. After completion of toning, the print must be thoroughly washed, and this can once again be done by following the Galerie washing sequence.

A sodium sulphide solution gives off the characteristic odour of hydrogen sulphide. To counter this, it is good idea to have on hand a dish of disinfectant, which can be poured down the drain immediately after the toner has been discarded.

Deterioration of base

The paper base and baryta coatings used for 'ordinary' photographic papers have always been subject to very tight standards of purity and consistency. Consequently, the paper base itself has rarely been a limiting factor in the life of a photographic print.

When water-resistant black-and-white papers such as Ilfospeed were introduced, it was confidently expected that they would prove more resistant to image deterioration than traditional papers, because it is much easier to remove residual fixer chemicals from a gelatin layer alone than from a gelatin layer combined with its fibre-based support. This prediction proved to be correct, but as field experience accumulated it was found that a quite different form of deterioration could occur, evidenced by cracking of the polyethylene layer beneath the image. The effect was not unlike the surface cracking that sometimes occurs with old oil paintings.

It is now known that cracking only occurred when a print had been exposed to rather exceptional conditions of light, heat or humidity, particularly if those conditions frequently changed. Under these special circumstances the polyethylene itself could begin to oxidise, and the oxidation could be accelerated by extremes of light or heat. Then, because the gelatin containing the image tried to swell in a humid environment and shrink in an arid atmosphere, it continually stressed the underlying polyethylene layer to which it was firmly attached. In the end, because the polyethylene became more brittle on oxidation, both the gelatin layer and the polyethylene layer began to crack.

Once the mechanism of the cracking was properly understood, it was seen that some way of preventing the polethylene from oxidising was necessary. Practical methods have now been found to achieve this improvement, so that prints made on current production of water-resistant black-and-white papers, when tested under severe accelerated aging conditions, prove to be as stable as a traditional paper such as Ilfobrom.

Bearing in mind that the image quality and surface characteristics of traditional paper can, in general, be matched with polyethylene-laminated papers, it seems probable that the additional convenience of using water-resistant papers will eventually make them preferable for any application.

7 Finishing and presenting the print

Very few prints, particularly those made from small negatives, are entirely free from defects immediately after processing. Fortunately the flaws are usually only small white areas caused by dust, hairs or scratches on one or both sides of the negative. The severity of the flaws is reduced when an enlarger is used with a diffuse light source, but even then some print finishing may still be required.

Print spotting

As with any other meticulous task done by hand, spotting cannot be learned from instructions but only by practice. However, there are some basic requirements and tips that may help at the outset. First of all, really good working light is absolutely essential for print finishing of any kind. After all, the areas being worked on are usually tiny and the fine point of the brush or pencil must be directed extremely accurately if the result is to be satisfactory. Even those with good near sight will need all the help they can get from the working light; for those whose close-up vision is not so good, a hand-held or headband magnifier may be necessary.

Most print spotting, that is the filling in of white spots or lines, is done with a brush rather than a pencil, because pencil will not 'take' to a glossy or silk-surfaced paper. Pencil will work well with the 'tooth' accorded by matt-surfaced papers, but it is then inclined to show up rather conspicuously whenever the pencil marks catch the light.

The great advantage of working with dye to spot a print is that if done well it is almost undetectable, because the dye enters the gelatin of the image layer and leaves no surface change to be caught by reflected light. There are several proprietary spotting and retouching dyes available, sometimes sold in sets of three or even six different shades to match a variety of image colours ranging from blue-black to sepia. For most purposes the so-called 'neutral' dye is adequate, although mixing of two or more dyes is necessary for warm-tone papers.

The size of brush best suited for spotting is a matter of opinion and preference, and sometimes two or more sizes may be needed for different purposes. Generally nothing larger than size 0 to 00

277

will be required, but manufacturers seem not to conform to a standard, so any recommendation cannot be precise. However, it is certain that the best-quality sable is essential if spotting is to be satisfying rather than a mere chore. A poor-quality brush cannot be made to behave, and there can be no satisfaction in using it.

From all the advice given on the art of spotting, one recommendation emerges: use an almost dry brush. This may seem contradictory, given the need to dip the brush in the dye solution in order to get started, but it simply means that all surplus dye should be removed before the brush is applied to a print. If surplus dye is not removed from the brush and an attempt is made to spot the print while the brush is wet, a drop of dye quickly forms around its tip as soon as the brush contacts the surface of the print; immediately the drop covers a circular area, regardless of the size and shape of the defect that needs to be filled in.

The brush therefore has to be repeatedly wiped free of surplus dye, by stroking it on a paper handerkerchief for instance. Rolling the wet brush while it is in contact with the absorbent paper not only removes the surplus dye but makes the tip of the brush nicely pointed and ready for use. Rather than use dye straight from its bottle, when it would often be too dense for immediate use, some finishers pour out a small amount into a white palette or saucer and then let it dry out completely, leaving a concentrated residue. Some of this dried concentrate can then be picked up on a moist brush and diluted in a little water to provide just the density required, as judged by constant testing on a scrap of paper or waste print. A drop of wetting agent in the water makes it easier to apply dye to the print.

When areas larger than mere dust spots have to be disguised, they are best filled in by 'stippling' rather than 'painting' dye on to the surface of the print, so that very many separate 'touches' of dye merge into what appears to be a uniform density.

Although spotting done with water colour is not as visible on the surface of the print as work done in pencil, it is usually slightly more noticeable than when dye has been used. If it were not for this slight disadvantage, water colour would probably be used more than anything else for spotting prints. Several companies, including Paterson, Jobo and Rowi, offer kits comprising tubes or pans of watercolour to suit blue-black and warm-tone images. The kits also include a palette and at least one brush. As with dyes, the brush used to apply watercolour needs to be moist and not wet; the actual density of colour applied again depends on the amount of water used for dilution. In the same way that dye can be concentrated by allowing all the water to evaporate from a small pool in a saucer, so water colour can be painted, full strength, on to a piece of smooth card; after it has dried, it provides a surface from which small amounts of colour can be lifted off with a moistened brush to be transfered directly to a print. In the US, Eastman Kodak sells spotting colours in the form of black, brown and white watercolour discs, from which colour can be lifted with a moist brush.

If the slightly matt surface in areas that have been spotted with water colour is thought to be too obvious, a better match with the rest of the print can sometimes be obtained by adding a little gum to the watercolour. This is easily done with a brush and the gummed flap of an envelope.

Knifing

Removing dark spots and blemishes from a print is not as easily done as filling in white spots, and with RC papers it is more difficult than with fibre-based prints because 'knifing' or scraping away the spot is hardly ever possible without disturbing the underlying polyethylene layer. Dark blemishes on a matt-surfaced paper such as Galerie 5K can be beautifully and undetectably removed with a knife. A glossy-surfaced print is a different matter, although evidence of scraping can be lessened by the subsequent application of a little gum.

Etching or scraping away part or all of the silver from some tiny area of a print calls for a lot of practice and a suitable knife or blade. There are a lot of handicraft knives available, such as those made by X-Acto and Swann-Morton; they usually have interchangeable blades with either pointed or curved ends suitable for use on either tiny spots or larger areas. Some practised workers prefer to use a razor blade for etching or scraping away silver density from a print. The double-edged type of blade is a favourite because it can be broken in two to make two separate working edges. One end of each piece of blade can be bound with tape for protection and to make it easier to hold. The slight flexibility and extreme sharpness of a scraper improvised in this way makes it very 'sympathetic' in use.

Scraping dark marks from RC prints is seldom a happy experience, and such corrections are generally best done by chemical treatment.

Local bleaching

Farmer's reducer (ferricyanide/hypo) can be used to lighten or remove dark areas of a print, but the working solution decomposes rapidly, making it difficult to control the rate of reduction of density. Some people therefore prefer to make a separate application of ferricyanide followed by treatment with hypo to remove the silver ferrocyanide. The best concentration of ferricyanide to use depends mostly upon judgement and experience, but also upon the density of the area to be removed: a solid black or merely some density of grey. However, if too strong a bleach is used the worst that can happen is removal of all the silver from the area being treated; the blank then has to be spotted back to match the surrounding density, something that some print finishers do as a matter of course.

The broad terms (pale yellow or deep yellow) used to describe different concentrations of potassium ferricyanide in solution are not much help to a beginner, who would do better to mix a range of three or four different-strength ferricyanide solutions and try them out on a scrap print to get the feel of them. A stock solution of potassium ferricyanide can be made up by dissolving a teaspoonful of the orange-coloured crystals in half a litre of water. This 'strong' solution is seldom used without dilution, and for the purposes of the tests it may be diluted with 5, 10 and 20 parts of water.

There are several methods of working with separate ferricyanide and hypo solutions to lighten or remove density from a print, but here is one way. Assuming the print has been dried already, soak it for five minutes or so in a hypo bath, before laying it on a flat sheet of glass or plastic material and wiping away all surface hypo with a sponge. If the print is taken straight from the fixer after being processed, do the same, making sure that the surface of the print is free of all droplets. Then, using whatever strength of ferricyanide solution was indicated by the preliminary tests, apply bleach to the area needing reduction with a sable brush of suitable size and immediately blot the area with a folded paper towel or napkin. The hypo retained in the image layer will react with the ferricyanide and a reduction in density will result within 10 or 15 seconds. As each stage of reduction is completed, assess the result. If necessary, repeat the application of ferricyanide followed by immediate blotting off to prevent any spread of the bleaching action. If the rate of reduction proves to be inconveniently slow, perhaps because the spot to be removed is very dense, one of the stronger solutions of ferricyanide can be tried. When sufficient reduction has eventually been achieved, the print is simply washed for about twice the time necessary for all traces of the yellow ferricyanide stain to disappear.

Another 'home-made' bleach that can be used for the after-treatment of prints is a copper-sulphate/potassium-bromide solution. About five grams of each of these two chemicals dissolved in 100 ml of water forms a working solution, which can be applied to the print with a brush. Dense spots need more than

280

one application, and the 'wet and blot' procedure described above should be used to prevent spread of the bleaching action. When all the black silver in the area concerned has been converted to silver bromide, it only remains to fix and wash the print.

In an emergency, even household bleach can be pressed into service. There are also proprietary solutions for locally removing or reducing the density of prints, but these have no particular advantages in use, and always require the print to be fixed and washed after the local treatment.

Background control

Whenever a completely blank background is required for a subject and the original negative is too small (as it so often is) to allow all background detail to be painted out with a liquid opaque, the work may have to be done on the enlargement.

After the print has been dried, the central subject that is to be retained must be protected by painting it with a coloured rubber solution such as Maskoid, Liquid Frisket or some similar product of the kind used by commercial artists. Alternatively a wax pencil may be used, but that has to be removed with a solvent, whereas the layer of rubber can be peeled or rubbed off the print very easily.

When the central subject has been carefully protected, any surrounding densities are removed with the aid of Farmer's reducer. The print can then be washed and dried before the masking is removed from the surface of the print.

Surface lacquer

In early days of pictorial photography, prints for exhibition were often 'worked-up' by hours of patient attention with pencil or brush, so that work on the surface of the print became all too obvious. To disguise the evidence of such excessive handwork, the surfaces of prints were waxed. This not only tended to cover up the surface marks, but also made the shadows look richer and the blacks blacker.

Today, much the same effect can be achieved by spraying the surface of a matt or semi-matt print with an aerosol lacquer. This offers the additional advantage of protecting the silver image from atmospheric sulphur, thereby enhancing its stability.

Mounted prints

There are two reasons for mounting a photographic print: one is to protect it from wear and tear and the other, of greater interest to the hobbyist and exhibitor, is to enhance its appearance. There is little doubt that a good print looks even better when it has been mounted so that it is truly flat and is separated from its surroundings by unobtrusive margins.

Some scientific work on the influence of surrounds on the appearance of black-and-white prints led E. Breneman to report: 'Changes in the relative luminance of the surround have a considerable effect on the apparent contrast among scene elements. When a dark surround is replaced by a light one, contrast is enhanced in the middle tones and highlights and reduced in the shadows.' Even leaving such considerations aside, there is something satisfying about viewing and handling a mounted print that usually makes the extra work worthwhile.

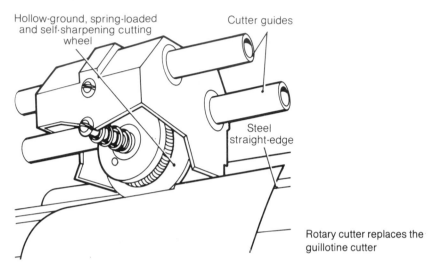

Hollow-ground, spring-loaded and self-sharpening cutting wheel

Cutter guides

Steel straight-edge

Rotary cutter replaces the guillotine cutter

In the same way as rotary glazing drums are rapidly falling into disuse, so guillotine cutters with their dangerous blades are fast disappearing from the photographic workroom. In their place, rotary wheel cutters with a simple, safe, horizontal action are now commonplace. However, a rotary cutter cannot handle card more than two or three millimetres thick, so thicker mounts and boards are generally cut with a trimming knife guided by a metal straight-edge. Two things make cutting card with a knife both easier and safer: a cutting mat made from 'self-healing' plastic material that shows no scores after being cut into, and a non-slip metal ruler with a rubber insert running its whole length so that it grips the surface on which it is being used.

Apart from temporary methods involving rubber solution or double-sided adhesive tape, there are several ways of mounting a photographic print, some of them having come into use since the widespread adoption of polyethylene-coated papers. The alternatives are:

1 Wet mounting with some form of water-miscible adhesive.
2 Dry mounting with heat.
3 Cold mounting with pressure-sensitive adhesive sheets.
4 Cold mounting with a spray-on adhesive.

282

Wet mounting   The simple materials and equipment required to mount a print with a water-miscible glue make it attractive to the hobbyist and sometimes essential for the professional. Wet mounting was a very common practice when all prints were made on fibre-based paper, but since the method cannot be used with polyethylene-coated papers, alternatives have been found. Water-based adhesive does not work with an impermeable print material because the glue cannot penetrate the back of the print to get a 'grip' on it. Furthermore, the water in the glue would take a very long time to migrate through the mount material, which is often hardboard or plywood.

However, there are times when wet mounting remains the only way to do a job. For instance, a print may need to be mounted directly on a wall or a partition, or wrapped around a cylindrical support or some kind. In neither of these cases would hot dry mounting be possible. The 'wet' method is also preferred for making large multi-sectioned murals, where the dimensional flexibility of a wet fibre-based print allows it to be stretched or squeezed just sufficiently for two parts of an image to be matched when their edges are butted together to make one large picture. For the hobbyist, one of the snags with wet mounting is that the finished result often curls badly because the print shrinks as it dries and takes the board with it. If the problem is too troublesome, it can be overcome by mounting a scrap print of the same size on the back of the board.

Dry mounting with heat   Dry mounting photographs with heat has always been the preferred professional method, although the hobbyist is usually precluded from using it by the relatively high cost of a press. An alternative for the hobbyist is to use a domestic electric iron; this can work satisfactorily with prints up to 20×25 or 25×30 cm (8×10 or 10×12 in), but beyond that there is a risk that prints will be spoiled, often by creasing.

Paterson have the amateur in mind with their Thermal Print Mountant, which is simply brushed evenly on to the back of a print and then left to dry. When the adhesive is dry, the print is located on its mount and the two bonded together with the aid of a hot iron. The temperature of the iron, provided that it is not so hot as to damage the surface of the print, is said not to be critical.

At one time there was just one kind of mounting press and mounting 'tissue', but since the introduction of polyethylene-coated papers and the surface treatment of prints by laminated layers the variety of presses and heat-sensitive foils has been extended.

Mounting presses are described as either 'soft-bed' or 'hard-bed'. While the former type is mechanically adequate to apply sufficient pressure to bond two flat surfaces such as a print and a mount, the hard-bed construction is necessary to allow enough pressure to be applied when laminating a protective layer to a rough-surfaced print or to embed a photographic image layer into canvas.

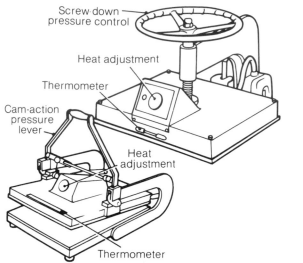

Screw-down pressure control

Heat adjustment

Thermometer

Cam-action pressure lever

Heat adjustment

Thermometer

'Hard-bed' (top) and 'soft-bed' mounting presses

All bench-top presses are open on three sides, so that even a 30 × 38 cm (12 × 15 in) platen can mount a 60 × 76 cm (24 × 30 in) print by taking four 'bites'. Larger industrial presses can handle 100 × 127 cm (40 × 50 in) prints in one operation, and have a hydraulic ram to apply the pressure. The smaller soft-bed presses are often operated by a simple cam-action lever, but the platen used for a hard-bed press is screwed down with a powerful threaded wheel.

If a vacuum is created, atmospheric pressure rather than direct mechanical force can be used to press a print into contact with a mounting foil and the foil into contact with a mount. The Vacuseal press works in this way, and overcomes the problems sometimes caused by creases or bubbles by extracting all air and moisture before bonding takes place.

Dry mounting tissue usually comprises a thin sheet of tissue paper coated on both sides with a dry adhesive that only becomes sticky when it is heated. Typically, a print/tissue/mount sandwich bonds together after about 30 seconds in a press at 80°C (175°F), although some tissues may require higher temperatures.

One or two precautions must be taken when dry mounting a print, since mistakes cannot usually be rectified. First, always ensure that both the print and the mount are quite dry, otherwise the finished sandwich will surely curl one way or the other.

Dryness can be ensured by placing first the print and then the mount between clean sheets of absorbent paper and putting them into the heated press for a short time to drive off any moisture. Second, always make sure that all four mating surfaces are scrupulously clean and that no fragments of card or mounting tissue are trapped between them, to become permanently sealed in. Third, always protect the surface of the image with a sheet of silicone release paper or engineer's drawing paper, while the print is being mounted.

If any air is trapped between a mounting board and a print on polyethylene-coated paper, there is no way in which it can escape after it leaves the mounting press, and there will be areas where the mounting tissue remains unattached to the print or the mount. One solution to this problem has been found by making a mounting tissue with a surface that is very slightly corrugated rather than perfectly smooth. The minute valleys thus formed in the tissue allow any air to be channelled to the edges of the print as pressure is applied but before bonding takes place.

Different kinds of mounting foils are now available, some of them having no paper core, but instead the foil itself is simply the layer of heat-sensitive adhesive material. These newer foils have another novel property in that they are slower to set after being heated. This means that if a mistake is made in positioning, a print

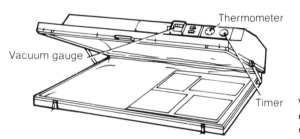

Vacuum mounting press ensures uniform pressure over whole print area

can be lifted off a mount up to five minutes after being removed from the press. Furthermore, one of these new adhesive layers (3M Promount 572) can be reheated so that a print can be removed from its support even years after it was originally mounted.

Ademco, a company whose name is synonymous with dry-mounting, realised that the materials used for mounting a photograph need to be quite inert if the life of the print is not to be impaired. They therefore produced an archival mounting tissue called Lamatec, which they say has 'successfully withstood artificial aging of up to approximately 170 years without causing embrittlement or discoloration of the laminated material'.

The time-honoured method of protecting images from dust and damp was to display them behind glass, which meant framing them. Now a clear plastic film, coated with adhesive on one side, can be laminated to the surface of a print in a hard-bed dry mounting press.

Cold mounting   Some people believe that improvements made in mounting adhesives that do not require heat to form a bond between two surfaces, but merely moderate pressure, have made the 'cold' method so easy that it will soon replace 'hot' mounting, at least for RC papers.

There are several different makes of cold mounting adhesive foils in both sheets and rolls, but they all work in much the same way and offer the considerable advantage of being repositionable. This means that a print can be relocated on, or even removed from, its mount at any time before the two are thoroughly pressed together by means of a roller squeegee or by being wound through a pair of spring-loaded rollers. The roller squeegeeing action, unlike pressure from a flat platen, tends to remove any air from the sandwich.

Increasingly, these cold mounting adhesives are being offered as an integrated part of a mount itself. Fixed sizes of prepared support material such as blockboard can be made ready for immediate use as soon as a protective layer of paper has been peeled off the adhesive surface. Provided that a print is made slightly larger than its mount, the surplus can easily be trimmed from the edges when the mounted print is placed face down on a flat surface.

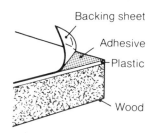

Prepared block allows quick and easy mounting

Spray-on adhesives are a more convenient way of providing an adhesive surface than spreading rubber solution, and can be either repositionable or immediate and permanent in action. However, the use of these aerosols is expensive for any but small prints, and the fumes they generate can be troublesome. In general, therefore, the spray-on method of obtaining a tacky surface is confined to small-scale occasional use.

'Splitting' RC prints   In what might be considered misguided attempts to simulate oil paintings, some portrait photographers have the image layers of their colour photographs embedded into sheets of canvas. The technique is made possible because the photographic image layer, together with its associated pigmented polyethylene underlayer, can be stripped away from the paper 'core' of an RC print. This flimsy image can then be transferred to almost any other support, even one with an irregular surface if sufficient pressure is applied. Small RC prints can be 'split' by hand, once delamination has been started at one corner, but the two parts of larger prints should be carefully rolled apart, using a smooth round rod or tube, about an inch or so in diameter.

8 Creative darkroom techniques

Andreas Feininger has said of print controls: 'Some, like printing through texture screens, introduce into the photograph a foreign element that I find objectionable. Others, like toning, vignetting or elaborate black border printing seem to me to be misguided attempts on the part of the photographer to enhance his pictures with the aid of attributes popularly associated with printing, in an effort to prove that Photography is an art. I find the resulting effects pitiful and ridiculous.'

Strong stuff, yet somehow inconsistent with Feininger's acceptance of such chance effects as reticulation, of which he says in one of his books: 'Reticulation, like an organic texture screen, gives the picture a feeling of graphic unity.'

If the Annual Ilford Print Awards, judged as they are by a different independent team every year, are any guide to good monochrome photography and printing, then toning, vignetting and the use of black borders are considered acceptable, since prints displaying these and other specialised forms of treatment frequently win prizes.

The modifications to a print that will convert it from being considered 'straight' can be divided into two groups. First, there are the effects that leave the basic characteristics of the image unchanged, while modifying the presentation by such treatments as toning to change the colour of the image or vignetting to isolate the central feature of a subject from a distracting background. Then there are the effects that drastically modify the characteristics of the image by such techniques as tone-separation, solarisation, or extreme enhancement of contrast or graininess.

Toning prints

Methods of toning with selenium and with sodium sulphide to enhance the resistance of an image to change are described in Chapter 6. But prints are also toned simply to enhance their aesthetic impact, since there are some subjects that seem to lend themselves particularly well to being represented by a coloured rather than a black image. Portraits and sunlit rustic scenes often look well when the print is sepia or brown, while seascapes and snow scenes can sometimes be made more interesting when they

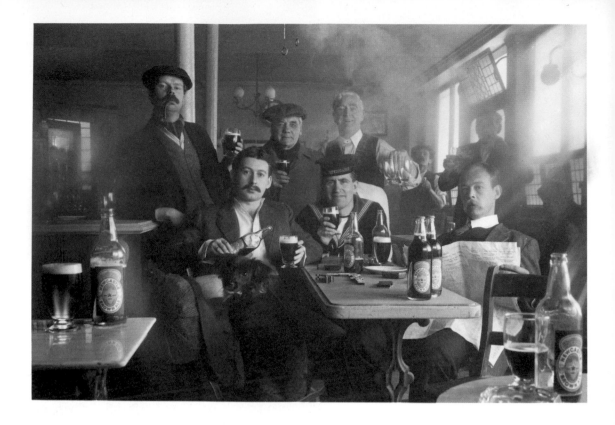

are toned blue. There are special cases too, such as the bar-room scene photographed by Derek Coutts for Newcastle Brown Ale, where the printer, Bill Rowlandson, really had little option but to tone his print brown.

Bill Rowlinson's award-winning print of a cleverly staged scene by Derek Coutts simply had to be sepia-toned

The processes of toning change the colour of a print by converting the neutral silver image into insoluble substances such as silver sulphide, which is brownish, or into coloured compounds of metals such as gold, uranium or iron. Gold and uranium yield colours ranging from reddish-brown to purple; iron gives the characteristic colour of prussian blue.

It must be stressed that printing papers do not react uniformly to toning treatments. In general, cold-tone originals respond less satisfactorily than warmer-toned papers. Furthermore, response is also influenced by the processing conditions under which the print was made. Preliminary testing with spare or waste prints is therefore advisable before any valuable print is committed to an untried combination of paper and toner.

Since methods of sulphide and selenium toning have already been described, this section considers one or two of the other metallic compounds to which a silver image can be wholly or partially converted in order to yield a reddish-brown or a blue

This simple holiday shot, by the author, serves well as an example of blue toning

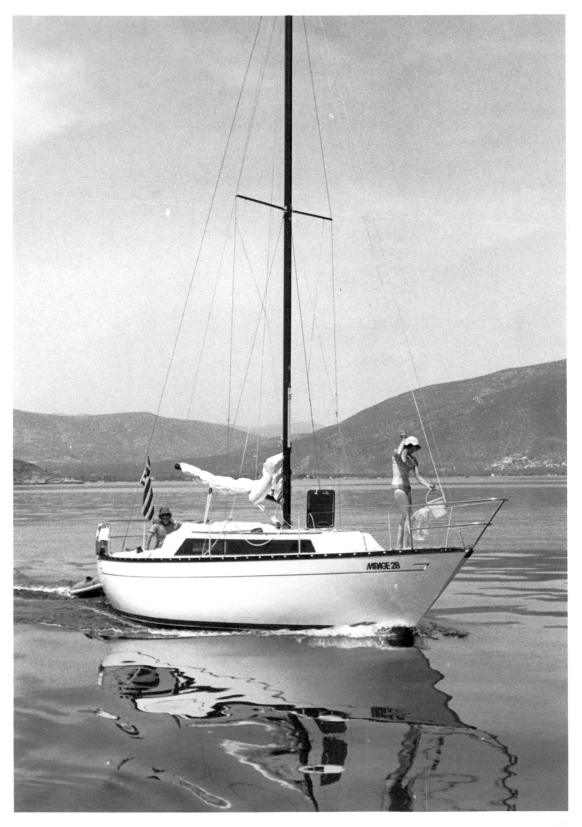

image. All these processes depend upon potassium ferricyanide oxidising the silver image to silver ferrocyanide before it is converted into an insoluble coloured ferrocyanide of whatever metal is being used.

Because the silver ferrocyanide formed as an intermediate step in the toning process is soluble in hypo, it is quite essential for all traces of fixer to have been washed out of a print before it is toned; this is of course easier to do with Ilfospeed or Multigrade prints than with Ilfobrom or Galerie.

Gold toning used to be recommended for obtaining a reddish-brown image colour, but it required that a print had already been through a sulphide toner. Also the high cost of gold has made the necessary solutions so expensive as to render the process unattractive for normal use. Uranium offers a less expensive alternative. It allows the formation of a range of tones between brown and yellowish-red according to the duration of treatment, i.e. the amount of red uranium ferrocyanide that is allowed to deposit on the image. Unfortunately a uranium-toned image is not as stable as the original silver image on which it depends. In particular, uranium ferrocyanide is soluble in alkaline solutions, so the changes of water used when washing the toned print need to be rendered slightly acid by the addition of a few drops of acetic acid.

A two-solution uranium toner can be made up as follows.

Bleach	potassium ferricyanide	10 g
	acetic acid (glacial)	25 ml
	water	500 ml
Toner	uranium nitrate	10 g
	water	500 ml

Thoroughly wash the print before bleaching it in the first solution. Then wash it again before toning it in the second. Leave the print to tone until its colour seems satisfactory, then transfer it to a tray containing slightly acidified water, followed by sufficient changes of water to remove all residual stain from white areas of the print.

Although single-solution iron toners have been proposed, a two-solution formulation such as the following is probably more reliable.

A	water	1000 ml
	potassium ferricyanide	2 g
	sulphuric acid (conc.)	4 ml
B	water	1000 ml
	ferric ammonium citrate	2 g
	sulphuric acid (conc.)	4 ml

Always add the acid slowly to the water, never the water to the acid. Mix equal parts of A and B just before use. When the desired tone has been reached, the print should be washed in acidified water, because iron ferrocyanide is soluble in alkaline solutions. In general, blue-toning tends to increase the visual density of a print and originals should therefore appear to be slightly lighter than normal. Here again, a few trials with scrap prints will repay the time taken.

A blue-toned print can be converted to green by treatment in the following solution of sodium sulphide.

water	1000 ml
sodium sulphide	5 g
hydrochloric acid	5 ml

Final washing should again be in changes of acidified water.

Although conversion of a silver image to some other metal compound that is coloured is the most usual method of toning a print, there are other ways of achieving the same end. Dye-toning, for example, is a process by which a silver image is converted to a colourless compound such as silver iodide, which can then be used to fix a dye of a chosen colour in an image-wise position before the mordant image itself is removed. This technique is more likely to work well with polyethylene-coated papers than with those having an unprotected fibre base from which it is difficult to remove residual dye.

Unorthodox development techniques can also be used to produce interesting effects, as evidenced by Lee Higham's study 'Quiet reflection', for the printing of which Gene Nocon won the Ilford Printer of the Year Award in 1980. The print was created by grossly overexposing a sheet of high-contrast paper and then underdeveloping it in a lith-type developer. The result is a fascinating picture with a mixture of yellowish highlights and brownish shadows.

Selective toning
Occasionally a subject is suitable for local rather than overall toning. For example, the 'print within a print' photograph by David Gepp, entitled 'Miss Evans, Talybont, with her grandfather', is made more interesting when the old photograph and its frame are sepia-toned while the remainder of the print is neutral. In the same way, Gene Nocon saw that Ed Pritchard's shot of a motorcyclist carrying a tyre would be greatly enhanced if the tyre remained black while the background was toned sepia.

Areas can be selectively toned simply by leaving them unprotected while the whole of the remaining areas of the print are

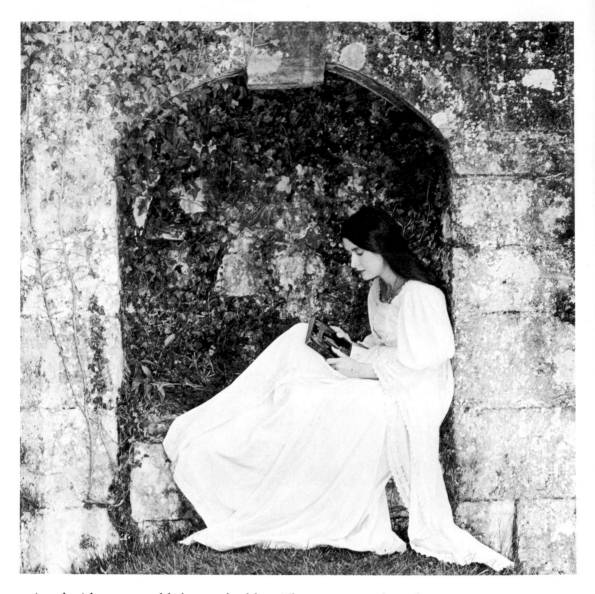

painted with a removable layer of rubber. There are a number of rubber solutions made for the purpose; they are usually coloured so that their location can be easily seen during application. When toning has been completed and the print is dry, the layer of rubber is easily stripped or rubbed from the surface.

It is even possible, but not often necessary, to simulate a colour print by applying several different toners to local areas of a suitable print. 'Cornish tin mine', by Tony Thomas, provides an example.

Vignetting
Vignetting is a technique that dates back to the very early days of photography; it was first used in 1853, albeit in contact and not

'Quiet reflections' won Gene Nocon the 'Printer of the Year' award in 1980. Taking Lee Higham's negative, Gene cleverly used a high contrast paper with a lith developer to create a subtle range of warm tones in the print

292

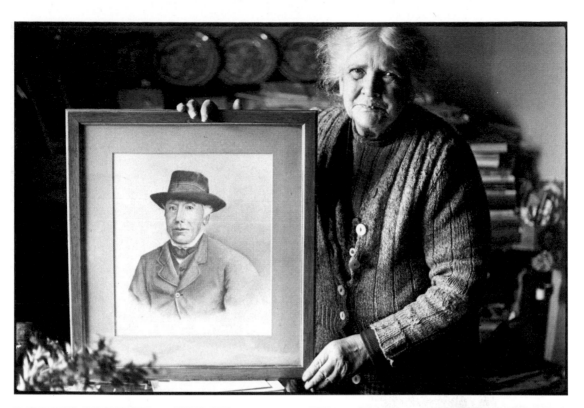

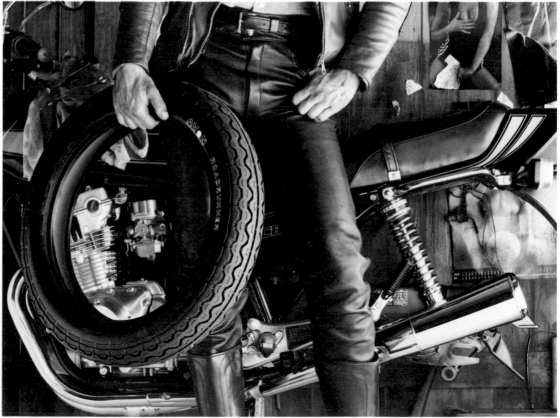

projection printing. Vignetted portraits were so popular at one time that special vignetting masks were made for the job, incorporating adjustable blades (rather like an iris diaphragm) that could be positioned to form apertures having different shapes and sizes to suit a wide variety of subjects.

When a vignetted image is made with an enlarger, the density gradient between the central image and the blank surround is made steeper or more gradual according to the position of the apertured mask in relation to the enlarger lens and the image plane. Usually, if the vignetting mask is held about midway between the lens and the paper, a satisfactory blend between image and surround results. If, in order to achieve more precise location of the vignetted image, the mask has to be held close to the paper, the edges of the aperture can be serrated by cutting it into a sawtoothed pattern to soften the transition between image and border.

As with any other form of dodging, the mask can be constantly moved or 'fluttered' to prevent its shadow forming a hard edge. Vignetting is usually applied to high-key portraits, particularly of children, although some landscape pictures can be given a 'period' look by the combined use of sepia toning and vignetting. Chris Baker's picture of an old railway cart in a yard is an example.

Effects filters in enlarging

Rodenstock have devised a Creative Print Set for use in conjunction with their Rogonar SC 50 mm and 70 mm enlarging lenses. The lenses are constructed with a slot in their barrels, into which any one of a range of filters can be inserted. The filters can be chosen to given soft-focus, graded and other effects, and their skilful use can be just as successful as filters used on a camera lens at the time of exposure.

Page 293: David Gepp's picture includes a framed photograph that was almost certainly sepia-toned in its original form. It seemed reasonable, therefore, to make it so in this print. Gene Nocon had the clever idea of sepia-toning all except the tyre in Ed Pritchard's study of a motorcyclist

Below, left: selected area of negative can be printed in isolation by placing opaque mask between enlarging lens and paper

Below, right: creative effects can be obtained by slotting filters between the elements of the specially constructed Rodenstock Rogonar enlarging lens

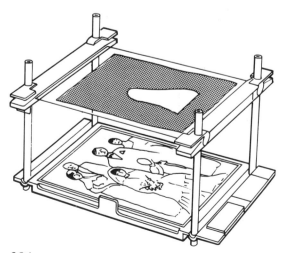

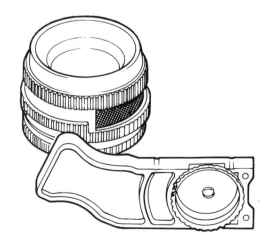

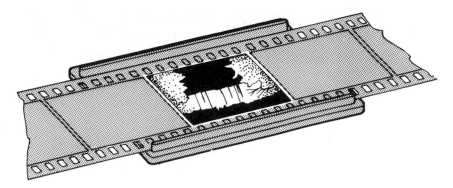

With negative carrier aperture slightly larger than negative image, black line can be formed around any print made from whole negative

Black line surround

It is generally agreed that a white border around a print sets it off effectively, and more prints are certainly made in this way than those that are 'bled-off' or borderless. Some photographer/printers consider that a black line between the image and the white border makes a further improvement. Denis Thorpe believes this is so, and most of his pictures are printed in this way (pages 298–299).

The easiest way of adding a narrow black line around an image is to draw it on the finished print in ink, using a ruling pen and a straight edge. If that method is thought to be cheating, another way is to arrange things so that the aperture in the negative carrier is just slightly larger in both directions than the negative image itself. This means that the whole of the negative image must be used, and composition must be decided at the time the exposure is made in the camera. It will be noticed that almost all Denis Thorpe's pictures have a 3:2 ratio corresponding to the 24 × 36 mm format of his negatives.

Another way of creating a black-line surround, without having to print the whole of a negative image, is to use a paper easel with four adjustable blades (such as the Saunders/Omega masking frame made in the US or the Leitz frame made in Germany). First, cut a stiff card to fit exactly within the image area defined by the blades when they have been set ready for the exposure. Expose a sheet of paper to the projected image, and then carefully place the opaque card in position within the blades of the easel. Next, move the blades outwards by a distance equal to the width of the black surround required. Finally, fog the uncovered line of paper by running a pen torch around the four sides of the print between the card and the blades.

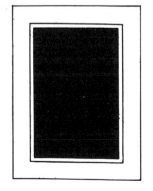

Mask for creating narrow white line with wide black print border; it must have opaque central area to protect separately exposed picture image

When the whole of the margin of a print is required to be black, the job is easier: locate the protective mask within the blades of the card before moving the blades outwards to clear the edges of the paper. Fogging the wider marginal areas can then be done with

295

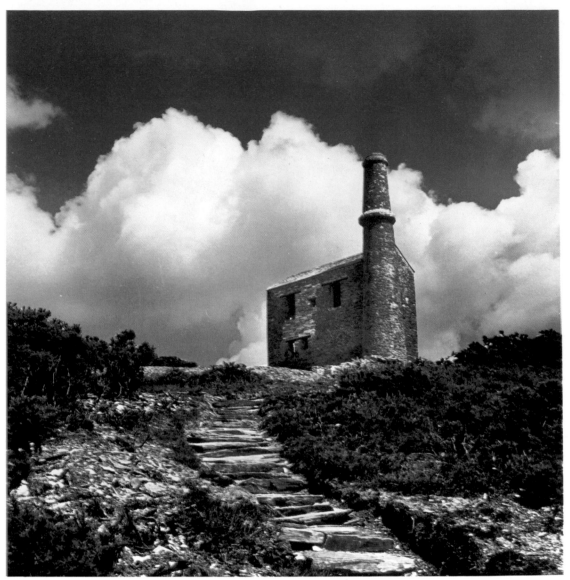

light from the enlarger after the negative has been removed from its carrier.

There are several ways of obtaining a thin white line within a wide black border on a print. One is to use a large masking negative having an opaque central area matching the image size of the finished picture, together with a surrounding black line. This mask is used in contact with a sheet of paper bearing the picture image when exposing the superimposed border.

Provided that its opaque patch has the same linear proportions as the required picture area, a smaller mask negative can be used to print the border image by projection. It is easier to do this if the picture negative is in one enlarger and the mask is already in position in a second enlarger.

By careful local application of several different toners, Tony Thomas has created a multi-coloured print from a monochrome original of his 'Cornish tin mine'

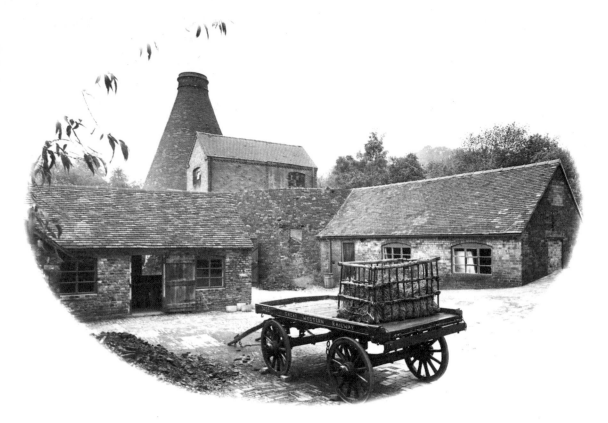

Sepia-toning and vignetting combine with the subject itself to give Chris Baker's picture a period look

Pages 298–299: Almost everyone seeing this picture is reminded of the work of the artist Lowry. As with so many of his photographs, Denis Thorpe composed the picture in the viewfinder of his Nikon, and then printed the whole of the negative

Combination printing

A popular application for combination printing is the addition of an interesting sky from one negative to the foreground of another. The technique is quite simple when the foreground subject is bold and simple in outline, because there may be no need to cut a mask for use during the secondary exposure. If on the other hand the division between the images required for the two negatives is at all intricate, masks must be cut and used carefully to protect first one part of the image from exposure and then the other part.

A frequent 'give-away' in a print that has been created from more than one negative is inconsistent lighting. Clouds are three-dimensional and usually display almost as much evidence of the direction from which they are lit as any foreground object; the two must therefore seem to be subject to the same source of light.

Other forms of combination printing can have a purely commercial purpose and simply require a soft-edged division of the area of the print into two or more parts. Malcolm Baker's print of Doug Hill's picture of a welder and the weld he has produced could have been done by combination printing, requiring no more than a card to be held in a position to protect first one part of the paper and then the other, during the two successive exposures. The correct exposure for each sector must be found by trial;

297

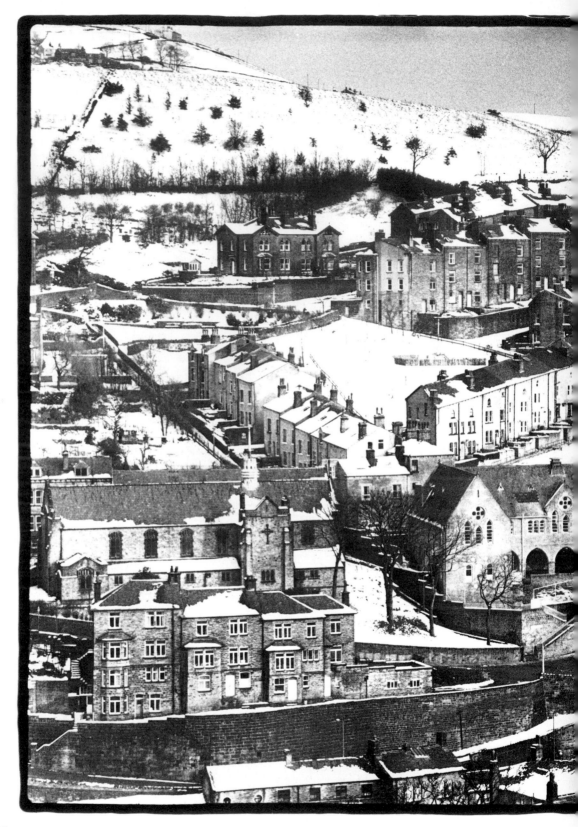

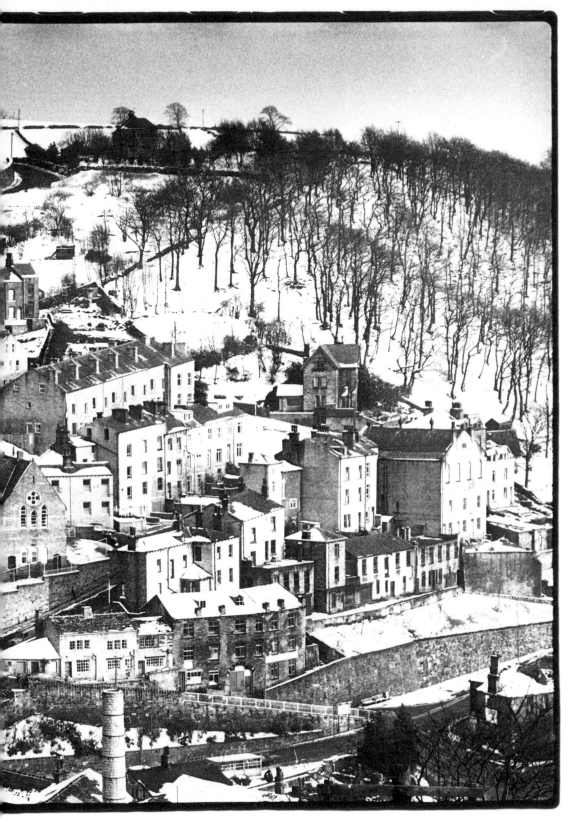

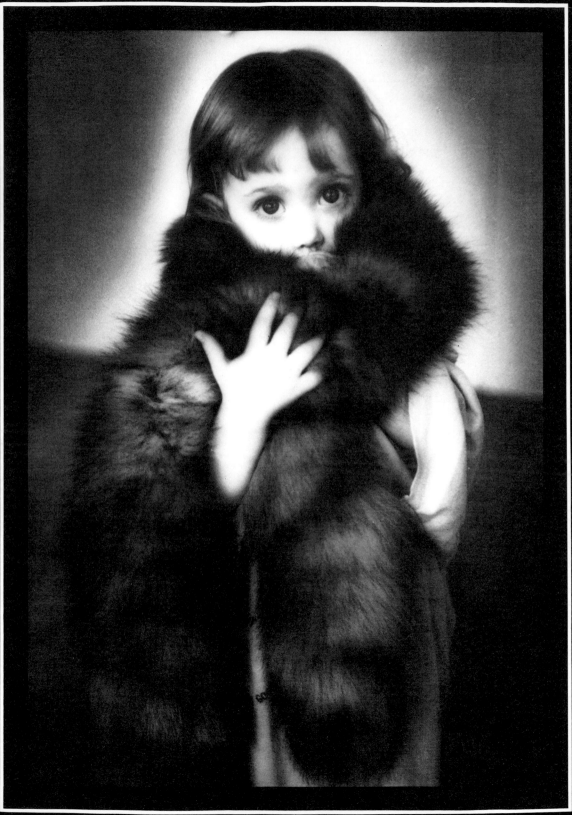

Many of the prints Larry
Bartlett makes from John
Downing's negatives are
given wide black borders
enclosing a narrow white
line

should the two negatives require different paper contrasts, this can easily be provided by Multigrade paper.

Creative use of dodging

Imaginative use of dodging can sometimes convert an ordinary picture into an award winner. The on-stage shot of singer Rod Stewart proves this. John Downing's negative produced a straight print that was competent but not outstanding, until Daily Express printer Larry Bartlett manipulated his print exposure so as to simulate the beam from a spotlight, and the picture took on another dimension.

Black-and-white prints from colour negatives

Theoretically, a black-and-white print should be made from a colour negative by using a panchromatic paper, but the inconvenience of making prints in complete darkness or very subdued greenish safelight is seldom justified by the relatively small improvement in tonal rendering that usually results. After all, provided that a blue/green sensitive paper such as Multigrade is used, the tone rendering will be much the same as if the subject had been photographed with an orthochromatic film or plate.

Most colour negatives are developed to the same gamma and in the same developer formulation (C41), so a negative of a typical outdoor subject usually prints quite well on glossy-surfaced Multigrade paper, perhaps with the aid of a pale magenta filter to increase contrast slightly. The exposure required is not very different from what would be expected when printing a black-and-white negative to a similar degree of enlargement. If graded paper is used (and often the resulting rendition of tones is quite satisfactory), grade 2 Ilfospeed or Ilfobrom serves very well.

Black-and-white prints from colour slides

While very good colour prints can be made from colour transparencies by direct exposure using the Cibachrome process, this takes more time and costs more than making a black-and-white print, which sometimes serves the purpose adequately. The easiest way of obtaining an enlarged black-and-white print from a colour slide is to make it by contact printing via an intermediate paper negative. Here again, slightly better tonal rendering results if Multigrade paper is used to make the large negative.

Unlike colour negatives, colour transparencies are processed to a gamma value slightly higher than 1.0, to allow for camera and projector lens flare and yet provide a screen brightness range that approximates that of the original scene. This means that the

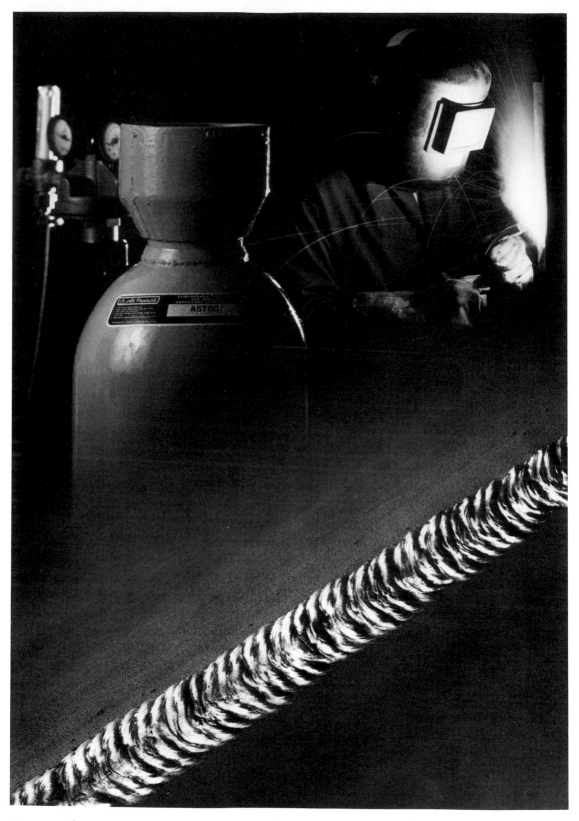

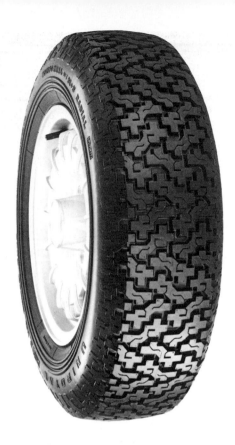

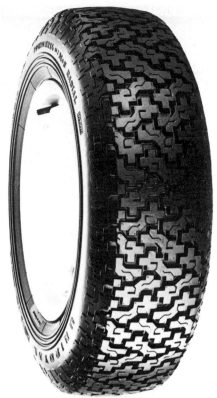

The combination of two images in one print, such as the welder and the weld in the picture (left) by Doug Hill, can sometimes be done in the camera, but usually it is more easily done by printing from two different negatives

Neither the soft print (above left) nor the hard print (above right) is really satisfactory; a combination of the two (right), producing a soft image of the wheel and a hard image of the tyre, is much better. The combined effect is obtained on Multigrade paper by exposing the area of the wheel through a yellow filter and the tyre through a magenta filter. This is very easily done with a Multigrade 400 enlarger head

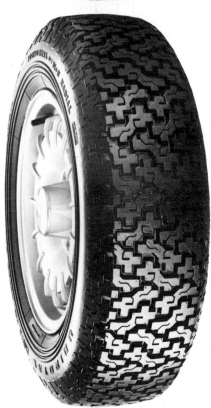

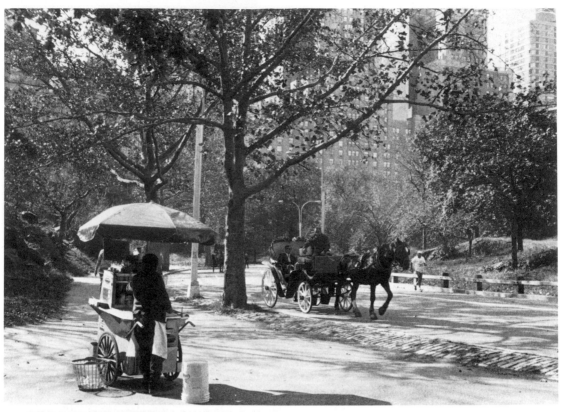

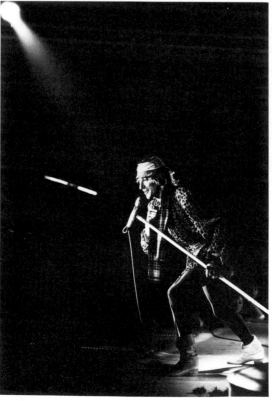

The smaller picture of Rod Stewart is a straight print from John Downing's negative. The award-winning version opposite was created from the same negative by Larry Bartlett, who held back the 'beam' of the spotlight while exposing the print

The black-and-white print above was made directly from a Kodacolor negative by the author, who used Multigrade paper for better tone rendering

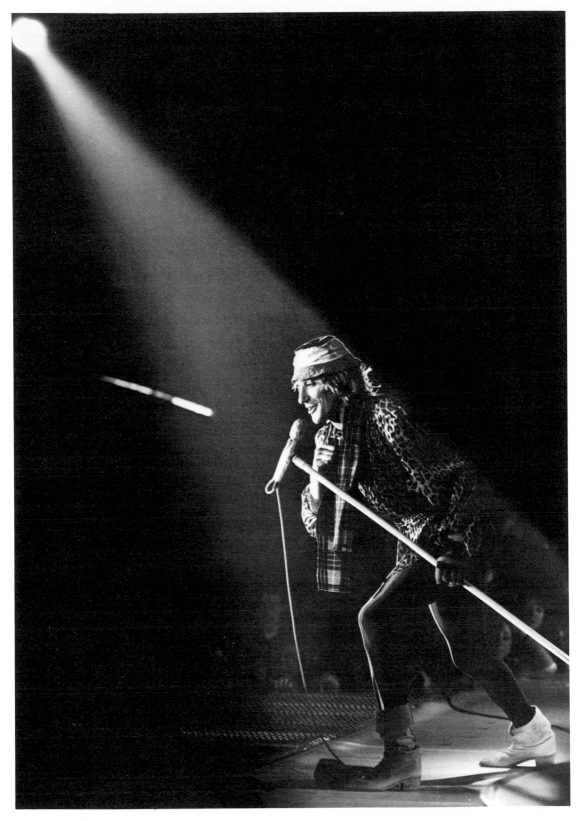

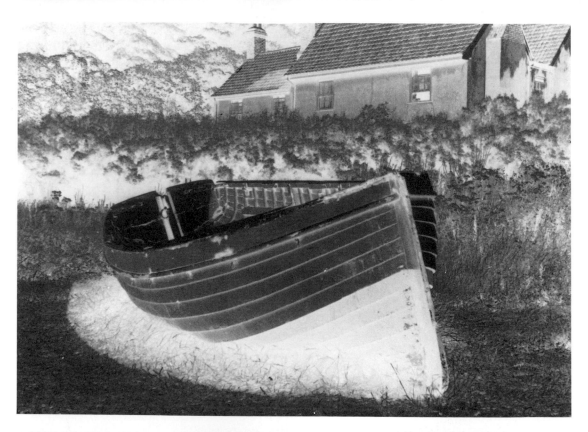

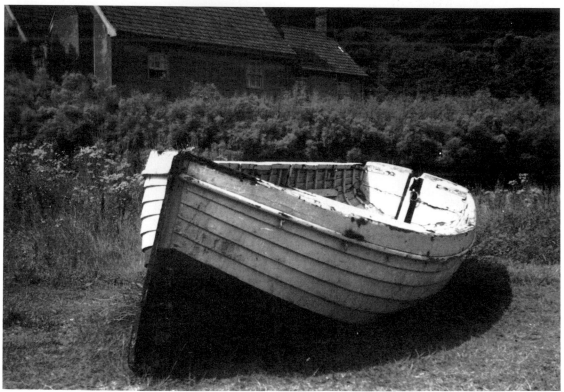

The reproduction at the top of page 306 is from a paper negative made by direct enlargement from a Kodachrome transparency on to Multigrade paper. A contact print on grade 0 Ilfospeed paper yields an excellent positive image

intermediate paper negative and the print made from it have to be made on low-contrast materials to avoid an excessively contrasty result. A suitable yellow filter, when used with Multigrade for the final print, usually yields a good result. Alternatively, grade 0 or 1 Ilfospeed or Ilfobrom can be used for the final contact print.

The opportunity to use pencil retouching and modification on the back of a paper negative and/or the paper positive from which it may have been made should not be overlooked, as it offers a convenient and flexible means of image control. When tested and found satisfactory, any pencil work (which is best done with a soft lead) can be prevented from smudging by means of a spray fixative such as is used by pastel artists.

High-contrast derivations
Because of the inherently high contrast of the material and the process, colour transparencies of long-scale subjects can easily be converted into extremely contrasty black-and-white prints if both the intermediate negative and the final print are made on grade 5 paper. Although it was made directly from a black-and-white negative, Denis Thorpe's against-the-light shot, 'Steam

By slanting the image within the print and converting it into a silhouette, Denis Thorpe and printer John Mallard greatly enhanced the impact of 'Steam enthusiasts'

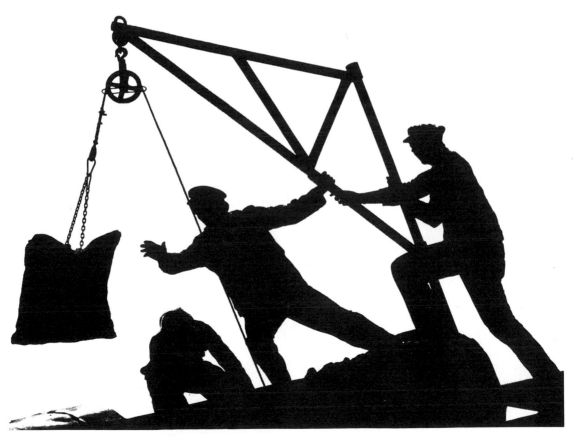

enthusiasts', became almost a silhouette when his colleague John Mallard used grade 5 to print it.

Other forms of derivation, including tone separation, tone-line conversion, enhanced grain and bas-relief effects, all involve the use of high-contrast line or lith films for the necessary intermediate images.

Tone separation   Division of the diverse densities of a continuous-tone negative into three or four different but uniform tones in a print is sometimes known as posterisation, perhaps because the result, with its three or four superimposed single-density images, is not unlike an artist's lithograph.

This form of tone separation involves the production of as many negatives as there will be tones in the finished print. They are best made via a fairly high-contrast, but continuous-tone, positive made from the original negative on a material such as Ilford Ortho cut sheet film. By using a high-contrast material such as Ilford Line film with appropriately adjusted exposure, first the light tones then the mid-tones and finally the dark tones of the subject can be 'extracted' from the continuous-tone positive. The three resulting negatives can then be printed in turn and in register on to the same sheet of paper, each exposure following the other so that the dark areas are exposed three times, the mid-tones twice and the light tones only once. Registration is usually achieve by punching holes in the negatives while they are accurately superimpsed and then locating them, together with a sheet of correspondingly punched RC paper, on registering pins during each exposure. Some experimentation is necessary to space the densities of the three tones to best advantage.

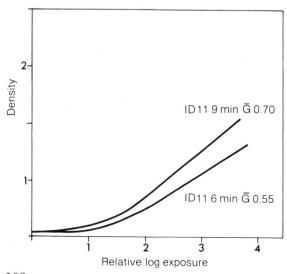

ID11 9 min $\bar{G}$ 0.70

ID11 6 min $\bar{G}$ 0.55

Density

Relative log exposure

Characteristics of Ilford Ortho cut sheet film developed in ID11 for six and nine minutes

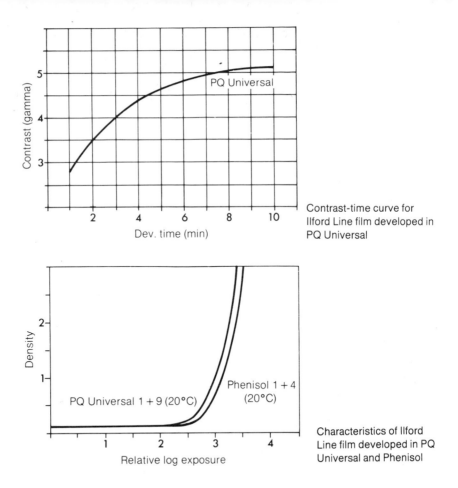

Contrast-time curve for Ilford Line film developed in PQ Universal

Characteristics of Ilford Line film developed in PQ Universal and Phenisol

Ilford Line is a high-contrast line film intended for use in process cameras and therefore relatively fast. It should be handled under an Ilford No. 915 (light red) safelight and developed for about three minutes at 20°C (68°F) in a developer such as Ilford Phenisol.

The Sabattier effect   The Sabattier effect is sometimes confused with solarisation, which is an unusual form of image reversal due to extreme overexposure. In 1862, Sabattier accidentally found that if a photographic film or paper is exposed to an image pattern, partially developed and then exposed to light before again being developed, then a positive image or a combined positive and negative image results.

Strange and interesting effects can sometimes be obtained by partially developing an image on grade 5 paper and then, after fogging the print by a carefully controlled exposure to white light, allowing development to continue. Quite often, however, the result looks just what it is, a fogged print; although by judicious treatment in a 'cutting' reducer, such as ferricyanide and hypo, it is

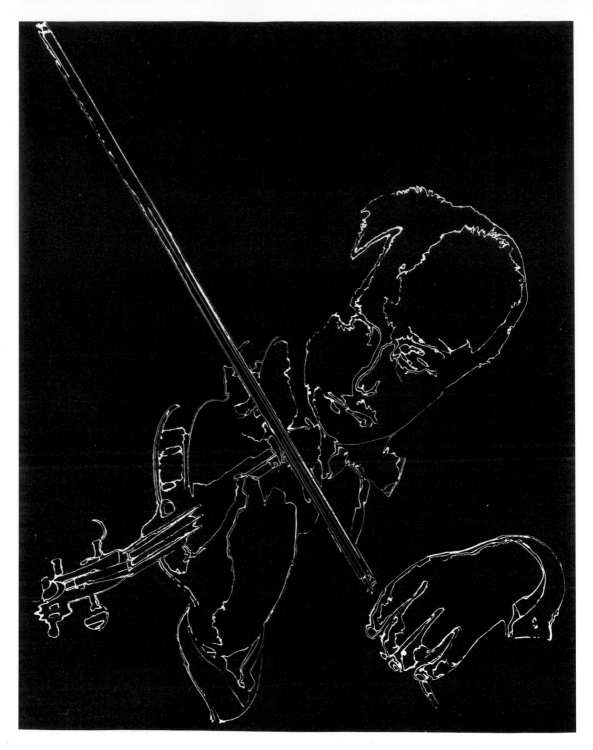

Tony Thomas knew that his
negative of a fiddler would
lend itself very well for
conversion to a line image
by use of the Sabattier
effect

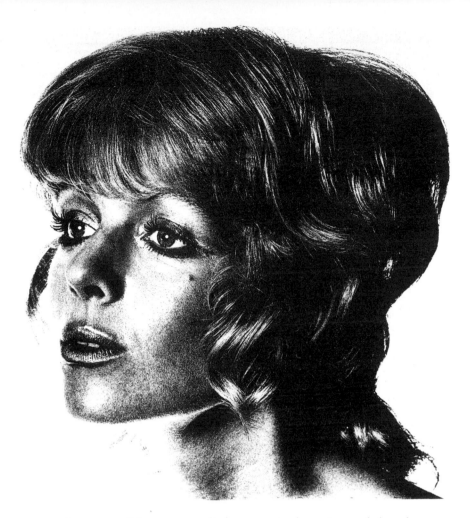

This striking portrait by Michael Barnett was achieved by using an intermediate positive to enhance both grain and contrast. But the subject must be suitable if this procedure is to succeed

sometimes possible to create light areas in the print and thereby make something of the result. In general, the Sabattier effect, together with associated Mackie lines, is more likely to be effectively formed when high-contrast intermediate films are used as translators of the original image.

The most problematical part of producing an image displaying the Sabattier effect is determining the amount of fogging required. If the lamp used for re-exposure is always the same and its distance from the film or paper is constant, a few tests quickly indicate the approximate exposure time required. The time taken for the first stage of development is another variable, but as a start it can be between 50 and 60 per cent of the time required for complete development with the particular combination of film or paper and associated developer.

Enhanced grain effects   Although photographers usually go to great lengths to restrict the graininess of the negatives they produce, graininess can, under some circumstances, be used as an interesting form of graphic representation. If it is decided before a picture is taken that the camera image is to be converted into a print emphasising the grain of the original negative, the film chosen should be a fast one and therefore relatively grainy. This is not essential, however, since the granularity of any negative image can be enormously exaggerated by the intermediate use of a high-contrast film such as Ilford Line developed in Phenisol. The portrait by Michael Barnett was taken on FP4 35 mm film; the grain was generated via an intermediate positive and negative, the print finally being made on Ilfospeed grade 5 glossy paper.

Enhanced tone rendering   Sometimes it is necessary to make a print from a negative of a high-contrast subject so as to yield a maximum of information in both shadows and highlights. Use of the softest grade of paper might at first seem to offer a simple solution, but in practice this often gives a somewhat dull and flat-looking result. A contrast-reducing mask would be a better answer, but making the mask is inconvenient and the time required may not permit it. There is another way in which a relatively contrasty paper can be made to yield good tone separation coupled with some beneficial edge effects of the kind described in connection with the XP1 film and process.

Some time ago, Leslie Thomson described what he called a 'hydraulic' method of print control. This amounts to using a grade 2 or 3 paper and an Amidol developer for part of the development period, followed by treatment in a still water bath for the completion of development. A suitable Amidol print developer would be:

sodium sulphite (anhydrous)	25 g
Amidol	6 g
potassium bromide	1 g
water to	1000 ml

This solution is already at working strength, but the developer does not keep well and should be made up as required. Amidol is chosen because it is active in neutral solutions and will therefore continue to work while the print is immersed in water.

Assuming that the developer would fully develop a properly exposed print in two minutes at 20°C (68°F), a print to be given the water-bath treatment should remain in the developer for only 30 to 45 seconds before being transferred to a dish of water at the same temperature as the developer. Neither the print nor the dish should be moved, so that growth of the image can continue, particularly in the highlight areas, by reason of the developer that was absorbed by the emulsion layer. After about two minutes, no further change will take place and the print can be fixed and washed as usual.

The apportionment between developer and water treatment has to be determined by trial. In general, the longer the print remains in the developer, the greater the large-area contrast; the shorter the immersion in developer, the more the whole print tends to uniform light grey, although with full detail. As Thomson explains: 'The water-bath print looks more evenly illuminated and softer in contrast than the normally developed one, but close inspection shows at least as much contrast in finer detail, sometimes considerably more. Some of the image is formed during the first short immersion, but the main purpose is to saturate the emulsion with developer. When the print is put in water, the developer tends to be used up promptly in the shadows, where development then ceases. In the highlights, there is developer enough to reduce all the silver needed for the image, and its action continues for several minutes. The shadows are therefore prevented from becoming too dark and the highlights receive full development.'

The 'edge effects' that arise in a print processed by the water-bath technique are explained by the fact that: 'The shadows receive a small spill-over of active solution from the well-endowed light areas, while in exchange the highlights receive restraining bromide from the developed shadows. Along the junctions,

Gelatin relief images formed by the bleach-etch process can be dyed in any colour required

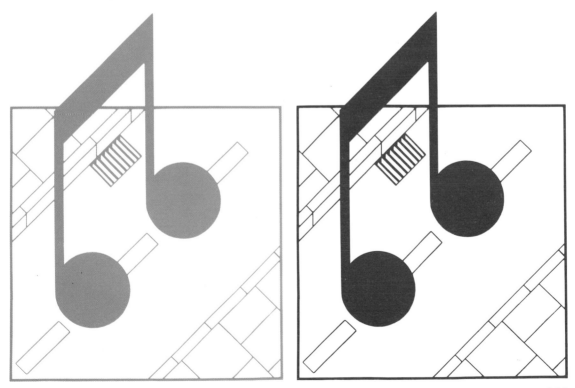

therefore, the shadows develop more completely and the highlights develop less than in the main sections of each area. This accentuated edge contrast is an essential feature of all two-bath development.'

The bleach-etch process
Besides their several other advantages, polyethylene-laminated papers offer the possibility of applying the bleach-etch process to yield a gelatin relief image that can be dyed in any desired colour. While the process cannot be used to produce continuous-tone images in colour, a black-and-white continuous-tone image can be superimposed on a coloured background; this can sometimes be useful for display cards and the like. Screen halftone images can also be used.

A positive original is necessary to produce a dyed positive result, and it is usual for the positive to be made on a high-contrast lith or line film to ensure clear-cut exposure that will penetrate the whole of the emulsion layer. This is important because the etching process, whereby the gelatin surrounding the silver image is softened and rendered soluble in warm water, must extend right through the emulsion layer so that no gelatin remains attached to

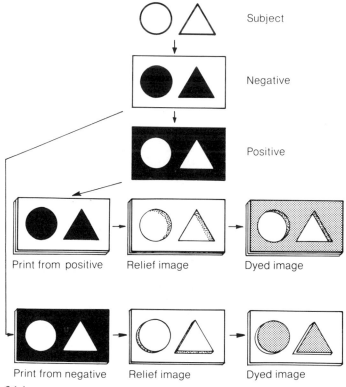

Subject

Negative

Positive

Print from positive   Relief image   Dyed image

Print from negative   Relief image   Dyed image

Principal stages in
bleach-etch process

314

the underlying polyethylene layer to take up dye and degrade the whites of the print.

A negative image, delineating the areas of the print that will eventually be clear, is developed in a developer such as Ilford Phenisol. The image must be developed fully before the print is fixed in a *non-hardening* fixer. Then the print is washed for two minutes or so before being transferred to a hydrogen peroxide bleach bath made up as follows:

A	cupric chloride	10 g
	acetic acid (glacial)	50 ml
	water to	1000 ml
B	hydrogen peroxide (20 volumes)	100 ml

For use mix 9 parts of A with 1 part of B. Note that '20 volumes' is simply an indication of the strength of the solution of hydrogen peroxide. If a 10 volume (3 per cent) solution is used, dilute with 5 parts of A. Hydrogen peroxide solution should be stored in a cool, dark place.

After a print has been immersed in the bleach-etch bath, the silver image will appear to be completely bleached in about one minute, but the print should remain in the solution for about twice this time.

The gelatin that has been softened by the peroxide can be removed in water at about 40°C (105°F) by using a soft brush or a swab of cotton wool, so that clear spaces are left where there had been deposits of silver.

Any dye that is soluble in water and combines with gelatin can be used. For small-scale and occasional use, domestic dyes such as Dylon cold-water dyes usually serve quite well and can be obtained from hardware stores. One small drum of dye dissolved in a litre (about a quart) of water dyes a very large number of prints.

Dyeing can sometimes be accelerated, and the density of the dyed image increased, if the etched print is immersed for a short time in a 1 per cent solution of acetic acid before it is dyed.

When a black-and-white silver image (whether line or continuous-tone) is to be superimposed on what will be a coloured area, the print is *not* fixed after being developed, but simply washed and then bleached directly. Then, before the softened parts of the image are washed away, the additional black-and-white image is printed, using a negative, on to an area of unused silver halide. The sensitivity of the original emulsion may have been changed by immersion in the bleach-etch solution, so tests are necessary to arrive at the correct exposure for the superimposed silver image. After development, the residual halides can be

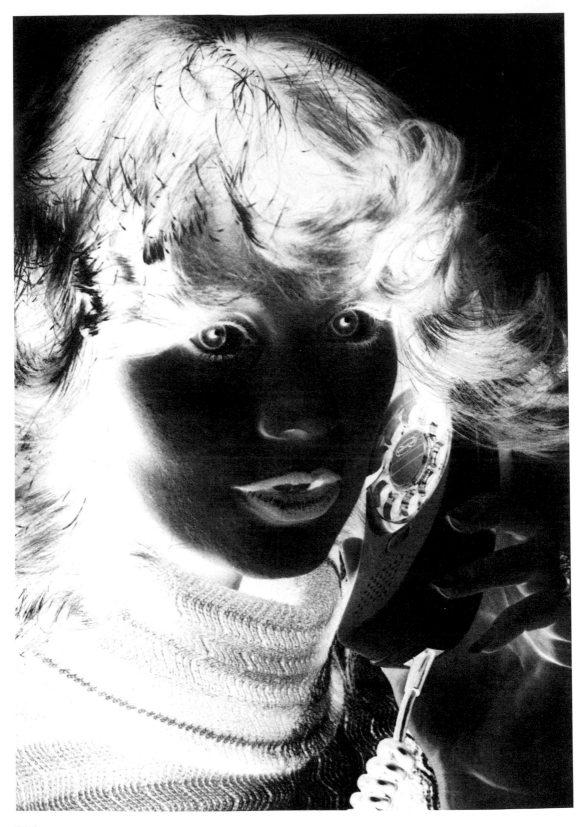

removed from the gelatin by fixing and washing in warm water, before the relief image is dyed.

Dyed prints

Sometimes, as for example with the guide print used for the jacket of this book, a useful or even striking effect can be achieved by overall or local dyeing of a black-and-white continuous-tone image. For the jacket photograph, the darkroom background was dyed orange while the projected image area and the windows of the Multigrade module were protected with a rubber-based stripping lacquer such as Maskoid. Then, after drying the print and removing the protective layer, the orange-dyed areas were in turn covered with a layer of rubber, while the baseboard image area was dyed magenta to represent the exposure of a contrasty print.

The negative print

At the conclusion of a book that has been almost entirely devoted to the techniques of producing a print bearing a positive image from a negative intermediate, it may seem odd to include a section on the production of negative prints. Nevertheless, quite powerful and striking graphic effects can be achieved by printing certain types of subject in the negative mode.

There are two quite easy ways of arriving at a black-and-white negative print. One is via a camera negative and an enlarged paper positive, the other is by working directly from a colour transparency.

By starting with a fine-grain high-resolution transparency material such as Kodachrome 25, excellent paper negatives can be made by direct projection printing on to Ilfospeed grade 0 paper or Ilfospeed Multigrade paper used with a yellow filter. When a black-and-white negative is the starting point, an enlarged paper positive print should be made and then used to produce the negative result by contact printing. Perfect contact is essential between the two sheets of paper during exposure of the negative print.

The grades of paper best suited for the job depend upon the original negative and the desired effect, but using grade 2 glossy Ilfospeed for both purposes usually yields an interesting result.

Index